CONTENTS

PROGRAM IN GW BASIC

PROGRAM IN GW BASIC

by

Ian Sinclair

Glentop Press Ltd

February 1989

Warranty

All programs in this book have been written expressly to illustrate specific teaching points. They are not warranted as being suitable for any particular application. Every care has been taken in the writing and presentation of this book but no responsibility is assumed by the author or publishers for any errors or omissions contained herein.

ISBN 1 85181 222 9

Published by Glentop Press Ltd
Unit 11
Stirling Industrial Center
Stirling Way
Borehamwood
Herts WD6 2BT

Originated directly from the publisher's word-processor disks by
NWL Editorial Services, Langport, Somerset, TA10 9DG
Printed in Great Britain by Bell and Bain Ltd., Glasgow

Preface

BASIC is a language that has existed in many more than the legendary 57 varieties, but now, some twenty years after the creation of BASIC, we seem to have accepted BASIC as the universal computer language. Though academics have always rejected the use of BASIC as a practical language, the fact remains that BASIC is one of the few languages in which nearly everything of a computing nature can be done. Many famous languages have weak spots, inability to handle strings easily, perhaps, or lack of good input/output disk filing routines, particularly random-access files. The more modern versions of BASIC are languages that allow the user to do in reasonably simple ways actions that are difficult and convoluted in other languages. For that reason, every small computer has always been provided with a version of BASIC, and many users have taken advantage of this to create programs for themselves.

Of the versions of BASIC that are available for IBM-PC™ compatible machines, GW BASIC (or the almost identical to the BASICA provided with many machines) is by far the commonest. This is an interpreted BASIC, which means that programs written in this BASIC are easy to try out, because you can alter the program each time an error appears and try it again.

This book is designed as an introduction to the features of GW BASIC, neglecting some of the features that would appeal mainly to the graphics enthusiast (like `PALETTE`, `GET` and `PUT`) and to the machine-code user (no `INLINE`, `PEEK` or `POKE`).

The aim has been to give the reader sufficient working knowledge and experience to be able to continue with only the manual as a further guide. I would like to emphasise that this book was written while I was using GW BASIC on a PC machine at my home, and that the listings of programs in this book were obtained from an EPSON printer that was connected to the computer. This might seem to be an unnecessary claim, but many books still appear in which the program listings have been re-typed, with errors appearing in many of them. Every program which appears in this book, and every example of programming commands, has been tested on GW BASIC. Nothing has been copied untested from the manuals, and where a command has operated in a way that is not obvious from the manual description, I have pointed out the difference.

I am greatly indebted to many people who made this book possible. I am particularly grateful to Eddy Maddix of Glentop Press for his efforts to keep me supplied with software and in converting this set of disks into a real book.
I am sure that the result of all this work will be a book that will match the capabilities of this excellent variety of BASIC.

Ian Sinclair

January 1989

Chapter 1

BEGINNINGS

At the risk of antagonising the reviewers who believe that every computer owner is already an expert, we need to start by asking what we expect a computer to do. The short answer is that it's a machine which can organise information for you. Give it a set of names and addresses, and it will store them, arrange them into alphabetical order, produce the address for a name that you type, and so on. Give it a list of names and payments to a club, and it will give you a list of who paid how much and who still owes. Give it a load of numbers in answer to questions about your earnings and expenses, and it will show you your correct tax code. Does this sound like a brainless machine? If it doesn't, that's because all of the organisation is done under the command of a program. The program is what we call the 'software' of the machine. Without a suitable program, the computer can do nothing. The machine itself is the brainless bit, the clever part is the program. So how do you go about writing a program?

It isn't as difficult as you might think. The reason is that there has been a lot of progress in this respect in the last twenty years. Once upon a time, computers were big machines which had to be programmed by skilled people who understood the number-code system (called machine-code) that the computer used. As time went on, programming languages were invented. A programming language is a way of instructing a computer by using command words which are English words. Even before microcomputers were dreamed of, there were several of these programming languages, but the most important one for us is BASIC. BASIC is short for Beginners All-purpose Symbolic Instruction Code. It was invented at Dartmouth College, USA, as a way of teaching computer programming. Since then, it has spread like wildfire to become the programming language that is used for each and every personal or home computer. It's still a good language for beginners in the sense that it's easy to learn, but it has also developed into a language that gives you a lot of control over your computer.

Your computer can use many varieties of BASIC, but one which is of particular use is called GW (sorry about this, but GW stands for Gee Whiz) BASIC. It's one of the more up to date varieties of BASIC, and yet it has been developed from one of the first versions of BASIC that was used in small computers, Microsoft BASIC. What that all boils down to is that GW BASIC is easy to use, reliable, and yet capable of getting the best from your computer. Unlike the older varieties, too, it will work on any PC machine that has the GW BASIC disk.

BASIC foundations

The BASIC language is built like any other language, with vocabulary and syntax. Vocabulary means the words that are used to form instructions to the computer. Syntax means the way that you have to use these words. Like any other language, BASIC has rules which you have to learn. What makes it so much easier for you to learn is that the words are mainly English words, and the rules are simple. In addition, your computer will tell you when you have disobeyed the rules!

To learn about BASIC, then, you have to learn what a number of words mean. There are about 220 of these words, and the meaning of many of them is fairly obvious. In addition, you have to learn the correct way to use each word. This is where you really come up against the 'brainless machine' bit. The computer can make use of a command which uses the correct word in the correct way. If you spell the word wrongly, use it in the wrong way, or use the wrong word, the machine can't do anything – so it stops. When it does this, a message will appear on the screen to tell you what happened. This is called an 'error-message', and from what it says, you should be able to find what went wrong.

If that makes it sound simple, that's because it is simple, and that's why it needs to be learned. Suppose, for example, you had a foreign friend who understood only about two hundred words of English. How would you make him understand, using only the words he knows, that you want him to do something like arrange words in alphabetical order or find how many members of the dominoes club have paid their subscriptions? The answer is that you have to break up these complicated actions into a lot of simple steps. You then have to describe each step in the words that your two-hundred-word friend understands. There's one big difference here, though. A human who knows a couple of hundred words of a language will pick up other words very quickly. A computer doesn't, so far, have this ability. Every instruction has to be made out of these important command words, the 'keywords' as we call them. A program consists of an arrangement of these keywords in such a way that something useful is done. A program might be educational, amusing, for business or leisure, working with words or with numbers, whatever you want it to be. Whatever it is, though, it still has to make use of these keywords, because that's all that the machine can make use of. You can't type instructions like *"Who ordered a dozen spob-tackers?"* or *"What will my payments be if I pay back one fifth of the mortgage?"*. These are questions for humans with human brains, not for computers. Computers have memory. They can store information and they can store instructions. They can't think what a new instruction might mean, though, which is why we have to write programs.

Interpreting and Compiling

Computer languages like BASIC can be arranged in two ways. One of these ways is called 'interpreted' and the other 'compiled'. The GW BASIC for your PC computer is interpreted. This means that the instructions which you have typed are held in the memory of the computer as a set of code numbers. When you run a program written in GW BASIC, the GW BASIC program must be present in the memory, and it will interpret each code number for an instruction and make it work. That means that the machine has to find what the code means, and then act on it. Acting on it means that the machine has to locate another set of coded instructions in its memory, and use these to direct the microprocessor, the 8086, which is at the heart of the computer. A language which uses interpretation is slow, because each command has to be looked up, in turn, as the computer comes to it. A compiler, by contrast, does the looking up once just after the program has been written. The instructions are then turned directly into the microprocessor codes. When a compiled program runs, then, there is no looking up to do, and the speed can be very much greater. In addition, a compiled BASIC program can be run like any of the programs that have `COM` or `EXE` extension names, just by typing its name. You don't have to have BASIC or GEM loaded in to run such programs. Many of the programs that are shown in the directory listing of disks that you buy as ending with `EXE` or `COM` are of this type, though they are usually compiled from other languages, such as *C* or *PASCAL*. For learning the language from scratch an interpreter is much better than a compiler because it allows you to alter the program when an error occurs, and try again. This sort of thing is never easy with a compiled program, which is why compilers are mainly used by professionals. As time goes on, too, you may feel that you need to use a faster-running language. The great advantage of the PC computer is that you have the choice.

Loading GW BASIC

I am assuming right from the start of this book that you have not made much use of a computer in this class with GW BASIC before, and that the actions of setting up your PC will have been carried out. The PC starts as a 'clean machine' meaning that when you switch it on, there is practically nothing in the memory. What is there consists of instructions that will make it load in further instruction codes from a System disk whenever you put such a disk into the drive. These instructions load in (or 'boot') the operating system that makes the computer usable, and the PC comes provided with two operating systems. The most common of these is called MS-DOS and is used for most of the serious business programs that are written for PCs.

You start GW BASIC by typing the name GW with the disk in the currently used drive. Some versions of GW BASIC use the name BASICA, because GW BASIC is identical in form to the BASICA of the IBM machine, so that BASICA has to be typed rather than GW. A look at the manual or the disk directory will decide which of the two you have. This file must be loaded before you can type, load, save or run a program in GW BASIC, because it provides all the interpreting actions.

Direct commands

GW BASIC allows you to control the computer in two ways. One way is by delivering direct commands. These are commands that are intended to be obeyed at once, and they use the same BASIC keywords as would be used in programs, though not all of the 220-odd keywords can be used as direct commands. A direct command can be issued at any time when the normal `A>`, `B>` or `C>` prompt is showing – the letter is determined by which disk drive you are currently using. If you now type an instruction, like `PRINT 1001`, and press **RETURN**, the screen shows the instruction, and the number `1001` appears on the next line down. The command `PRINT` means 'print on to the screen', and it is executed whenever the **RETURN** key is pressed. To delete everything from the screen, type `CLS` and press **RETURN**. This is a direct command to delete everything from the screen, and it can also be used as a program statement to clear the screen.

If you want to repeat this or any other direct command, you need to type the whole command again. Because of this, the use of direct commands in GW BASIC is confined to just a few essential actions, however the really important instructions are those which form a program and which remain stored in the memory of the computer until it is switched off or until something else is loaded in.

Program instructions

To type program instructions requires the use of the screen as an editor, like a word-processor used without a printer. When you start up (boot) any type of BASIC, the screen is used purely for writing program instructions. When you use GW BASIC you type these lines with each program line numbered in the sequence that they are to be executed because such a number is the only way that GW BASIC can distinguish between a direct command and a program line. Any GW BASIC instruction(s) written without a line number are commands, instruction(s) with a line number are program instructions or statements. You can, for example, type a line that starts with the number 50, and this line will be placed between line 40 and line 60, no matter where or when you typed it. Chapter 11 deals with the editing methods of GW BASIC.

GW BASIC listings can be used with two versions of compiled BASIC: Turbo BASIC and QBASIC.

Loading and Saving

Typing program instructions into the computer would be of little use if we could not save the programs on disk and recall them for later use. Practically all varieties of interpreted BASIC use the word `LOAD` to mean reading a program form a disk, and `SAVE` to mean recording a program on disk, and these words are used by GW BASIC. Since the ability to save and load reliably is very important, these two actions need to be checked out before we go any further. First of all, we'll look at how load and save are carried out in GW BASIC. This requires a short test program, and it's a good time to introduce one of the useful extras of GW BASIC, automatic line numbering. Typing `AUTO` **RETURN** or pressing **Alt-A RETURN** will present you with the number 10 on the screen, and each time you press the **RETURN** key to signal the end of a BASIC line, a new number will appear. The numbers start at 10, and rise in units of ten, though

```
10 REM
20 REM
30 REM
40 REM
```

Figure 1.1
A very simple test program to practice editing, saving and loading.

you can alter this by using the methods shown in Chapter 11. The appearance of the line numbers is cancelled by pressing the **CTRL BREAK** keys.

With this automatic line numbering on, type the test program shown in Figure 1.1. You can then show how it is stored by typing `LIST` **RETURN**, or by pressing **F1** and **RETURN**. Notice that if you typed `rem` in lower-case (small) letters these will have been converted into upper-case (capital) letters. All BASIC instruction words are converted in this way, and it's good practice always to type in lower-case so that you can check for mis-spellings simply by looking to see if the words appear in upper-case or not when you `LIST`. This is not much of a program – `rem` means *reminder*, and is ignored by either an interpreter or a compiler – it's used to start a reminder line so that you know what your program is supposed to do at this point. With the four lines typed in, make two savings. Press the **F4** key, which will bring up the word `SAVE"` with a quote mark. Now type your filename, perhaps `b:test.bas"`, so that the whole line looks like this:

```
SAVE"b:test.bas"
```

– and then press **RETURN**. Obviously, if you are using a single drive you might want to put your programs on the same disk as GW BASIC, or place a fresh formatted disk into the drive. If you don't use `b:`, then drive A will be taken as the default.

In addition, since saving the program on to a disk does not delete the program, we can save another version. This time, the line should appear as:

```
SAVE"b:testa.bas", a
```

with the 'a' added following the closing quote. The 'a' is not part of the filename, but is a command to GW BASIC to make the program be saved in ASCII codes rather than in the shorter internal codes of GW BASIC in which `REM` is represented by a single number rather then by three ASCII codes. To see the difference, remove the program disk and leave GW BASIC by typing `system` **RETURN**. Put your program disk into the current drive and type:

```
TYPE test.bas
```

This produces a few meaningless shapes caused by the code numbers. Now try

```
TYPE testa.bas
```

and see the difference. This time you see the program just as it appeared on the screen during listing. Using the comma and 'a' following the filename during saving saves in ASCII code, so that the program can be read with `TYPE` or with a word-processor. Because of this, you should always save in this form, rather than in the more compressed coding that you get when you omit the final `a`. No matter which method you used for saving, GW BASIC can read your program files when you use `LOAD"b:test.bas"` or `LOAD"b:testa.bas"`. Make sure that you can reliably save and load, because until you can do this there is little point in typing programs.

Chapter 2

INPUTS AND OUTPUTS

Chapter 1 will have broken you in to the idea that BASIC takes its orders from you when you type them on the keyboard. You will also have found that a direct command in GW BASIC is obeyed when the **RETURN** or **ENTER** key is pressed. From now on, we'll use just the word **RETURN** to mean this key, whatever it happens to be labelled on the keyboard. You will also know that you can use the command `LIST` (then press **RETURN**) which prints your program instructions on to the screen. One useful command action of GW BASIC is that you can clear the screen by pressing the key that is marked **Home** at the same time as the **Ctrl** key. This has also the effect of placing the cursor at the top left hand corner of the screen. The messages at the bottom of the screen are not erased in this way, however. You can get the same screen clearing effect by pressing the **CTRL** key along with the 'L' key. Pressing **CTRL** and **L** together is usually written as **CTRL L** to save space. As your familiarity with the computer keyboard increases, you will want to make full use of the GW editing commands, and these are explained in Chapter 11.

Now there are two ways in which you can use a computer. One way is called *direct mode*, and it means that you type a command, press the **RETURN** key, and the command is carried out at once. This can be useful, but the more important way of using a computer is in what is called *program mode*. In program mode the computer is issued with a set of instructions, with a guide to the order in which they are to be carried out. A set of instructions like this is called a program. The difference is important, because the instructions of a program can be repeated as many times as you like with very little effort on your part. A direct command, by contrast, will be repeated only if you type the whole command again, and then press **RETURN**. The set of command words that can be used, along with the rules for using them, make up what is called a 'programming language', which in this case is BASIC.

Let's now take a look at the difference between a direct command and a program instruction in GW BASIC. If you want the computer to carry out the direct command to add two numbers, 1.6 and 3.2, then you have to type:

```
print 1.6 + 3.2
```

(and then press **RETURN**). You have to start with `print` (or `PRINT`), or its abbreviation ?, because a computer is a dumb machine, and it obeys only a few set instructions. Unless you use the word 'print', the computer has no way of telling that what you want is to see the answer on the screen. It doesn't recognise instructions like '`GIVE ME`' or '`WHAT IS`', only a selection of words (about 140 of them) that we call its *reserved words* or *instruction words*. `PRINT` is one of these words. So that you can recognise these reserved words more easily in this book they and their associated instructions are shown in this `evenly spaced` typeface (also used for showing you what to type into your computer, and what you will see on its screen). They will generally be shown in upper-case, but you know by now that you can type them in either upper-case or lower-case. You will always see them in upper-case when you `LIST` your GW program.

When you press the **RETURN** key after typing `PRINT 1.6 + 3.2`, the screen shows the answer, `4.8`, under the command. This answer is not printed at the extreme left hand side of the screen, it's placed one space in, and the word '`O.k`' appears under this answer. The '`O.k.`' is a 'prompt', a reminder that the computer is ready for another command. The space is there to allow for the presence of a + or – sign if it is needed. Once this command has been carried out, however, it's finished.

A program in GW BASIC does not work in the same way. A program is typed in, but the instructions of the program are not carried out when you press the **RETURN** key. Instead, the instructions are stored in the memory, ready to be carried out as and when you want. The computer needs some way of recognising the difference between your commands and your program instructions. With GW BASIC this is done by starting each program instruction with a number which is called a line number. This must be a positive whole number, the type of number that is called a positive integer. We looked at this idea briefly in Chapter 1.

The `PRINT` instruction, then, is the way that we get the computer to provide information to us. With very few exceptions, all computer uses involve three things, inputs, processes, and outputs. The hard part about programming is not

```
10 PRINT 5.06+6.08
20 PRINT 9.2-4.7
30 PRINT 3.3*3.9
40 PRINT 7.6/1.4
```

Figure 2.1

A program that illustrates the use of the four arithmetical actions.

learning the language of BASIC, it's learning how to get what you want from these three actions. For the moment, we'll leave inputs aside, and concentrate on outputs and a bit of processing. Processing means doing whatever we want to do with numbers or words. It can be as simple as adding two numbers, or as complicated as putting a set of names and addresses into alphabetical order of surname. It can mean producing shapes and colours on the screen, and moving them about. It can mean producing sound, either sound effects or music, to go with the screen displays. Summing it all up, it means all of the actions that make a computer so interesting and so useful.

Let's start programming, then, with the arithmetic actions of add, subtract, multiply and divide. Computers aren't used all that much for calculation, but it's useful to be able to carry out calculations now and again. In addition, you are much more likely to recognise the sort of instructions that use numbers than the ones which are used to work with words. Figure 2.1 shows a four-line program which will print some arithmetic results. The process here consists of four bits of arithmetic, each with an output.

Take a close look at this, because there's a lot to get used to in these four lines. To start with, the line numbers are 10, 20, 30, 40 rather than 1, 2, 3, 4. This is to allow space for second thoughts. If you decide that you want to have another instruction between line 10 and line 20, then you can type the line number 15, or 11 or 12 or any other whole number between 10 and 20, and follow it with your new instruction. Even though you have entered this line out of order, the computer will automatically place it in order between lines 10 and 20. If you number your lines 1, 2, 3 then there's no room for these second thoughts, though you can change line numbers if you have to by using the editing commands. This idea of having line numbers that go in tens is so common that it's built into GW BASIC in the form of the `AUTO` command (see Chapter 12).

The next thing to notice is how the number zero on the screen is slashed across. This is to distinguish it from the letter O. The computer simply won't accept the zero in place of the letter 'O', nor the O in place of a zero, and the slashing makes this difference more obvious to you, so that you are less likely to make mistakes. The zero that you see on the keyboard is not slashed but it is on a different key, and is differently shaped. Type some zero's and O's on the screen so that you can see the difference. Unfortunately, due to the vagaries of typesetting it has proved impossible to use slashed zeroes in this book – so keep your wits about you when typing in from the listings!

Now to more important points. The star or asterisk symbol (*) in line 30 is the symbol that BASIC uses as a multiply sign. Once again, we can't use the x that you might normally use for writing multiplication because x is a letter. There's no divide sign on the keyboard either, so BASIC, like all other versions, uses the slash (/) sign in its place. This is the diagonal line which is on the same key as the question mark, not the one which slopes the other way, and which is placed at the left hand side next to the Z key..

So far, so good. The program is entered by typing it, just as you see it. You don't need to leave any space between the line number and the P of PRINT, because GW BASIC will put one in for you when it displays the program on the screen. You don't need to leave a space following PRINT either, and you can type ? in place of PRINT. GW BASIC is very tolerant about this sort of thing, so don't be surprised when you see a program listing in this book which shows words run together. There are some places where you must leave spaces, and we'll deal with these as we come to them. Getting back to the program example, you will have to press the **RETURN** key when you have completed each instruction line, before you type the next line number. You should end up with the program looking as it does in the illustration. When you have entered the program by typing it, it's stored in the memory of the computer in the form of a set of code numbers. There are two things that you need to know now. One is how to check that the program is actually in the memory, the other is how to make the machine carry out the instructions of the program. with GW first.

The first part is dealt with using the command LIST that you know already. You can use the **Ctrl-L** keys to wipe the screen first if you like, then type LIST (or press **F1**) and press the **RETURN** key. When you press the **RETURN** key, and not until, your program will be listed on the screen. You will then see how the computer has printed the items of the program on the screen, with spaces between the line numbers and the instructions. To make the program operate, you need another command, RUN. Type RUN (or press **F2**), then press the **RETURN** key, and you will see the instructions carried out. To be more precise, you will see:

```
11.14
4.5
12.87
5.428571
0.k.
```

That last line should give you some idea of how precisely GW BASIC can carry out its arithmetic. When you follow the instruction word PRINT with a piece of arithmetic like 2.8 * 4.4, then what is printed is the result of working out that piece of arithmetic. The program doesn't print 2.8 * 4.4, just the result of the action 2.8 * 4.4.

This program has done two of the main computer actions, process and output, for you. The only input has been the program, and we can't alter any of these numbers in the program without altering the program itself. Try writing a program of this type for yourself, and see how the BASIC carries out the calculations and displays the answers. All of this is useful, but it's not always handy to get just a set of answers on the screen, especially if you have forgotten what the questions were. BASIC allows you a way of printing anything that you like on the screen, exactly as you type it, by the use of what is called a 'string'.

Figure 2.2 illustrates this principle. In each line, some of the typing is enclosed between quotes (inverted commas) and some is not. Enter this short program and run it. Can you see how very differently the computer has treated the instructions? Whatever was enclosed between quotes has been printed exactly as you typed it. Whatever was not between quotes is worked out, so that the first line, for example, gives the unsurprising result:

```
2+2=4
```

Now there's nothing automatic about this. If you type a new line:

```
15 PRINT "2+2=";5*1.5
```

```
10 PRINT "2+2=";2+2
20 PRINT "2.5*3.5=";2.5*3.5
30 PRINT "9.4-2.2=";9.399999-2.2
40 PRINT "27.6/2.2=";27.6/2.2
```

Figure 2.2

Mixing arithmetic with items that are to be printed on the screen as shown.

then you'll get the daft reply, when you RUN this, of:

```
2+2= 7.5
```

The computer does as it's told and that's what you told it to do. Only a loony could believe that computers would take over the world – after all, screwdrivers didn't!

This is a good point also to take notice of some other points. The line 15 that you added will have been fitted into place between lines 10 and 20 if you are using GW BASIC – use LIST if you don't believe it. No matter in what order you type the lines of your program, the computer will sort them into order of ascending line number for you. Note also that the computer has put a space between the '=' and the number. This doesn't always happen, and this space is reserved for a minus sign. If we want to make sure that a number with a minus sign is separated from the '=' sign, we need to add a space between the '=' and the final quote-marks. Another important point about this example is that it shows how to make a program display what is being done. As before, the command word PRINT has to be used to make things appear on the screen, but by using quotes, we can make the computer print whatever we want, not just the results of some arithmetic. Try making the computer print some answers for yourself, using this form of program. Finally, though I typed the number 9.4, the computer has substituted 9.399999 in the listing – a peculiarity of GW BASIC.

With all of this accumulated wisdom behind us, we can now start to look at some other printing actions. PRINT, as far as BASIC is concerned, always means print on to the screen, and you can obtain the word by using **Alt-P**. There is a complete set of the **Alt**-key plus letter codes, and a list is shown in Appendix A. For activating a paper printer (hard copy, it's called), there's a separate instruction LPRINT (and LLIST for program listings). It's not an indication of Welsh design – the L once meant 'line' in the days when printers for computers were huge pieces of machinery that printed a whole line at a time. These instructions are useful to you only if you have a printer connected – but if you are using a machine in this class you are almost certain to have a printer.

Now try the program in Figure 2.3. In GW BASIC, you can try typing the lines in any order that you like, to establish the point that they will be in line-number order when you list the program. When you RUN the program, the words appear on three separate lines. This is because the instruction PRINT doesn't just mean print-on-the-screen. It also means 'take a new line', and start at the left hand side. You will also find, incidentally, that when the words on the screen reach the line above the bottom line, then all the lines apart from the bottom one

```
10 PRINT"This is"
20 PRINT"the famous"
30 PRINT"GW BASIC"
```

Figure 2.3
Illustrating how each PRINT item takes a new line.

appear to move up, and the top line disappears. This is the action that is called 'scrolling', and it's the way that the machine deals with displaying lots of lines on a screen which holds only 25 lines altogether, counting the bottom line. In this example, the words have been placed between quote marks, and they have appeared on the screen just as we typed them, but with no quotemarks showing. This, then, is the sort of programming that is needed when you want to display instructions or other messages on the screen. The real problem, as you'll see when you try it, is of getting the messages to look really neat. Nothing looks worse than printing which has words split, with half of a word on one line and the rest on the next line. Even at this stage, it's possible to make your printing look neat with some care. If you type the `PRINT"` part, then type the words that you want, and continue typing without touching the **RETURN** key until you reach a position on the screen which is directly underneath the quotemark. If you are in the middle of a word, then erase this word by using the **DEL** key. Now type a second quotemark, and then press **RETURN**. Start another line now, using `PRINT"`, and then type the rest of the message in the same way. If you never cross the point where a letter comes directly under a quotemark on the line above, you will never split a word across a line end. The listings in this book are prepared to 40 characters per line so as to fit easily into this book, so you will find many examples in which words that appear to take a couple of lines will fit into one line on your screen.

Now the action of selecting a new line for each `PRINT` isn't always convenient, and we can change the action by using punctuation marks that we call print modifiers. Start this time by acquiring a new habit. Type `NEW` and then press the **RETURN** key. This clears the old program out, and you might also like to use the **Ctrl-L** keys to clear the screen. If you don't use the `NEW` action, there's a chance that you will find lines of old programs getting in the way of new ones. Each time you type a line, you delete any line that had that same line number in an older program, but if there is a line number that you don't use in the new program it will remain stored. In Figure 2.3, for example, the line 15 that you added would be left in store even when you typed a new line 10 and a new line 20.

```
10 PRINT"This is ";
20 PRINT"the great ";
30 PRINT"Big BASIC."
```

Figure 2.4
Using the semicolon to suppress a new line.

Now try the program in Figure 2.4. There's a very important difference between Figure 2.4 and Figure 2.3, as you'll see when you run it. The effect of a semicolon following the last quote in a line is to prevent the next piece of printing starting on a new line at the left hand side. When you run this program, all of the words appear in one line. It would have been a lot easier just to have one line of program that read:

```
10 PRINT "This is the great Big BASIC "
```

to do this, but there are times when you have to use the semicolon to force two different print items on to the same line. We'll look at that sort of thing later in program examples. Meantime, look also at how I have placed a space between the last letter and the last quote mark in lines 10 and 20. The semicolon doesn't just order the computer to prevent a new line being taken, it also forces it to place one item right up against another. If you left no spaces, the words 'is' and 'the' would be printed as 'is the', and 'great' and 'Big' as 'greatBig'. Try removing the spaces, and see for yourself. Turn to Chapter 12 to read how to edit out a space or any other character if you want to avoid having the type the whole line again.

Rows and Columns

Neat printing is a matter of arranging your words and numbers into rows and columns, so we'll take a closer look at this particular art now. To start with, we know already that the instruction PRINT will cause a new line to be selected, so the action of Figure 2.5 should not come as too much of a surprise. Line 10 contains a novelty, though, in the form of two instructions in one line. The instructions are separated by a colon (:), and you can, if you like, have several instructions following one line number in this way, taking several screen lines. You can put instructions together in this way almost indefinitely, but it makes the line cluttered and very difficult to read. In a 'multi-statement' line of this

```
10 CLS:PRINT"This is BASIC"
20 PRINT:PRINT
30 PRINT"-ready to work for you."
```

Figure 2.5
Clearing the screen, and using two program statements in one line.

type, BASIC will deal with the different instructions in a left-to-right order. The instruction CLS should not surprise you either – this clears the screen, and makes the printing start at the top left hand corner. It's the same action as the **CTRL-HOME** or **CTRL-L** keys, but done automatically within the program. Another point about Figure 2.5 is that line 20 causes the lines to be spaced apart. The two PRINT instructions, with nothing to be printed, each cause a blank line to be taken. There are other ways of doing this, as we'll see, but as a simple way of creating a space, it's very handy. Remember, to save typing, that you can type ?, and the machine will convert this into 'PRINT' for you! Now try for yourself a program which will put words on different lines like this. Remember that you have 24 lines to play with on the full screen.

Figure 2.6 deals with columns. Line 20 is a PRINT instruction that acts on the numbers 1, 2, 3 and 4. When these appear on the screen, though, they appear spaced out just as if the screen had been divided into four columns. The mark which causes this effect is the comma, and the action is completely automatic. The comma is on the key next to the letter 'M', and if you use the apostrophe on the key next to the semicolon key, you will not get the same effect. The two can sometimes look rather alike on the keyboard, but completely different on the screen. As line 30 shows, you can't get more than five columns in this way. Anything that you try to get into a sixth column will actually appear on the first

```
10 CLS
20 PRINT 1,2,3,4
30 PRINT 1,2,3,4,5,6,7,8
40 PRINT"one","two","three","four"
50 PRINT"one","two","three","four","five","six","seven","eight"
60 PRINT"This item is too long","two","three"
```

Figure 2.6
Using commas in a PRINT line to create columns.

column of the next line down. The action works for words as well as for numbers, as lines 40 and 50 illustrate. When words are being printed in this way, though, you have to remember that the commas must be placed outside the quotes. Any commas that are placed inside the quotes will be printed just as they are and won't cause any spacing effect. You will also find that if you attempt to put into a column something that is too large to fit, the long phrase will spill over to the next column, and the next item to be printed will be at the start of the next line. Line 60 illustrates this – the first phrase spills over from column 1 into column 2, and the word 'two' is printed starting at the third column. Note also the difference between numbers and words. A word starts in the first position of a column, but a number always starts one space in, leaving room for that + or – sign. The column size is fixed at 14 characters.

Commas are useful when we want a simple way of creating up to five columns. A much more flexible method of placing words on the screen exists, however. This makes use of the command word `TAB` (short for 'tabulate') to position the cursor anywhere along a line, as Figure 2.7 illustrates. For the purpose of using `TAB`, we need to remember that the screen is normally divided into a grid of 80 divisions across and up to 25 down (Figure 2.8). By normally, I mean the situation when you have switched on the computer and done nothing to alter the screen arrangement, like typing `WIDTH 40` to make the screen width 40 characters per line rather than 80. These screen column and line numbers use a range of 0 or 1 to 80 across and 0 to 24 down. When you are entering programs, however, you can use only 24 lines down the screen, so that you have to keep to the numbers 0 to 23 rather than 0 to 24. The word `TAB` can be used only in a line that has started with `PRINT`, and has to be followed by the number of the position, in brackets, with `TAB(0)` and `TAB(1)` being taken as the same position, the left hand side of the screen. If you omit the brackets, the `TAB` instruction is ignored. If you omit a space between `PRINT` and `TAB` you will get an error message. In the example, line 10 clears the screen, and line 20 shows the Left and Right positions on the screen. I have used L and R rather than printing numbers 1

```
10 CLS
20 PRINT TAB(0)"L";TAB(79)"R"
30 PRINT TAB(37)"Centre"
40 PRINT TAB(5)"Start paragraph here..."
50 PRINT TAB(1)"Tab 1 position"
```

Figure 2.7
Tab-taster

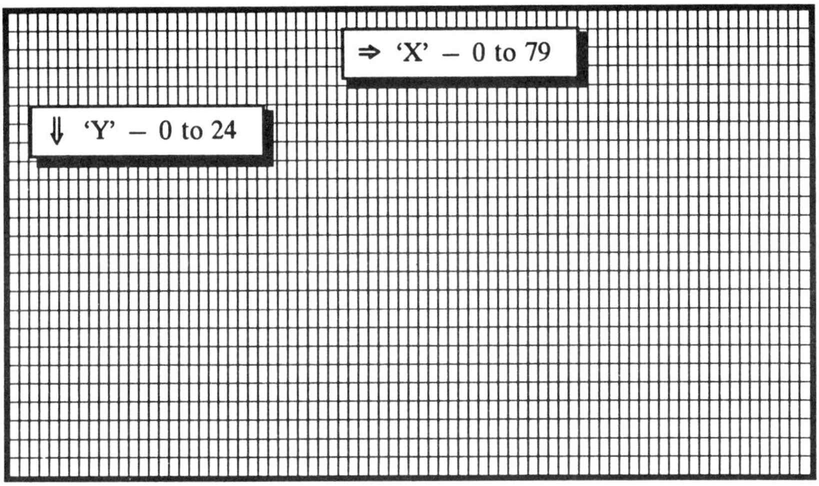

Figure 2.8
The normal screen arrangement, consisting of 80 columns in each line and 24 or 25 lines.

and 80, because the number 80 would have to be printed using TAB(78)! Why? Because a number is printed with a space in front, so the number '80' would take three spaces, TAB positions 78, 79, and 80. Line 30 prints the word 'Centre' near the middle of the screen, and we'll look later at how to calculate the correct tab number for centering a word or phrase. Line 40 simply shows TAB being used to 'indent' a line, which means put a space between the first word and the left hand side. Finally, line 50 illustrates that TAB(1) gives the same position as TAB(0).

Figure 2.9 shows some more secrets of TAB. To tab across a line, you need to use numbers that lie between 0 and 80, but you can use larger numbers. These will *not* have the effect of getting you to a different line, only to some TAB position in the existing line. The actual position is the tab number that remains after you have divided the number by 80. For example, if you use TAB(200), then 200/80

```
10 CLS:PRINT"Top line"
20 PRINT TAB(2)"A"
30 PRINT TAB(5)"TAB(5)";TAB(3*80+5)"Where is this?"
```

Figure 2.9
When the TAB argument exceeds 79, the position is on the same line.

1. **Count the number of characters in the phrase.**
2. **Divide this amount by 2.**
3. **Subtract from 40.**
4. **Use this as the TAB number.**

Figure 2.10
The method of centring a word or phrase in a line.

is 2 and 40 remaining, so the effect is of TAB(40). The listing also shows that you can use an 'expression' inside the TAB brackets. An expression is a bit of arithmetic that has to be worked out, in the example it is 3*80+5. The 5 is the real TAB number here, since the other part of the expression is a multiple of 80.

Oh, yes, how did I position the word 'CENTRE' at the centre of a line in Figure 2.7? This is done by calculating the correct 'across' number for the TAB instruction. The method is shown in Figure 2.10. You have to count up the number of characters that you want to print centred. By characters, I mean letters, digits, spaces and punctuation marks. You then subtract this from 80, and divide the result by 2. Take the whole number part of the answer – forget about any half left over-, and this is then the correct number to use with TAB. Later, you'll see that we can use letters in place of numbers in the TAB and other instructions. This allows us to centre words without all the fuss of counting letters – but that's more advanced programming than we should be thinking about at this point. Right now, you might like to think about how you could display the words 'MY ADDRESS' centred on the screen, with your address shown neatly printed lower down the screen. When you have achieved this, you will have learned quite a lot about the use of TAB.

Figure 2.11 shows a different way of spacing out figures and letters on the screen. This uses the SPC command, and though you might think that it's pretty much the same as TAB, its use isn't. Figure 2.11 shows how. When you TAB the numbers, the first letter of each word is placed in the correct TAB position. Note, incidentally, that you can have more than one TAB in a line. I have shown a

```
10 PRINT TAB(2)"BIG";TAB(20)"BASIC"
20 PRINT TAB(2)"BIG";SPC(20)"BASIC"
```

Figure 2.11
Comparing the actions of TAB and SPC.

semicolon used to separate the second TAB, but this isn't necessary. In line 20, though, I have used SPC(20). This has the effect of putting 20 spaces between the end of 'BIG' and the start of 'BASIC'. That's quite different from having the 'B' of 'BASIC' on the number 20 TAB position. The rule is that you use TAB when you want neat columns, with the first letter of each word starting in the correct place. You use SPC if you want to fix the amount of space between words, even if the words are of different lengths. Not many versions of BASIC allow you as much choice as this! Line 20 shows a semicolon between the end of 'BIG' and the SPC. Once again, this isn't necessary, and you can omit it. I like to use it because it makes it easier to see where the next part of the instruction is placed.

Palace of varieties

So far, our computing has been confined to printing numbers and words on the screen. That's covered two of the main aims of computing, processing and output, but we have to look now at some of the actions that go on before anything is printed. One of these is called assignment. Take a look at the program in Figure 2.12. Type it in, run it, and contrast what you see on the screen with what appears in the program. The first line that is printed is line 20. What appears on the screen is:

```
2 times 23 is 46
```

but the numbers 23 and 46 don't appear in line 20. This is because of the way we have used the letter X as a kind of code for the number 23. The official name for this type of code is a *variable name*.

Line 10 assigns the variable name X, giving it the value of 23. Assigns means that wherever we use X, not enclosed by quotes, the computer will operate with

```
10 CLS
20 X=23
30 PRINT"2 times";X" is";2*X
40 X=5
50 PRINT"X is now";X
60 PRINT"and twice X is";2*X
```

Figure 2.12
Using a variable name, and the effect of changing the number assigned

the number 23 instead. Since X is a single character and 23 has two digits, that's a saving of space. It would have been an even greater saving if we had assigned X differently, perhaps as X=2174.3256, for example. Line 20 then proves that X is taken to be 23, because wherever X appears, not between quotes, 23 is printed, and the 'expression' 2*X is printed as 46. We're not stuck with X as representing 26 for ever, though. Line 30 assigns X as being 5, and lines 40 and 50 prove that this change has been made.

That's why we call X a *variable* – we can vary whatever it is we want it to represent. Until we do change it, though, X stays assigned. Even after you have run the program of Figure 2.12, providing you haven't added new lines or deleted any part of it, you can type PRINT X (or PRINTX, or ?X), and pressing **RETURN** will show the value of X on the screen.

This very useful way to handle numbers in code form can use a 'name' which must start with a letter. You can add to that letter other letters or digits, but not spaces or punctuation marks. You can, however, use the decimal point (.) to make a variable name out of two words. As examples N, name.of.it, and N532 are all names that you can use for number variables, and each can be assigned to a different number. Just to make it even more useful, you can use similar 'names' to represent words and phrases also. The difference is that you have to add a dollar sign ($) to the variable name. If N is a variable name for a number, then N$ (pronounced en-string or en-dollar) is a variable name for a word or phrase. The computer treats these two, N and N$, as being entirely separate and different. The variable names that you can use can be as long as you like, subject to the rules above – but remember that you might have to type them many times over in a program. In general, it helps if the names remind you of what the variable is used for, so that names like Total.less.VAT are a lot more useful than names like T or N5. One thing you always have to look out for, however, is using reserved names such as NAME itself, or TAB or PRINT. No name which is used by BASIC as a command can be used as a variable. By joining words with dots, you ensure that your names are not of this kind, and the same is true of single letter names or letter-number names.

```
10 CLS:ITSNAME$="Modern"
20 A$="BASIC"
30 B$="rules"
40 C$="O.K."
50 PRINT TAB(20);ITSNAME$
60 LOCATE 11,5
70 PRINT"The ";ITSNAME$;" ";A$
80 LOCATE 7,12
90 PRINT ITSNAME$;" ";A$;" ";B$;" ";C$
```

Figure 2.13
String variables and the use of LOCATE. The name of a string variable is distinguished by the use of the dollar sign, often called the string sign.

Serenade for strings

Figure 2.13 illustrates *string variables*, meaning the use of variable names for words and phrases. It also illustrates a very different way of placing things on to the screen without using TAB. LOCATE is a command which is used to control the cursor position. LOCATE has to be followed by a space, and then by up to two numbers, and these numbers have to be separated by a comma. Of these numbers, the second one is just the ordinary TAB number that you have used already. You can, in fact, use LOCATE with just one number, but not omitting the comma, and it will work just like TAB. For example, LOCATE, 5:PRINT"HERE" works like PRINT TAB(5)"HERE". The difference is that TAB must follow PRINT, but LOCATE must come before a PRINT instruction. The first number is a line number, and you are allowed to use numbers between 1 and 24 here. The big difference between LOCATE and TAB, apart from allowing the use of a number to select the screen line, is that LOCATE can put the cursor where you like. If you try to use TAB to move from right to left or up the screen instead of down, you are doomed to fail. LOCATE, however, will put words or numbers anywhere you like, in any order. You can put words at the bottom of the screen, and then work up, if you fancy that sort of thing. You can also place new words over old, which can be rather useful, as we'll see.

Lines 10 to 40 carry out the assignment operations, and lines 50 to 90 show how these variable names can be used. Notice that you can mix a variable name, which doesn't need quotes around it, with ordinary text, which must be surrounded by quotes. You have to be careful when you mix these two, because it's easy to run words together. Note in line 70 how a space has been left between the 'e'of 'The' and the quote. If you omit this space, you will see this part of the phrase printed. In line 50, using TAB(20) gets Modern placed quarter-way across the screen. Line 60 then uses LOCATE 11, 5. The 5 part tabulates so that the phrase in line 70 will be indented, and the 11 selects the eleventh line of the screen. Notice that lines 70 and 90 have had to use spaces between the variable names. This has been done by typing a quote, then pressing the spacebar, then typing another quote. Notice also that we can print on line 11 and then move up to print on line 7. If you use LOCATE with only the line number, as LOCATE 6, then you have a very convenient 'vertical tab' command.

You can use a string variable name for longer phrases if you like. The limit to the number of characters that you can assign to a string variable, however, is 255. Remember that you can type these string variable names as a$ and b$, and the computer will convert them to upper-case. It won't convert anything that you have typed between quotes, though. There wouldn't be much point in printing messages in this way if you wanted the message once only, but when you continually use a phrase in a program, this is one method of programming it so that you don't have to keep typing it. Remember, however that you need to avoid reserved words, and remember also that the computer converts all letters, other than letters enclosed in quotes, into upper-case. If you assign a variable name of N, followed by a variable name of n, then the computer treats N and n as being identical. You can't make N=3 and n=2, and if you try this, then only the assignment which you most recently made will stick.

Getting some input

So far, everything that has been printed on the screen by a program has had to be placed in the program before it is run. Our programs have just consisted of a bit of processing and some output, but with no input apart from whatever was placed in the program. We don't have to be stuck with restrictions like this, however, because the computer allows us another way of putting information, number or name, into a program while it is running. A step of this type is called an *input* and the BASIC instruction word that is used to cause this to happen is also INPUT.

Figure 2.14 illustrates this with a program that prints your name. Now I don't know your name, so I can't put it into the program beforehand. What happens when you run this is that the words:

```
10 CLS
20 LOCATE 2,5:PRINT"What is your name"
30 INPUT NAM$
40 LOCATE 6,3
50 PRINT NAM$;" - this is your life!"
```

Figure 2.14

Using INPUT to assign a string variable from the keyboard. You do not need to use quotes, and the end of the string variable is marked by using the **RETURN** *key.*

```
What is your name
```

are printed on the screen, positioned by the `LOCATE` instruction in line 20. On the line below this you will see a question mark. The computer is now waiting for you to type something, and then press **RETURN**. Until the **RETURN** key is pressed, the program will hang up at line 30, waiting for you. If you're honest, you will type your own name and then press **RETURN**. You don't have to put quotes around your name, nor worry about spaces between parts of your name, simply type it in the form that you want to see printed. When you press **RETURN**, your name is assigned to the variable `NAM$`. The program can then continue, so that line 40 uses `LOCATE` to move the cursor to screen line 6. Line 50 then prints the famous phrase with your name at the start. You could, of course, have answered *Mickey Mouse* or *Donald Duck* or anything else that you pleased. The computer has no way of knowing that either of these is not your true name. Even if you type nothing, and just press **RETURN**, it will carry on, with no name at all. Don't listen to the nutters who tell you that computers know everything! Now that you can type something that can be assigned to a variable, and then use the variable later, you can use all three computing actions. Could you now design a program that asked for your name, and assigned it, and then asked for your address, and assigned that? Could you then arrange it so that it then cleared the screen, and printed your name and address? You now know all of the commands that are needed.

We aren't confined to using string variables along with `INPUT`. Figure 2.15 illustrates an `INPUT` step which uses number variables `A` and `B`. The same procedure is used. When the program hangs up with the question mark appearing, you can type a number and then press the **RETURN** key. This time, though, the question mark will appear on the same line as the message. This is because there are semicolons following the `PRINT` messages in lines 10 and 30. The action of

```
10 CLS:PRINT"Enter a number ";
20 INPUT A
30 PRINT"...and another number, please";
40 INPUT B
50 PRINT:PRINT"The product is ";A*B
```

Figure 2.15
Using INPUT with number variables, in this example keeping the answer on the same line as the question.

pressing **RETURN** will assign your number to A, and allow the program to continue. Lines 30 and 40 then get another number from you, and line 50 proves that the program is dealing with the numbers that you entered. This is a simple example of the computer used with input, process and output. The input steps get your numbers and assign them, the process is just multiplication, and the output is the action of printing the product. You could design a program for yourself which added or subtracted or divided numbers to order in this way. When you use a number variable in an INPUT step, then what you have typed when you press **RETURN** must be a number. If you attempt to enter a string, the computer will refuse to accept it. Some computers stop running at this point, but this BASIC simply prints 'Redo from start', and this gives you another chance of typing a number and pressing **RETURN** again. If your input step uses a string variable, then anything that you type, providing it contains no commas, will be accepted when you press **RETURN**.

The way in which INPUT can be placed in programs can be used to make it look as if the computer is paying some attention to what you type. Figure 2.16 shows an example – but with INPUT used in a different way. This time, there is a phrase following the INPUT instruction. The phrase is placed between quotes,

```
10 CLS
20 INPUT"Type your name, please ";NAM$
30 PRINT
40 PRINT"Thank you, ";NAM$;" - "
50 PRINT"I'm very pleased to meet you."
```

Figure 2.16
Printing a phrase with INPUT – the phrase is put between quotes as it would be if you had used PRINT.

```
10 CLS
20 INPUT"Name and number, please ";NAM$,NUM
30 PRINT:PRINT
40 PRINT"The name is ";NAM$
50 PRINT"The number is ";NUM
```

Figure 2.17
Using a single INPUT statement for two quantities – you must type the first quantity, then a comma, then the second quantity before pressing **RETURN.**

and is followed by a semicolon and then the variable name NAM$. This line 20 has the same effect as the two lines:

```
10 PRINT "Type your name, please";

20 INPUT NAM$
```

and again the question mark appears on the same line as the question, and your reply is also on the same line – unless the length of the name causes letters to spill over on to the next line. Incidentally, you can use a comma in place of a semicolon after the text, like:

```
INPUT"What is your name ", NAM$
```

– and the difference will be that no question mark is printed when the computer is waiting for you to type something and press **RETURN**.

The use of INPUT isn't confined to a single name or number. We can use INPUT with two or more variables, and we can mix variable types in one INPUT line. Figure 2.17, for example, shows two variables being used after one INPUT. One of the variables is a string variable NAM$, the other is the number variable NUM. Now when the computer comes to line 20, it will print the message and then wait for you to enter both of these quantities, a name and then a number. There is just one correct way of entering these quantities, which is to type the name, then a comma, and then the number. Pressing the **RETURN** key will then assign the two variables in one operation, and the computer will continue on its way. If you type only the name and then press **RETURN** you will get the 'Redo from start' message, so that you will than have to type the name again, then a comma, then the number before pressing **RETURN** again. When the inputs are accepted, the name and number will be printed again in lines 40 and 50.

```
10 CLS
20 PRINT"Enter a name that contains a comma and a full-stop"
30 PRINT"Like Cadwallader, Hiram P."
40 LINE INPUT NAM$
50 PRINT "The name is "; NAM$
```

Figure 2.18

If you need to enter something that might contain commas, then LINE INPUT will accept whatever you type until you press **RETURN.** *Only one item can be entered.*

Now suppose that you wanted to write a program that would total sets of four numbers for you. You could have an INPUT step which used four variable names. Remember that you can have names like N1, N2, N3, and N4 if you like. You could write such a program now. Remember to clear the screen, and print some sort of message to remind you what to do. You'll need an INPUT to get the numbers assigned to variables, and then a PRINT step to say what is being printed, and then print the sum of the numbers. Can you make this look neat? One more point. When you use INPUT, you can't type anything which contains a comma, because the machine will assume that this means another variable is being used. If you want an INPUT step to accept anything that you type, then use LINE INPUT in place of INPUT. This is illustrated in Figure 2.18, in which you can enter a name like:

```
Forshaw, Eric M.
```

without getting any error messages. You can even include quote marks in such names, like:

```
Snow, David "Fluffy" G.
```

and everything you type will be included into the string.

Reading the data

There's yet another way of getting data into a program while it is running. This one involves reading items from a list, and it uses two instruction words READ and DATA. The word READ causes the program to select an item from the list. The list is marked by starting each line of the list with the word DATA. The items

```
10 CLS
20 READ NAM$
30 PRINT NAM$;
40 PRINT" is valued at ";
50 READ NUM
60 PRINT NUM
70 DATA Word-processor disk,185
```

Figure 2.19
Using READ and DATA to assign items read from a list to variable names.

of the list can be separated by commas, and they can be strings (with no quotes) or numbers. Each time an item is read from such a list, a '*pointer*' is altered so that the next time an item is needed, it will be the next item on the list rather than the one that was read the last time round. We'll look at this in more detail in the form of examples later, but for the moment we can introduce ourselves to the READ..DATA instructions. Figure 2.19 uses these instructions in a very simple way. Line 20 reads the first item on the list and assigns it to the variable NAM$. This is printed in line 30, with the semicolon keeping printing in the same line so that the phrase in line 40 follows it. The semicolon at the end of line 40 once more keeps the printing in the same line, and line 50 reads the number which is the second item in the list. This is assigned to the variable name NUM (we could just as easily have used NAM$ again, because anything can be assigned to a string) and printed in line 60. This is a good example of why it is so useful to be able to keep printing in one line with semicolons. You can print each bit as it is read, and still end up with a complete line. Note that you don't need any quotes around the name in the DATA line 80. You do, however, have to be careful about how you match your READ and your DATA. If you use a number variable in the READ, like READ A, then what is in the DATA line being read must be a number. If you use a string variable, as in READ A$, then it doesn't matter whether your DATA line contains a number or a string. Remember, though, that if you read a number using READ A$, then you can't carry out any arithmetic on that number. Later on, we'll see how a number in this form can be converted back to number for so that you can carry out arithmetic. If a string in your DATA line must contain a comma, then the whole string has to be surrounded by quotes. For example, if you had one name James Taylor and another Forbes, E.G., then these would have to put in as:

```
DATA James Taylor, "Forbes, E.G."
```

The READ..DATA instructions really come into their own when you have a long list of items that are read by repeating a READ step. These would be items that you would need every time that the program was used, rather than the items you would type in as replies. We're not quite ready for that yet, so having introduced the idea, we'll leave it for now.

The USING modifiers

The PRINT instruction can be made even more useful by adding the word USING. This is a more advanced topic, and if you are reading this book for the first time with no previous experience of BASIC, it's just as well to skip the rest of this chapter. You can come back to it later, when you have more experience with placing text and numbers on the screen. The thinking behind USING is that you often want numbers or strings to be arranged in a particular way. We call this *formatting*, so that USING is a formatting instruction. Suppose, for example, that you were writing a program which had to calculate the amount of VAT on a price. This means finding 15% of the price, and adding this amount of tax on. It's simple enough, but what do you do when the result looks silly? For example, the VAT at 15% on a price of 2.13 is 0.3195. Now you can't add these up to get 2.4495 and print this as a price. Formatting offers one of several ways to get rid of this problem. We might, for example, want to print the final price to two decimal places only, as 2.45. This is where print-formatting comes into its own. We can use symbols in place of the digits of a number to show the computer how we want the number printed. These symbols are placed into a string, and this string or string name is used following PRINT USING.

Figure 2.20 shows how this can be used. Line 10 gets a quantity from you, and assigns it to the number variable PRE.VAT. Line 20 then assigns VAT=.15. This

```
10 INPUT"Price, please ";PRE.VAT
20 VAT=.15
30 VAT.BURDEN=PRE.VAT*VAT
40 FORM$="##.##"
50 PRINT"Total is $";
60 PRINT USING FORM$;PRE.VAT+VAT.BURDEN
```

Figure 2.20
Print formatting with the USING statement. This example shows a formatting string being used to round quantities to two decimal places.

is done rather then using the number .15 in the calculation, because it makes life a lot easier if the tax rate changes. In a long program, finding one line that reads VAT=.15 is much easier that finding each place where the figure .15 has been used. Line 30 then calculates the amount of VAT, assigned to VAT.BURDEN. Line 40 assigns FORM$ to "##.##". This means that a number is to be printed with at least two digits before the decimal point, and only two following. Lines 50 and 60 then print the result. You'll see that if you enter 2.13 as a price, you get the result 2.45. If you enter a price which uses more than two places of figures before the point, then the result is printed with a % sign in front. This is just a reminder that the number is greater than you allowed for. Try altering line 40 to read FORM$="####.##", and then see how the result of entering 2.13 is printed. The spacing is there because you have requested it in the format. Note that the currency sign is the dollar. This is because the printer I am using can print pound signs only by making use of the hashmark (#), and if I make the change, then the FORM$ will appear to be made of pound signs. For working on screen, you can place a pound sign into line 50 in place of the dollar that has been illustrated.

Now there are a lot of formatting marks that can be used in this way, and your manual will probably list them all. At the moment, the only other important one is the one that places a currency sign in the correct place. If you use a formatting string such as $$###.##, then the effect is to place one dollar sign in front of the number. In this case, no spaces are left between the $ sign and the first digit, because this is the formatting for cheque printing, and you wouldn't want to leave a space between the pound sign and the rest of the numbers. Figure 2.21 shows this in action. Line 10 shows six hashmarks in the formatting string, but you'll see if you try small amounts in the INPUT line, that each sum is printed with no space between the dollar sign and the first number, though there is a

```
10 CLS:FORM$="$$######.##":VAT=.15
20 INPUT"Sum due, less tax ";SUM
30 TOT=SUM+VAT*SUM
40 PRINT:PRINT
50 PRINT"Please pay ";USING FORM$;TOT
```

Figure 2.21

Formatting with a floating dollar sign, to ensure that the dollar sign is placed immediately ahead of the money sum with no gaps. GW BASIC is of U.S. origin, and makes no provision for using currency signs other than the dollar.

space between the word 'pay' and the dollar sign sufficient to allow for a sum of six figures of dollars. Now you can start to design the output stage of that accounts program – so long as the quantities are in dollars!

Chapter 3

QUANTITIES OF NUMBERS

So far, we have looked at how a number can be printed and how it can be assigned to a variable name. A lot of the uses for computers make use of numbers (particularly games programs), and so we have to know something about how BASIC deals with numbers. The more specialised instructions that are needed by engineering and scientific programs, however, have been left to the end of this chapter, so that you can take them or leave them. In general, unless your programming is likely to be concerned with engineering or scientific problems, you can leave them.

We can use numbers in programs in two different ways. One way is the use of numbers as constants. A constant is a number whose value can be put into a program at the programming stage, and never changed. You might, for example, be writing a program that deals with VAT at 15%, so that the number .15 keeps appearing. The other way of dealing with numbers is to assign them to variable names. For most purposes, this is a better way of dealing with them than the use of constants. There are two reasons for this. The first reason, one which we have already looked at, is that a variable can be changed easily. Suppose that you have a program in which the amount .15 occurs a dozen times. It's a lot easier to have a line which reads `VAT=.15` early in the program, and which uses `VAT` rather than .15 each time a calculation is carried out. That way, you type the value once only, and if the rate of tax changes (usually meaning increases), then you only have to alter the line that reads `VAT=.15`, not all the places in the program where `.15` is used. That's a very great advantage. The other point is one that we're coming on to, that a variable can often need less memory for storage than a constant.

BASIC allows you to use three different types of number variables. At first, when you are fairly new to computing, the differences do not seem to be very important. Later on, though, you will find that if you are aware of these differences, you can take advantage of them to make your programs run more efficiently. The differences concern the amount of memory that is needed to store each value, the time that the computer takes to work with each value, and the precision of working with each value. The three types of variables are integer, real and double-precision.

Integer variables

An integer variable is one that uses a name which starts with a letter, as usual, and can have any other letters or digits following. It ends with the percent sign, `%`, so that names like `Notit%`, `X2%`, `TOT%` are all valid integer names. Unlike other number variables, though, integer variables obey very strict rules. The value that is assigned to an integer variable must not contain any fractional part. You can correctly assign `A%=5`, for example, but not `A%=5.5`. If you do use `A%=5.5`, then you will find from using `PRINT A%` that the value which has actually been assigned is 5 and the fraction has been completely ignored. In addition, integer variables can use only a limited range of values, from –32768 to +32767. If, for example, you try to assign `A%=- 32800` or `A%=42000` you will get the message '`Overflow`' when the program tries to carry out this command. Overflow means that there isn't enough memory to take the number, because an integer number uses very little memory, less than any other kind of variable. An integer variable value needs only two bytes of memory for storage, though each integer will, in fact, need more than that because one byte is kept to place a code for the variable type, and others are used for the characters of the variable name, one byte for each character.

Because so little memory is used for storage, any program which can make use of only integer variables will run faster and take up less memory than a program which uses the other variable types. If you can be sure that your programs will use only integer number variables, there are two ways that you can take advantage of this. One is to remember to place the integer mark, %, after each number variable name. The other, which is easier when you are using a large program, is to define all of your integers in advance. You can do this by using `DEFINT`. For example, if your program starts with:

```
10 DEFINT J-N
```

```
10 DEFINT A-Z
20 PART=45
30 QUEST=12
40 DEBIT=PART/QUEST
50 PRINT"Int. division gives 45/12 as"; DEBIT
60 PRINT"Normal division gives 45/12 as";PART/QUEST
70 PRINT"The remainder of 45/12 is";PART MOD QUEST
```

Figure 3.1
Arithmetic with integers. Note how the first line declares that any variable name will be an integer, unless this is overruled by the use of a $, ! or # sign.

then any variable name which starts with J, or with K, L, M, or N, will be an integer. This includes names like NOTE2, JJCM, LOQ, KIM, and so on. It's the first letter that counts here. You can over-ride the action of DEFINT if you like by using one of the other symbols. For example, even if you have used DEFINT J-N, you can still assign a number like K1!=101.76. In this case, K1! is a *single-precision* or *real* number, not an integer.

Integers can be used with any arithmetic action, but it's better to stick to addition, subtraction and multiplication. The reason is that division, along with actions like taking square roots, can give results which can contain fractions. Integer numbers cannot make use of fractions, so something has to give. Take a look at Figure 3.1 to illustrate this. Lines 20 to 40 assign integer values to integer variable names. Because the first line has used DEFINT A-Z, all number variables are integer variables. Line 40 has assigned DEBIT as the result of dividing PART by QUEST. Now this result is not an integer, so if it is assigned to an integer variable, the fractional part will be ignored, as line 50 shows when the program runs. The PRINT action, however, is not the same as assignment, and so the correct value is printed in line 60. If you use division in a program that makes use of integer variable, then, you can PRINT the result, but you can't be sure that it will be correct if you assign it to an integer variable. The inability to use fractions, however, does not make integers completely useless for division, because MOD will find out the remainder after a division. The syntax is A MOD B, which will give the remainder after A has been divided by B. This is illustrated in line 70.

It's surprising how many numbers that you deal with are integers. The most obvious use is in a count, but integers can be used for other calculations. If you have a program which deals with small sums of money, for example, you can convert each amount to pennies and then use an integer variable. The program will not be able to handle a sum of more than 32767 pence, which is £327.67, but this can sometimes be quite useful.

Real number variables

A real, or single-precision, number variable can be marked in two different ways. One way is to make use of the exclamation mark (!) following each variable name. Names like Added!, BC2X!, H2! are all valid real number variable names. The alternative is to define a range of variable names as single-precision. This is done by using DEFSNG. For example, DEFSNG A-Z will define all number variables as single-precision, unless some other mark is used following the variable name. A variable like this needs four bytes to store the value in GW BASIC so that only six of the figures of the number to be stored precisely, and a seventh rounded, so that if you assign a number which uses more figures than 6, it will be approximated. For example, if you assign A!=1234567890, then this value will be stored as 1.234568 and 1,000,000,000, meaning that 1.234568 will be multiplied by 1,000,000,000 to give the (approximately) correct value. Figure 3.2 illustrates this, and also shows that numbers which cannot be stored in precise form, like 1/11 and 10/11, will still give the correct answer when added. Numbers of this single-precision kind, then, are perfectly accurate only for values up to 999999 and down to -999999. You can still get accurate results with numbers like 134000000, because the zero's are not 'significant', they are not the part of the number that is coded into six digits. Similarly, numbers like .00000012 are stored accurately, because once again, the zeros are not part of the number that has to be stored in coded form. A lot of computers use a different form of coding

```
10 CLS
20 DEFSNG A-Z
30 DEMO=1234567890#
40 PRINT DEMO
50 A=1/11:B=10/11
60 PRINT A+B
```

Figure 3.2

Single-precision arithmetic. When you specify in a program line a number that is really too large to be represented precisely, the # sign appears when you LIST to remind you that you could get more precision by using a double-precision number.

which allows a larger number of figures, but is not so accurate for any numbers. The BASIC system ensures that arithmetic which uses single precision numbers will be carried out with good accuracy if the numbers contain six significant figures or less. The differences in the ways that some versions of BASIC use to store single-precision numbers and round them for presentation means that there will sometimes be small differences between the number outputs from identical programs if you compare different BASICs. Note that in the listing, the number 1234567890 is terminated with a hashmark. This was not typed – it is put there by the machine when the program is listed as a reminder to you that a number of this size cannot be stored with perfect precision.

Double precision

A variable name which ends with the hashmark (#), or which has been selected by the use of `DEFDBL A-Z`, is a double-precision variable. A variable of this type needs eight bytes to contain the number value. This allows numbers to be stored precisely up to a maximum of fourteen significant figures. If you use no marking for a number variable, it will be a single-precision variable, so that the use of double-precision has to be a deliberate choice. You would use this only when such accuracy was needed – it seldom is – because the use of double precision arithmetic slows down the action of the computer considerably. As it is, the method that is used for storing either single or double precision numbers is comparatively slow in action compared to the methods that are used for some other varieties of BASIC, but at least you don't get 1/11 + 10/11 giving 0.999999. Throughout this book, then, we'll use only as much precision as we need, so you will see the use of the % marks in a lot of the programs in which the default single-precision is not needed. None of the programs here require double-precision arithmetic.

Handling numbers

The amount of computing that we shall cover in this book will persuade you that computers aren't just about numbers. For some applications, though, the ability to handle numbers is very important. If you want to use your computer to solve scientific or engineering problems, for example, then its ability to handle numbers will be very much more important than if you bought it for games, for word processing or even for accounts. It's time, then, to take a very look at the number abilities of BASIC. It is a comparatively brief look because we simply

```
10 CLS
20 X=5
30 PRINT"Value of X is ";X
40 X=X+1:PRINT
50 PRINT"Now after x=x+1, x is";X
```

Figure 3.3
Incrementing a number in BASIC, the fundamental counting action.

don't have space to explain what all the mathematical operations do. In general if you understand what a mathematical term like Sin or Tan or Exp means, then you will have no problems about using these mathematical functions in your programs. If you don't know what these terms mean, then you can simply ignore the parts of this section that mention them.

The simplest and most fundamental number action is counting. Counting involves the ideas of incrementing if you are counting up and decrementing if you are counting down. Incrementing a number means adding 1 to it, decrementing means subtracting 1 from it. These actions are programmed in a rather confusing-looking way in BASIC, as Figure 3.3 shows. Line 20 sets the value of variable `X` as 5. This is printed in line 30, but then line 40 *increments* X. This is done using the odd-looking instruction:

```
X = X + 1
```

meaning that the new value that is assigned to `X` is 1 more than its previous value. The rest of the program proves that this action of incrementing the value of `X` has been carried out.

The use of the = sign to mean 'becomes' is something that you have to get accustomed to. When the same variable name is used on each side of the equality sign, this is the use that we are making of it. We could equally well have a line:

```
X = X-1
```

and this would have the effect of making the new value of `X` one less then the old value. `X` has been decremented this time. We could also use `X = 2*X` to produce a new value of `X` equal to double the old value, or `X = X/3` to produce a new value of `X` equal to the old value divided by three. This two-way use of the equality sign is a peculiarity of all versions of BASIC, and one which is avoided in other languages. Typically, other languages use methods like x==x+1 or x:=x+1 to indicate this 'becomes' action, reserving the single equality sign to mean equality only.

Number operations

An operation means some action that is carried out on the value of a variable. For example, if variable X has been assigned with a value, then 2*X is an operation, the operation of multiplying the value of X by two. Similarly, X-1, X/2 and X+3 are all operations which are carried out on the value of X. Another important operation that is often carried out on numbers is raising to a power (also called exponentiation). The ^ symbol is used by BASIC for this purpose, so that 5^2 means five to the power two, or five squared, and its value is 25. To take another example, 3^3 is three to the power three, or three cubed, whose value is 27. You can use fractional or negative powers in this way. The meaning of a fractional power is a root, so that 4^(1/2) means the square root of two, and 27^(1/3) means the cube root of three. We make use of square roots so often, however, that a special operator SQR can be used in place of ^.5, so that you can type SQR(4) in place of 4^.5 or 4^(1/2). The result, whether you use PRINT SQR(N) or X=SQR(N) will be a single-precision number. A negative power means the inverse of the power of the number, so that 5^-2 means one over five squared, which is 1/25, and 3^-3 means one over three cubed, which is 1/27. A less obvious operation is X=-X. This means that the value of X is to be made negative. If X had the value of +5, then the action of X=-X would make X equal to –5; if X had the value of –5, then X=-X would make the value +5. This operation is called negation, or unary minus.

These operations can be carried out on numbers, or on variables which have been assigned to number values. Number operations cannot be carried out on string variables, however. Figure 3.4 lists the operations which are of importance

Anything contained in brackets.	**(x)**	*highest priority*
Raising to a power (exponentiation).	^	
Multiply and divide.	* /	
Add and Subtract.	+ –	*low priority*

Figure 3.4
Some of the number operators in order of precedence.

Bracketed items
Exponentiation
Negation (using negative sign)
Multiplication and floating point division (* and /)
**Integer division using **
Modulo (remainder) using MOD
Addition and subtraction
Relations (<,< =,=,> =,>,< >)
NOT
AND
OR and XOR

Figure 3.5
The full order of precedence for operators.

to you at this stage. These operations are given in order of precedence, and this is the next subject that we have to devote some attention to before we leave the subject of number operations.

When we deal with one operation at a time, programmed in separate lines, the order in which operations are carried out is strictly the order of the line numbers. For example, if you program:

```
10 X=12.5
20 Y=2.4*X
30 Z=Y-4
```

– then the order of actions is assignment, then multiplication, and then subtraction. It may not be so easy to see what would happen if you programmed `Z=2.4*X-4z`. As it happens, this gives the same answer, because `X` is multiplied by 2.4, and then 4 is subtracted. You could imagine, however, that the command could be interpreted as subtracting 4 from `X` and then multiplying the result by 2.4. Take another example – what would you expect to be the result of:

```
5.4-2.2*3+4.6/1.5-2.2*1.2
```

If your reply is –.7733333333333, then you have taken the numbers in the correct groupings (and your calculator is a good one!). You do not carry out the operations in the order in which they are written. Instead, you carry them out in the order of precedence, which is multiplication, division, addition and subtraction, ***MDAS*** if you need a short way of remembering it. What this means is that multiplication and division steps are always carried out first, and then the addition and subtraction steps. The computer will always use this order of precedence unless you over-ride it by the use of brackets. Figure 3.5 shows the full order of precedence including unary minus and exponentiation operations. Note that the equality (=) has quite a low order of precedence.

There are often times when you want to impose an order of precedence which is not the same as that of the machine. For example, you may want to subtract 4 from the value of `X` and then multiply by 2. If you programmed this as `2*X-4`, you would not achieve this, because the order of precedence would ensure that the value of `X` was multiplied by 2 before the number 4 was subtracted. Similarly, if you typed `X- 4*2`, the computer would multiply 4 by 2, giving 8, before subtracting this value from the value of `X`. If you want to make the computer carry out a subtraction before a multiplication, then you have to enclose the subtraction in brackets. By typing `(X-4)*2`, you force the operation of `X-4` to be carried out first, and the multiplication second. This is because the use of brackets has a higher order of precedence than multiplication. Whatever you have placed within the brackets will be carried out in normal order of precedence. For example, if you have:

```
(5-1.2*X)-(4+1.6/Y)
```

then the order of actions will be to work out the contents of the brackets first, in normal precedence. The value of `X` will be multiplied by 1.2, and this result will be subtracted from 5. The value 1.6 will be divided by the value of `Y`, and 4 will be added. The value of the result of the second bracket will then be subtracted from the value of the result of the first bracket to obtain the final result. When one set of brackets is contained inside another (nested brackets), then whatever is enclosed in the innermost brackets will be carried out first. When this has been done, the action of the outer brackets will be executed, and following that, anything that was placed outside all the brackets. This order of precedence of brackets applies to all operations, not just to number operations as we shall see illustrated later when we deal with strings.

Formula translation

The first uses of computers were for solving equations, and one of the first useful computing languages was *Fortran*, an abbreviation of FORmula TRANslation.

Fortran is still used to some extent in mainframe computers, but BASIC is just as capable of working with formulae, and many other computing languages have been devised with similar capabilities. If all that you wanted to do was to work out one single answer from a formula, then a calculator would be the quickest and most obvious method. Where the computer becomes essential is when the formula is a large and tedious one, and a very large number of answers have to be worked out.

Take a simple example first, Figure 3.6. The quantities A and B represent the lengths of the shorter sides of a right-angled triangle (remember Pythagoras in the days when schools taught real mathematics?) and C represents the length of the longest side. These sizes are strictly related by this formula, which states that C squared equals A squared plus B squared. The value of C is thus found by taking the square root of each side of the equation, so that C is equal to the square root of the sum of A squared added to B squared. Suppose that we have

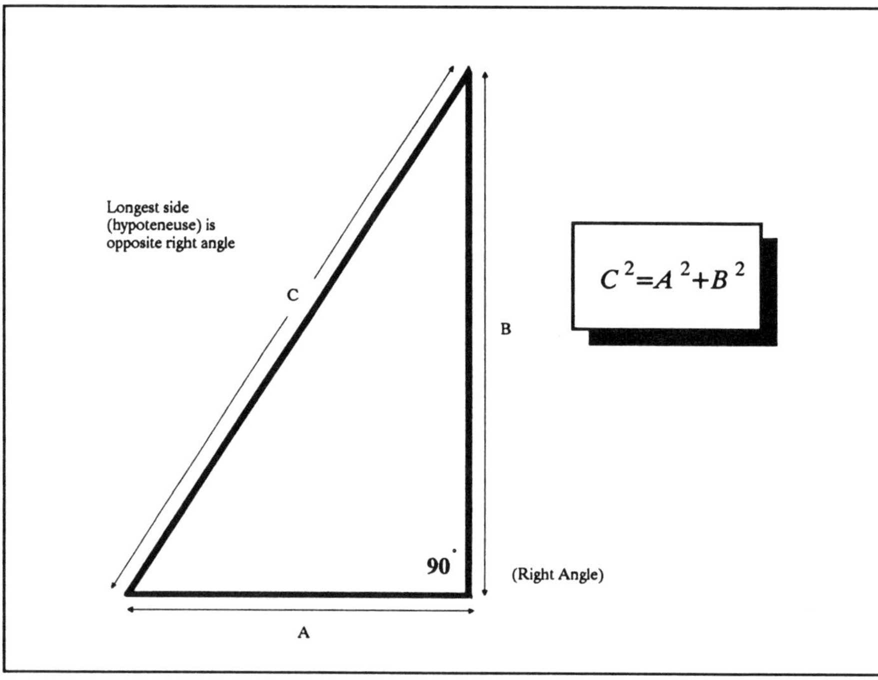

Figure 3.6
Pythagoras' formula for finding the size of one side of a right-angled triangle when the other two sides are of known sizes.

assigned number values to variables A and B, how do we type a line which will give the value of C?

The important thing to remember is precedence. The square root action will always take precedence over addition, so that if we program this as :

```
C=SQR(A^2)+B^2
```

then the value of A will be squared and then rooted, leaving it unchanged, and added to the value of B squared. This is not what we want. What we have to do is to carry out the addition of the squares completely within brackets, and have the SQR preceding the brackets:

```
C=SQR(A^2+B^2)
```

so that the squaring is carried out first, then the addition, and finally the square root action.

Formula translation will very often include the use of trigonometric quantities such as the sines, cosines and tangents of angles. It is important to remember that these trigonometric actions will have very high precedence, so that a number value for a SIN, COS or TAN will be found even before anything else inside a bracket is worked out. SIN, COS, TAN, and all of the others are called functions of angles, meaning that they are a method of finding a value for a number. The computer uses many of these functions, each of which is said to *return a number.* By this, we mean that the result of the action will always be a number if the function has been used correctly. BASIC assumes that the values of angles will be in units of radians, and Figure 3.7 shows the relationship between radians and the more commonly used degrees for angular measure. GW BASIC has no built-in converter for getting radian values from degrees, or degrees from radians, and no pre-assigned numeric value for PI.

The radian is defined so that pi radians are equal to 180 degrees. This makes the radian equal to about 57.296 degrees. To convert in the opposite direction, one degree = 0.01745 radians.

Figure 3.7
Degree and radian measure for angles.

Number functions

Figure 3.8 illustrates the use of some of these number functions. A number function in this sense is an instruction which operates on a number to produce another number. Line 10 picks the value of 2.5 for X. Line 20 then prints the value of X squared, meaning X multiplied by X. This is programmed by typing X^2, and the character which the PC computer uses for this is on the '6' key. To get the square root of the number that has been assigned to X, we use the instruction word SQR. An alternative is X^.5, but SQR(X) is easier to type and remember. For other roots, like the cube root you can use expressions like X^(1/3) and so on. LOG(X) produces the natural logarithm of X. This is not the type of logarithm that you may want, and to find the ordinary (base 10) log, you have to divide this result by log(10). This needs some other alterations if you are working with the logarithms of fractions, but you'll have to consult a textbook of mathematics for that one, there isn't room here.

Figure 3.9 illustrates the various number functions that can be used, with a brief explanation of what each one does. Some of these actions will be of use only if you are interested in programming for scientific, technical or statistical purposes. Others, however, are useful in unexpected places, such as in graphics programs. We'll look at a few of them now, though, because they will be used in many of the program examples that follow. RND is a function that is particularly important in a lot of games and graphics programs. RND means random, and if you assign X=RND, then what you get is a number which has been picked at random, and which is something between 0 and 1. It will never be quite zero, or quite 1, however. The main problem when RND is used is to ensure that it does not produce the same sequence of numbers each time the program runs. This is because the number is calculated from a starting number which is called a *seed*.

```
10 CLS:X=2.5
20 PRINT"x squared is";X^2
30 PRINT
40 PRINT"Its square root is";SQR(X)
50 PRINT
60 PRINT"Its natural log. is";LOG(X)
70 PRINT"and its ordinary log is";LOG(X)/LOG(10)
```

Figure 3.8

Some of the number functions in use. Note that the argument (the number that is being operated on) is always contained in brackets.

The argument of a function of this kind is the number (or string) contained in the brackets that follow the keyword.

`ABS()`	Absolute value, stripped of – sign.
`ASC()`	ASCII code for first character of string.
`ATN()`	Angle in radians whose tangent is supplied.
`CDBL()`	Convert number to double-precision format.
`CEIL()`	Round number up to next larger integer.
`CINT()`	Convert number into integer form (if possible).
`COS()`	Give cosine of argument (angle in radians).
`CSNG()`	Convert number into single-precision form.
`CVI()`	Convert number in random access file form into integer form.
`CVS()`	Convert number in random access file form into single-precision form.
`CVD()`	Convert number in random access file form into double-precision form.
`DEFINT`	Declare letters for integer variables.
`DEFSNG`	Declare letters for single precision variables.
`DEFDBL`	Declare letters for double precision variables.
`EXP()`	Exponential (e) raised to power of argument.
`FIX()`	Strip fractions to give integer.
`INT()`	Convert to integer by rounding.
`LOG()`	Give logarithm to base e of argument.
`RANDOMIZE`	Provide starting number ('seed') for random number generation.
`RND`	Provide random fraction.
`SGN()`	Sign of number.
`SIN()`	Sin of argument (angle in radians).
`SQR()`	Square root of argument.
`TAN()`	Tangent of argument (angle in radians)

Figure 3.9

A full list of the number functions of GW BASIC. Many of these will be of little use to you unless you specialise in mathematical work.

Normally, the seed will be the same each time a program runs. To get around this, make one of the early instructions in a program:

```
RANDOMIZE TIMER
```

– and this will have the effect of setting a different seed each time you use the program, because TIMER is a number variable that is used in the clock actions. Don't worry if this expression appears to be baffling at present, the action will be clearer when you have worked your way through the book.

Another function that comes in useful here is INT. INT causes only the integer part (the whole number part) of a number to be used. It's a way of chopping off fractions, and it's very often found used along with RND. For example, suppose you want a random number which lies between 1 and 10. The method of getting this is:

```
X%=INT(RND(1)*10+1)
```

The RND part will generate something greater than 0 and less than 1. Multiplying by 10 will give something which can take values from less than 1 to less than 10. Adding 1 gives a range of just over 1 to less then 11. Taking INT then gives a range of 1 to 10.

SGN is a function that can return –1, 0, or +1. It is used in the form X%=SGN(Y). If Y is negative, then X% will be –1. If Y is positive, X% will be +1. If y is zero, then X% is also zero. It's a good way of finding out what the sign of a number is. You might, for example, want a routine that rejected negative numbers, perhaps because you wanted to take square roots.

There are three functions that deal with number precision problems. A typical problem is that one single-precision number has to be divided by another, and because the quotient is likely to take more places of decimals than either number, you want the quotient as a double precision number. You might think you could get round this by using, for example, res#=num1/num2, where num1 and num2 are the single-precision numbers and res# is the double-precision result. It doesn't work out, however, because dividing one single-precision number by another always gives a single-precision result, no matter what type of variable we assign it to. To get around this, you can use CDBL to convert single to double precision, so that the assignment:

```
res#=CDBL(num1)/CDBL(num2)
```

will provide the correct degree of precision for res#. As it happens, if we had used CDBL(num1)/num2 we would get the same effect, because having one quantity in double precision will ensure that the other one will be converted automatically.

The two other conversion functions of this type are CINT (convert to integer) and CSNG (convert to single precision).

Defined Functions

The predefined or intrinsic functions such as SIN, COS and TAN, which are programmed into the BASIC machines, are often all that will be needed to solve an equation. A few varieties of BASIC, including our BASIC, allow an extension of the use of functions, which is the creation of a new function from existing ones. This is a particularly useful way of programming a formula, and it is known as a *user-defined function*.

The use of a user-defined function is particularly helpful in a program which makes a lot of use of an action. Suppose, for example, the we frequently need to find the root of the sum of squares in a program. Instead of programming C=SQR(A^2+B^2) each time, we define a function of our own, which will be called RT. If we want to find the root of the sum of A^2 and B^2, then all we need to do is to use the function RT. This is done in the form FN RT(A, B). The FN part is used to indicate to the computer that a defined function is to be used. RT indicates which (of possibly more than one) function is to be used, and A and B are the numbers (or parameters) which the function will need to use. The important thing about a defined function as used in BASIC is that you are not confined to the use of variable names A and B. Your variables could be X and Y, or P and Q, any pair of variable names that you like. The only condition is that both of the variables must have been assigned with number values before the defined function is called into use. By making use of a defined function, then, a formula can be typed once only, and then subsequently used in a program by making use of a function name such as RT. You must be sure that the name which you pick is not the name of an existing function such as SIN, COS, TAN etc.

Figure 3.10 shows a very simple example of a defined function in use. Line 20 starts with DEF to indicate to the computer that this is the definition of the function. This is followed by the name of the function, FN RT, and the parameter name which will be used, N in this example. This definition of what FNRT is must be made before the function is used. Some versions of BASIC allow such a definition to be put at the end of a program, but for our BASIC you must place it near the start, certainly before the function is used. Line 30 then asks you for a number, and line 50 prints the value of the square root of this number. This is because FN RT was defined as SQR(N), the square root of a number. The important point here is that the definition in line 20 uses a variable N, but when

```
10 CLS
20 DEF FN RT(N)=SQR(N)
30 INPUT"Number, please";A
40 IF SGN(A)=-1 THEN A=-A
50 PRINT"The square root is";FN RT(A)
60 GOTO 30
```

Figure 3.10

A simple defined function that finds a square root – but allows you to use negative or positive numbers.

we use the function, the variable name is A. This is a very important point about defined functions, and one which makes them very useful. If the function were able to make use of only the variable names N, then any other variable value that we wanted to use would have to be reassigned. For example, if our value were held as variable X, we would need a line such as:

```
1000 N=X
```

before we could find the root value. Using the form of defined function that BASIC permits avoids this extra action, which is called passing variable values. The action of finding roots repeats, because of the GOTO 30 command in line 60. This ensures that the lines 30 to 60 are repeated until you press the **CTRL** and **BREAK** keys together.

Now look at another slightly more complicated defined function, in Figure 3.11. This time, the defined function works out the square root of the sum of two squares, using two numbers which in line 20 are referred to as variable names A and B. Line 20 also gives the definition of the function as equal to SQR(A^2+B^2), the familiar root of the sum of the squares. The definition of the function must be completed in one line. In line 30, two numbers are asked for. When you type the two numbers and use **RETURN**, the next line will print the value of the root of the sum of the squares. Note once again that the numbers are represented by variable names NUM1 and NUM2, and we can 'call' the function by using FN HYPOT(NUM1, NUM2), even though the definition used variable names A and B. The use of a defined function is a very useful way of making the computer carry out the actions of applying a formula to a set of numbers. The numbers are assigned to variable names, and then put into the defined function formula by using an instruction such as FN formula(A, B, C, D), using as many variables as you need numbers to put into the formula. The only thing that you have to

```
10 CLS
20 DEF FN HYPOT(A,B)=SQR(A^2+B^2)
30 INPUT" Two numbers, please";NUM1,NUM2
40 PRINT"Third side is ";FN HYPOT(NUM1,NUM2)
50 GOTO 30
```

Figure 3.11
A defined function for finding the longest side (the hypotenuse) of a right-angled triangle.

watch is that you use the correct number of variables. If your `DEF FN` formula used four variables, then your `FN` formula must also use four, no more, no less. In addition, if the order of numbers is important you must keep to it.

Tests and approximations

When you make use of number functions in formulae, or to create defined functions, you always have to be careful about approximations. If you don't mark number variables with a # or % sign, then you will be working with single-precision numbers, and the accuracy will be good enough for all but the most exacting requirements. What you have to watch, though, is that you have got the formula correct, and that you have programmed it correctly. If you have spelled an instruction word wrongly, or used it in the wrong way, then you will get a '`Syntax error`' message when the program runs. If you have made a mistake in programming the formula, but have used the instruction words correctly, there will be no error messages. The answers, however, will be wrong! You won't know this unless you test the program, using numbers that will produce an answer that you know. For example, if you are testing a defined function for the root of the sum of squares, you would test with numbers like 3 and 4, or 5 and 12. The result from 3 and 4 should be 5, and if you get anything else then something is not correct. Testing like this is very important if the formula is a complicated one, because if you can't rely on the computer to give correct results there isn't much point about using a computer!

Numeric arrays

So far, we've looked at variable names for numbers with the idea that we might be using just a few numbers in our programs. Suppose that we want to use hundreds of numbers, though? Just to give an example, suppose we are keeping records of the amounts of money that are paid into a Christmas Club fund. There might be a couple of hundred members of the Club, and each one will contribute a different amount. How do you keep records of this? You can't very well use a different variable name, like `A`, `B`, `C` ... for each member. This would use up too many letters, and you would find it difficult to keep track of the variable names. An application like this requires a rather different use of a number variable.

This new use is a number or numeric array. A numeric array just means a set of numbers that you want to keep together as a set. Examples such as Christmas Club payments, subscriptions, examination marks, scores in League matches, are all numbers that belong to a set. The computer allows you to use just one variable name for a set like this. You then distinguish between one item and the next by using a 'reference number', which is called a 'subscript'. The subscript number follows the variable name, within brackets. For example, you might want to use the variable name of SUBS for subscriptions to a club. The first member's subscription is assigned to variable `SUBS(1)` (pronounced *subs of one*), the next to `SUBS(2)` (*subs of two*) and so on. The important point is that the number, 1, 2, or whatever, can be a numeric variable. We can refer to `SUBS(X)`, and make `X` equal whatever we like. If you want to find what member number 27 paid this year, just make `X=27` and `PRINT SUBS(X)`, and it's on your screen!

This very different way of handling numbers in lists is something that we'll come back to. The reason is that arrays are best handled by a program that allows actions to be repeated, and we're not at this stage yet. Watch out for more in Chapter 5.

Chapter 4

STRINGS ATTACHED

In Chapter 3, we took a look at numeric functions. If numbers turn you on, that's fine, but string functions are in many ways more interesting. What makes them that way is that the really eye-catching and fascinating actions that the computer can carry out, are so often done using string functions. A string means any collection of up to 255 characters, the sort of thing that we put between quotes in a PRINT action, or assign to a string variable name like A$, or BC$. What's a string function, then? As far as we are concerned, a string function is any action that we can carry out with strings. That definition doesn't exactly help you, I know, so let's look at an example, in Figure 4.1.

This shows two strings, A$ and B$, being assigned in lines 20 and 30. A$ is assigned the string value "One" and B$ is set to "Two" – remember that you

```
10 CLS
20 A$="one"
30 B$="Two"
40 PRINT A$+B$
50 A$="12":B$="34"
60 C$=A$+B$
70 PRINT C$
```

Figure 4.1
Concatenating strings, which means joining one string to the end of another.

must use quotes in an assignment like this. Line 40 shows what you get for A$+B$. What is printed on the screen is:

```
OneTwo
```

the two strings run together. The + sign, then, is a kind of operator for strings, but the operation is not addition in the way that we add numbers. To distinguish it, this use is called *concatenation*, which sounds like something that happens on the tiles at night. The rest of the program shows that concatenation works in the same way even if the strings are of number quantities. If you PRINT A$ or PRINT B$ after line 50 has been run, you will see 12 for A$ and 34 for B$, but C$ is 1234, not 46. The + is not an addition sign as far as strings are concerned, it is a joining sign. Concatenation can be useful if you have carried out actions on two different strings and you then want to join them. Suppose, for example, that you have a mailing list program, and to save on memory space you allow names of up to ten characters only. When a name is entered, you don't chop off all the characters after the tenth. This would result in JONATHAN MILKMAN being chopped to JONATHAN M because the space counts as a character. The more sensible method is to separate the surname from the forename, and chop each to ten characters. Both parts of JONATHAN MILKMAN then can be joined again. If the surname is long, as with SILAS PREPONDERANCE, then the name appears as SILAS PREPONDERA, which is enough to recognise it.

Now for some other string functions. Figure 4.2 shows a program that prints:

```
BIG BASIC
```

as a title. What makes it more eye-catching is the fact that the word is printed with twelve asterisks (*) on each side. The asterisks are produced by a string function whose instruction word is STRING$. STRING$ means 'make a string out of', and it has to be followed by two items placed within brackets and separated by a comma. The first of these items is the number of identical characters that

```
10 CLS
20 A$=STRING$(12,"*")
30 PRINT TAB(23)A$+"BIG BASIC"+A$
```

Figure 4.2
Using STRING$ and concatenation to frame a title.

you want to put into this string. The second item is the character itself. In this example, we've used the * character, and it has had to be placed between quotes.

STRING$ is a useful way of creating strings of one character, and it's particularly useful when we come to look at graphics characters. There are two more points about the use of STRING$. The first is that you can't create a string of more than 255 characters, so that the first number in a STRING$ expression has to be 255 or less. If you attempt to use a larger number, you will get the 'Illegal function call' error message. The other point about STRING$ is that the second item in the brackets can be a number, with no quotes. Each character that is used by the BASIC computer is represented by a code number, using what we call ASCII code. The letters stand for *American Standard Code for Information Interchange*, and the ASCII (pronounced Askey) code is one that is used by most computers. Figure 4.3 shows a list of the main ASCII code numbers and the characters that they produce on an average printer. In place of the asterisk that we have used between quotes in Figure 4.2, then, we could have used the number 42, making the instruction into STRING$(12,42), which is shorter.

The number characters of normal ASCII code extend only from 32 to 127. The code numbers above 127 are used by BASIC for other purposes, and we can select how we make use of them. Figure 4.4 gives a flavour of this, something that we'll investigate in much more detail in Chapter 7. By using the number 215 in the STRING$ command in line 20, we select a centipede *pattern* rather than a letter *character*, so producing a more effective looking frame for the name.

The long and the short of it

String variables allow us to carry out a lot of operations that can't be done with number variables. One of these operations is finding out how many characters are contained in a string. Since a string can contain up to 255 characters, an automatic method of counting them is rather useful, and LEN is that method. LEN has to be followed by the name of the string variable, within brackets, and the result of using LEN is always a number so that we can print it or assign it to a number variable. Since the number is always an integer, it should be assigned to an integer variable unless the program is a very short and simple one.

Figure 4.5 shows a useful example of LEN in use. This program uses LEN as a way of printing a string called T$ centred on a line. This is an extremely useful routine to use in your own programs, because its use can save you a lot of tedious counting when you write your programs. The principle is to use LEN to find out

Code/Char		*Code/Char*		*Code*	*/Char*
32	<space>	64	@	96	‘
33	!	65	A	97	a
34	"	66	B	98	b
35	# or £	67	C	99	c
36	$	68	D	100	d
37	%	69	E	101	e
38	&	70	F	102	f
39	’	71	G	103	g
40	(	72	H	104	h
41	)	73	I	105	i
42	*	74	J	106	j
43	+	75	K	107	k
44	,	76	L	108	l
45	-	77	M	109	m
46	.	78	N	110	n
47	/	79	O	111	o
48	0	80	P	112	p
49	1	81	Q	113	q
50	2	82	R	114	r
51	3	83	S	115	s
52	4	84	T	116	t
53	5	85	U	117	u
54	6	86	V	118	v
55	7	87	W	119	w
56	8	88	X	120	x
57	9	89	Y	121	y
58	:	90	Z	122	z
59	;	91	[	123	{
60	<	92	\	124	|
61	=	93	]	125	}
62	>	94	^	126	~
63	?	95	_	127	DELete

Figure 4.3

The ASCII code numbers and the corresponding characters. Values from 128 to 255 are also used, but have no ***standard*** *interpretation.*

```
10 CLS
20 A$=STRING$(12,215)
30 PRINT TAB(23)A$+"BIG BASIC"+A$
```

Figure 4.4
Making use of some of the numbers between 128 and 255 in the ASCII set.

how many characters are present in the string T$. This number is subtracted from 80, and the result is then divided by two. If the number of characters in the string is an odd number, then the number 'TB' will contain a .5, but this is completely ignored by TAB when the string is printed. Note how brackets have been used in line 20. The easiest way of writing a line like this is to start at the innermost brackets. For example, you know that you need to find the length of the string, T$, so you write LEN(T$) first. You have to subtract this from 37, so you then add this, to get 37 – LEN(T$). The whole of this, not just LEN(T$), must be divided by two, so you must place brackets around it, to get (37-LEN(T$))/2, which is then assigned to TB. You will find that this 'inside to outside' approach pays off when you have to work with lots of brackets. If you are uncertain about using brackets, be thankful that you are programming in BASIC, and not in the language called *Lisp*! The whole process of centering could be done in one line, but I have shown it in three lines so that you can see what the steps are. In Chapter 6, we'll look at ways of re-writing actions like this so that they can be called up when we want them, just like another instruction word. We should also start now to be more fussy about number variable types, and we could start by using TB% in this example, since this must be an integer.

```
10 CLS:T$="BASIC Computing"
20 TB=(80-LEN(T$))/2
30 PRINT TAB(TB)T$
40 REM You can assign anything you like to T$
```

Figure 4.5
Using LEN to print a string centred on a line. If your string is more than 80 characters long, you will have to split it into pieces of less than 80 characters and print them separately.

By the left: Slice!

The next group of string operations that we're going to look at are called slicing operations. The result of slicing a string is another string, a piece copied from the longer string. Note that this is a copying process, nothing is removed from the longer string when the copy is made. The piece that is copied can be printed or assigned as you please. String slicing is a useful way of finding what letters or other characters are present at different places in a string.

All of that might not sound terribly interesting, so take a look at Figure 4.6. The strings A$ to E$ are assigned in lines 20, 30 and 40. There's a new instruction in line 50, in the form of SPACE$. SPACE$ is a way of assigning a string which consists of spaces, as many as the number that is enclosed in the brackets. It's a simple and useful way of creating spaces, which saves having to use lines like:

```
100 SP$="                              "
```

which are not easy to follow because you have to count the number of spaces for yourself, or:

```
100 SP$=STRING$(5,32)
```

In this example, line 50 assigns just one space to the variable S$, so that we can use it to space words. Line 60 then prints some slices from each string on the screen. Now how did the letters BASIC appear? The instruction LEFT$ means 'copy part of a string starting at the left hand side'. LEFT$ has to be followed

```
10 CLS
20 A$="Battersea":B$="After"
30 C$="Surgery":D$="Intensive"
40 E$="Care"
50 S$=SPACE$(1)
60 PRINT LEFT$(A$,1)+LEFT$(B$,1)+LEFT$(C$,1)+LEFT$(D$,1)
  +LEFT$(E$,1) +S$+"Computing"
```

Figure 4.6

String slicing with LEFT$, and the use of SPACE$ to create a space. Despite the name, slicing is a copying action, but it copies only a portion of the original.

```
10 CLS
20 INPUT"Surname, please ",A$
30 B$=LEFT$(A$,5)
40 PRINT"Short form is ";B$
```

Figure 4.7
Extracting a part from a name. This routine is often used to speed up the action of searching for a name in a list.

by two quantities, within brackets and separated by a comma. The first of these quantities is the variable name for the string that we want to slice, A$ in the first example. The second is the number of characters that you want to slice (copy, in fact) from the left hand side. The effect of `LEFT$(A$,1)` is therefore to copy the first letter from '`Battersea`', giving '`B`'. The next `LEFT$(B$,1)` copies the '`A`' from '`After`', and so on. The last part of line 60 then adds the word '`Computing`' to these letters. How about trying for yourself a program which asks for your forename and surname, and then prints your initials?

You aren't confined to printing or assigning just one letter, of course. Suppose that you are working on a mailing list program for the local darts club. The names and addresses which are printed on the letters will be complete, but to save your typing finger(s), you want to be able to list the names on the screen using just the first five letters. You can then command the computer to find an address by just typing the first five letters of the surname. The part of this problem that we can solve easily now is the first five letters bit. Figure 4.7 shows how this would be arranged. Line 20 asks for a surname to be typed, and line 30 then uses `LEFT$(A$,5)` to copy the first five letters of the name. In this example, no attempt has been made to do any more, and later on, we'll look at ways of controlling this better, so that all of the names can be kept in a list, and the first five letters copied as required. One thing at a time, if you please.

Eyes right

String slicing isn't confined to copying a selected piece of the left hand side of a string. We can also take a copy of characters from the right hand side of a string. This particular facility isn't used quite so much as the `LEFT$` one, but it's useful none the less. Figure 4.8 illustrates a simple use of this instruction to

```
10 CLS
20 READ D$
30 PRINT"Part No. is ";RIGHT$(D$,6)
40 DATA PD1Q-747-164027
```

Figure 4.8
Slicing from the right-hand side of a string using RIGHT$. The number is the number of characters counted from the right hand side.

avoid having to use the whole of a complicated code number. Take a look, for example, at the code number on your telephone bill. There are other serious uses like this. You can, for example, extract the last four figures from a string of numbers like 010-242-7016. I said a string of numbers deliberately, because something like this has to be stored as a string variable rather than as a number. If you try to assign this to a number variable, you'll get a silly answer. Why? Because when you type

```
N = 010-242-7016
```

then the computer assumes that you want to subtract 242 from 10 and 7016 from that result.The value for `N` is –7248, which is not exactly what you had in mind! If you use `N$="010-242-7016"` then all is well.

Middle cut

There's another string slicing instruction which is capable of much more than either `LEFT$` or `RIGHT$`. The instruction word is `MID$`, and it has to be followed by three items, within brackets, and using commas to separate the items. Item 1 is the name of the string that you want to slice, as you might expect by now. The second item is a number which specifies where you start slicing. This number is the number of the characters counted from the left hand side of the string, and counting the first character as 1. The third item is another number, the number of characters that you want to slice, going from left to right and starting at the position that was specified by the first number.

It's a lot easier to see in action than to describe, so try the program in Figure 4.9. Line 20 assigns to `A$` the phrase `"Using Common putty."`, and line 30 then assigns a new string, `B$` which is made out of slices from `A$`. The first slice uses

```
10 CLS
20 A$="Using Common putty."
30 B$=MID$(A$,7,3)+MID$(A$,14,3)+MID$(A$,3,3)
40 PRINT B$
```

Figure 4.9

Portions can be sliced from the middle of strings using MID$ with two numbers. The first number is the position of the first character sliced, counting from the start, the second number is the number of characters to be copied.

`MID$(A$,7,3)`. If you count the characters in `A$`, including spaces, you'll find that the seventh character is the '`C`' of '`Common`'. Remember that the counting for `MID$` starts at 1, not at 0 like so many other counting actions. The slice starts with the '`C`', and is of three characters, '`Com`' from this part of the phrase. The other two slices also take three characters each, to make up the word '`Computing`', and this is what appears on the screen.

One of the features of all of these string slicing instructions is that we can use variable names or expressions in place of numbers. Figure 4.10 shows a more elaborate piece of slicing which uses an expression, along with a random number. Line 20 ensures that the numbers are more truly random, and the action all starts innocently enough in line 30 with a request for your name. Whatever you type is assigned to variable `NAM$`, and in line 40 the length of this string is found and assigned to L%. Line 50 then generates a number, at random, which will

```
10 CLS
20 RANDOMIZE TIMER
30 INPUT "Your surname, please ",NAM$
40 L%=LEN(NAM$)
50 R%=INT(RND*L%)+1
60 COD$=MID$(NAM$,R%,1)
70 PRINT"Todays code letter is ";COD$
```

Figure 4.10

Extracting a letter at random from a name. The use of INT makes certain that the random number is rounded down – if this is omitted the number range can be from 1 to L% + 1.

lie between 1 and L%. We saw how this was done in Chapter 3, so the principles should be familiar by now. This random number, assigned to R%, will be a whole number because an integer variable can hold only a whole number. It is used in line 60 to select one of the letters from your name, and line 70 informs you that this letter is your code letter for today. It's a simple example, but the point is important – that whatever appears in the number part of MID$ (or LEFT$ or RIGHT$) can be a number variable. Could you now take this piece of program, and alter it so that you got a group of letters of random length. The number of letters should not be more than half the number of letters of your name, so that for Taylor, you might get AY or YLO or YLOR for example.

Tying up more strings

It's time now to look at some other types of string functions, starting with two that are important when your program handles numbers. The first of these is VAL, and it's used to convert a number that is in string form back into ordinary number form so that we can carry out arithmetic. Suppose, for example, that we have NR$="3.4". NR$ is a string, and if we carry out PRINT NR$+"2", then the result is 3.42, not 5.4. This is because numbers which are in string form cannot be added, and no other form of arithmetic is possible either. If you have a number in this form, then you can convert by using VAL. You can, for example, use A=VAL(NR$) to convert the number from its string form in NR$ to single-precision variable form as usual, you can choose whether to use an integer, single-precision or double-precision number variable. Remember that if you don't specify, the form will always be single-precision.

Having looked at VAL, we can now account for an expression that can be used in RANDOMIZE, in which:

```
RANDOMIZE(VAL(RIGHT$(TIME$,2)))
```

is used to RANDOMIZE on the number of seconds in the time.. The string name TIME$ gives a value for time in hours, minutes and seconds, unlike TIMER which is a number of seconds. Don't expect this time to be correct unless you have specifically set it, because it has not been read from the battery-powered clock of the PC (if you have one), it simply starts when BASIC is loaded. You can synchronise the TIME$ of BASIC to the clock of the computer by running the appropriate program before you start running BASIC. This is ideally done with a disk that will load in the MS-DOS operating system, carry out the action, and

```
10 N$="22.5":V=2
20 CLS:PRINT
30 PRINT N$;" times ";V;" is";V*VAL(N$)
40 PRINT
50 V$=STR$(V)
60 PRINT"There are ";LEN(V$);" characters in ";V$;"!"
70 PRINT
80 PRINT N$;" added to ";V$" is not ";N$+V$
```

Figure 4.11
Conversions between number and string form, using VAL and STR$.

start BASIC as well, and Appendix B shows how, when you are ready for it. Note that this type of action is not part of GWBASIC.

There's an instruction that does the opposite conversion from number form to string form: STR$. When we follow STR$ by a number, number variable, or expression within brackets, we carry out a conversion to a string variable. We can then print this as a string, or assign it to a string variable name, or use string functions like LEN, MID$ and all the others. Figure 4.11 illustrates these processes – with a warning! Lines 10 to 30 show that we can do arithmetic on N$ if we use VAL with it. Line 50 converts the number variable V into string form, using the string name of V$. Now V has been assigned to the number 2 in line 10, and we would expect just one character to be present in the string. Line 60 reveals that there are two. The reason is that when we use STR$ to convert a number into string form, a space is left at the left-hand side of the string in case we want to put in a sign, + or –. This space is, of course, an invisible extra character, which explains why 2 appears to consist of two characters, and 42 of three characters. Line 80 shows the strings being concatenated, just to emphasise the difference between string variables and number variables.

The reason why

You may by now be wondering why on earth we might want to use numbers in string form, when we have all this carry-on about converting between string form and number form. One reason is that string form is often very convenient. Just to give an example, you can enter anything in string form, using something like INPUT X$. If you have INPUT X, then what you enter must be a number, and only a number. You can't, for example, enter 27A. If you do, then you'll just get the usual 'Redo from start' message to remind you that only a number is acceptable, and 27A isn't an ordinary number. Now if it's only you that will use the program, this might be acceptable, but if a non-programmer uses it, then this error message might cause a lot of confusion. If you use an input which is to a string variable, then items like 27A *will* be accepted. You can then use VAL to extract the number part. This use of VAL, however, works only if the string starts with a number. You can extract the number 27 from 27A, but not from A27. If you type A27 as your answer, then VAL will give the number 0. When a reply consists of mixed numbers and letters, you will have to make use of MID$ or RIGHT$ to get rid of the letters before you use VAL. That's something that we'll come back to when we deal with loops in Chapter 5.

There's another reason for needing VAL. Up until now, we've used INPUT as our only way of getting a value into a program when it is running. INPUT, you remember, causes the program to hang up until you press the **RETURN** key. There's another way of getting a character from the keyboard, though, which uses a different instruction word, INKEY$. The important point about this one is that it has to be assigned to a string variable. You can use K$=INKEY$, but not K=INKEY$. The other point about INKEY$ is that it 'scans the keyboard'. This means that at the instant when the line that contains K$=INKEY$ is executed, the computer checks to find if any key is being pressed. If no key is pressed, the computer makes K$ equal to a blank string and goes on its merry way. If you want to make use of K$=INKEY$ to get something from the keyboard, then, you have to arrange for the instruction to be repeated until a key is pressed. Figure 4.12 shows this in action. Line 30 assigns K$ to INKEY$, so that the computer

```
10 CLS
20 PRINT"Press any key..."
30 K$=INKEY$:IF K$="" THEN 30
40 PRINT"Your key was ";K$
50 PRINT"Number value is ";VAL(K$)
```

Figure 4.12
Detecting a key being pressed. Line 30 will repeat until a key has been pressed to provide a value to INKEY$.

will test the keyboard at this point. If K$ is a blank string, we want this action to repeat, and this is done by the test which reads:

```
IF K$="" THEN 30
```

This means that if K$ is a blank string because no key was pressed, the next line should be line 30. This makes line 30 repeat until K$ is no longer a blank. Note how a blank string is typed as a pair of quotes with nothing between them – you just tap the quotes key twice to get this. The program will therefore hang up, repeating line 30, until you press a key. You only need to press one key, and unlike INPUT, you don't have to follow it with pressing the **RETURN** key. Lines 40 and 50 then show the effect of what you have done. This is where VAL is really essential, because K$ is a string. If you want to use a number value here, then you can assign something like V%=VAL(K$). V% must be an integer, because INKEY$ allows you one key only, and one digit key can't give you a fraction. Note, however, that the use of INPUT$(1), dealt with at the end of the chapter, can often be more convenient than INKEY$.

Why should we need STR$? Let me give you just one example. Suppose you have a program which accepts numbers. These might be catalogue numbers of gifts, for example. Now when the computer lists are printed, we might want numbers like 1, 12, 123 to be printed out as 0001, 0012 and 0123 respectively, using four characters. It's quite difficult to arrange this if the program prints number variables, but it's simple if you use strings. Figure 4.13 illustrates what I mean. Line 20 gets a number from you, and you should try the effect of numbers like 3, 45, 624, 1234 and so on, keeping to numbers of four digits or less. In line 30, the number is converted to string form as V$. Line 40 takes the length of this string, and subtracts 1. This, remember, is because STR$ always places a

```
10 CLS
20 INPUT"Number, please ";V
30 V$=STR$(V)
40 L=LEN(V$)-1
50 V$="0000"+RIGHT$(V$,L)
60 V$=RIGHT$(V$,4)
70 PRINT V$
```

Figure 4.13

Padding a number to a given size with zeros, an action that is possible only if the numbers are in string form.

blank space before the first digit of the number. We don't want to have this when we print the number, so we subtract 1 from L. The string is then concatenated with the string "0000" in line 50, and only the number part of V$ is added. This is done by using RIGHT$(V$,L). For example, if N=23, then LEN(V$) will be 3, and L=2. Line 50 will then take the last two characters of V$, "23" and add them to "0000", to get "000023". Line 60 then takes the last four digits of this, which are "0023", and this is printed in line 70. Note how a variable name like V$ can be reassigned several times in the course of a program like this. You could, of course, use different variable names at each stage of the process, but it's more economical to reassign the same name, and it makes things easier to follow. This is because you know that V$ is always being used to hold the quantity that you are working with. There are lots of other manipulations like this that become easy when STR$ is used. Another example would be adding letters to a number. Could you design a piece of a program that asked for your name and your age, and then took the first three letters of your name and joined them to your age to give a code like TAY44?

ASC and CHR$

If you look back at Figure 4.3, now, you'll remember that we introduced the idea of ASCII code. This is the number code that is used to represent each of the characters that we can print on the screen. We can find out the code for any letter by using the function ASC, which is followed, within brackets, by a string character or a string variable. The result of ASC is a number, the ASCII code number for that character. If you use ASC("BASIC"), then you'll get the code for the 'B' only, because the action of ASC includes rejecting more than one character. Figure 4.14 shows this in action. Line 20 asks you to press any key, and line 30 contains an INKEY$ to get the character from the keyboard.

```
10 CLS
20 PRINT"Press a key, please ";
30 K$=INKEY$:IF K$="" THEN 30
40 PRINT"ASCII code is ";ASC(K$)
50 GOTO 20
```

Figure 4.14

How ASC will obtain the ASCII code for a letter. If you use ASC with a word or phrase, only the code for the first character will be found.

```
10 CLS
20 LOCATE 10,2
30 INPUT"Number, please ";N
40 PRINT:PRINT"Character is ";CHR$(N)
50 PRINT:PRINT"Press any key to proceed"
60 K$=INKEY$:IF K$="" THEN 60
70 GOTO 10
```

Figure 4.15

Looking at the characters that correspond to ASCII codes (including the range 128 to 255).

Line 40 then prints the ASCII code for whatever key has been pressed, by using `ASC(K$)`. When you run this, you will find that keys which don't produce anything on the screen will still give an ASCII code. Keys such as the spacebar, the **ESC**, **TAB** and **DEL** keys, for example, all give their own codes. You will also find that the **CTRL** key gives no code of its own, but when it is pressed along with another key, a new code is generated. Try the effect of the function keys keys as well. Each of these will give you a complete string of codes, corresponding to the word that is printed on screen when each key is pressed.

`ASC` has an opposite function, `CHR$`. What follows `CHR$`, within brackets, has to be a code number, and the result is the character whose code number is given. The instruction `PRINT CHR$(65)`, for example, will cause the letter **A** to appear on the screen, because 65 is the ASCII code for the letter A. Figure 4.15 is a short program that allows you to enter numbers, and see what their effect is on the screen. The numbers that can be used for this `CHR$` action extend from 0 to 255. Several of the numbers from 0 to 31 do not produce any visible character on the screen. These are 'action' code numbers, which produce *effects* like backspacing the cursor, clearing the screen and so on. Figure 4.16 lists these effects. The number 32 is the ASCII code for the spacebar, and the numbers from 33 to 254 will produce various characters, but 255 is blank.

One of the main uses of `CHR$`, which we shall investigate in Chapter 7, is in producing graphics shapes, the other is for coding messages. Every now and again, it's useful to be able to hide a message in a program so that it's not too obvious to anyone who reads the listing. Using ASCII codes is not a particularly good way of hiding a message from a skilled programmer, but for non-skilled users it's good enough. The codes can be kept in a `DATA` line, read in one by

The characters from 1 to 31 generally follow the pattern of the shapes shown in your computer manual. The exceptions may include:

CHR$()	*Effect*
7	**Sound beep**
9	**TAB 8 spaces along**
10	**Take new line**
11	**Go to top left hand side of screen**
12	**Clear screen, cursor to top left hand corner.**
13	**Take new line**
29	**Backspace and delete**
30	**Move to start of line**

Figure 4.16
The effects of some of the codes 1 to 31 when used in CHR$.

one, converted in characters by using CHR$, and printed. This is something that we'll look at when we come to the subject of loops in the next chapter.

The law about order

We saw earlier in Figure 3.9, and we'll look again in the next chapter at how numbers can be compared. We can also compare strings, using the ASCII codes as the basis for comparison. Two letters are identical if they have identical ASCII codes, so it's not difficult to see what the identity sign, =, means when we apply it to strings. If two long strings are identical, then they must contain the same letters in the same order. It's not so easy to see how we use the > and < signs until we think of ASCII codes. The ASCII code for A is 65, and the code for B is 66. In this sense, A is 'less than' B, because it has a smaller ASCII code. If we want to place letters into alphabetical order, then, we simply arrange them in order of ascending ASCII codes.

This process can be taken one stage further, though, to comparing complete words, character by character. Figure 4.17 illustrates this use of comparison using the = and > symbols. Line 20 assigns a nonsense word – it's just the first six letters on the top row of letter keys. Line 30 then asks you to type a

```
10 CLS
20 A$="qwerty"
30 PRINT:INPUT"Type a word (lower case) ";B$
40 IF B$=A$ THEN PRINT"Same as mine!":END
50 IF A$>B$ THEN SWAP A$,B$
60 PRINT"Correct order is ";A$; " and then ";B$
70 END
```

Figure 4.17
Comparing strings to determine their order in an alphabetical list.

word, using upper-case (capital) letters. The comparisons are then carried out in lines 40 and 50. If the word that you have typed, which is assigned to B$ is identical to QWERTY, then the message in line 40 is printed, and the program ends. If QWERTY would come later in an index than your word, then line 50 is carried out. If, for example, you typed PERIPHERAL, then since Q comes after P in the alphabet and has an ASCII code that is greater than the code for P, your word B$ scores lower than A$, and line 50 swaps them round. BASIC does this by using the useful command SWAP. When SWAP is followed by two variable names, separated by a comma, it will do what the name suggests – swap the values. This is the command that has been used in line 50 following the IF test. Line 60 will then print the words in the order A$ and then B$, which will be the correct alphabetical order. If the word that you typed comes later than QWERTY, for example, TAPE, then A$ is not 'greater than' B$, and the test in line 50 fails. No swap is made, and the order A$, then B$, is still correct. Note the important point though, that words like QWERTZ and QWERTX will be put correctly into order – it's not just the first letter that counts. The SWAP command applies to number variables as well as to string variables.

There's one snag here to putting words into order – the ASCII codes discriminate between lower-case and upper-case, with the lower-case codes being 32 more than the upper-case ones. If, then you have the words Queen and king, the order of placing them will be Queen, then king, because Q comes before k in ASCII order.

Some variants of BASIC offer the ability to make comparisons in which both strings are converted to the same case without affecting the strings. For example, a line such as:

```
IF UCASE(A$)>UCASE(B$)
```

can be used in Borland's Turbo BASIC™ so that the order will be strictly alphabetical whether upper or lower-case is used. GW BASIC lacks this useful function, but a subroutine (see later, Chapter 6) can be written to carry out the action, though it's slow and cumbersome. A string defined function can be used to convert each letter in turn:

```
DEF FN UCASE$(X$)=CHR$(ASC(X$)+32*(ASC(X$)>96 AND
ASC(X$)<123))
```

String arrays

We looked briefly at the idea of numeric arrays in Chapter 3, showing how a single variable name could be used for a set of numbers. The same arrangement can be used for strings, and the only change that needs to be made is that a string variable name has to be used. We can, for example, use `A$(1)`, `A$(2)`, `A$(3)` and so on, to represent a set of strings, which might be the names of the members of the local Music Society (or the violinists, perhaps). A string array like this also has to be dimensioned so that the computer can set aside memory for storing the strings. If, for example, you wanted to use the array `A$` for up to item `A$(100)`, then you would need a line that read:

```
DIM A$(100)
```

This line would have to be carried out before you started assigning values to these `A$` elements. If you find in the course of a program that you need more array items, and you haven't dimensioned enough, hard luck! You cannot dimension the same array for a second time while the program is running. If your early line was `DIM A$(100)`, you cannot have a later line of `DIM A$(200)`. This is because the computer has set aside memory for the first dimensioning, and will have made use of the memory around this reserved piece. Attempting to re-dimension `A$` would cause the computer to clear some of the other parts of its memory, and this could result in the program being completely destroyed. When the computer comes across a second `DIM` statement about the same variable name, then, you get a '`Re-dimensioned array`' error message, and the program stops. BASIC allows you to use subscript numbers up to 10 without needing to use `DIM`. This allows you eleven items, because `A$(0)` can be used as well as `A$(1)` and so on. What you have to watch if you take advantage of this is that you do not use an array like this and then try to dimension it by a command like DIM A$(20). This also will cause the 'Re-dimensioned array' message. We'll look at examples of string arrays in use in Chapter 5.

String ends

There are, inevitably, a few commands that we haven't looked at yet, mainly because they haven't fitted in with the others. One of these is the interesting and useful one, INPUT$. This is not quite like INPUT, because it allows you to enter a preset number of characters, and they are not shown on the screen when you enter them. It's ideal for security codes, as Figure 4.18 shows. Line 30 contains the step A$=INPUT$(5). This means that only five characters can be accepted for this input, and the string of characters will be assigned to A$. The computer hangs up and waits for you when line 30 runs, but you don't need to press **RETURN**. Immediately you press the fifth key, the entry is complete, but without anything appearing on the screen. In this example, line 40 then checks that what you have entered is the correct password. It's a very useful way of getting an entry of the right number of characters. There's no need to count characters and use a test to detect the entry of the wrong number of characters. An extension to INPUT$ allows entry from tape or disk. The most common use for INPUT$, however, is as a substitute for INKEY$, because you can use K$=INPUT$(1), with no need to bother about detecting which key has been used.

Another useful function is FRE. If you type PRINT FRE(A), or FRE(A$), then the machine will print the number of bytes of memory that you can use. You can use any variable name in place of A$, and it doesn't need to be a variable name that is used or assigned in your program. A variable name used in this way is called a *dummy variable*. The amount of memory available may give you a nasty shock if you thought that your machine had 512K (524288 bytes) or even 640K

```
10 CLS
20 PRINT"Please type the 5-letter code"
30 A$=INPUT$(5)
40 IF A$<>"QSRBN" THEN PRINT"Incorrect - no entry":GOTO 10
50 PRINT"Pass, friend."
```

Figure 4.18
INPUT$ is useful for entering security codes, as this example shows, and can also replace INKEY$ for one-key replies.

of free memory! You can use FRE(A) to decide if you have to stop using a program because of lack of memory. By having a line such as:

```
IF FRE(A)<1000 THEN PRINT "No room - please save
data":GOSUB 5000
```

you can detect when memory is running short, and then save your data.

Finally, BASIC can make use of an excellent command, INSTR. This is used to find if one string is contained in another. It's used in the simple form:

```
X= INSTR (A$,B$)
```

to find if B$ is contained in A$. If it is, then X is the position number of the first letter of B$ that is found in A$. If B$ is not contained in A$, then X is zero. X will always be zero if B$ is longer than A$. You can, of course, use the form:

```
PRINT INSTR(A$,B$)
```

if you just want to see the number.

Figure 4.19 shows a simple example of this function in action. Lines 20 to 40 allocate names to strings, and lines 50 to 70 make the tests, so that you can see how they work out. Notice that the strings have to be exact for the function to work – it's no good looking for 'Bert' if what is contained in the string is 'bert' or 'BERT', for example.

```
10 CLS
20 A$="Albert Hall"
30 B$="Richardson, Bertram"
40 C$="Taylor, Jim"
50 PRINT"In ";A$" bert is located at ";INSTR(A$,"bert")
60 PRINT"In ";B$;" Bert is located at ";INSTR(B$,"Bert")
70 PRINT"In ";C$;" BERT is located at ";INSTR(C$,"BERT")
```

Figure 4.19

The INSTR$ function will detect if a given set of consecutive characters is contained inside a word or phrase – but the characters have to be identical and in the identical order.

To leave you with a thought, suppose you had a string:

```
A$="YESyesYUPyupSUREsureOKok"
```

and you asked for a yes/no answer. You could get `INSTR` to look through this. If the result of `X=INSTR(Answer$, A$)` is zero, then the answer wasn't any form of '*Yes*'. The snag, of course, is that the routine would accept something like *upSU* as a 'yes'!! The other point about `INSTR` is that you can specify at which character in the string you start the search. This is done by putting in a number as the first item within the brackets. The other items are used as before, with commas between them. For example, if you had:

```
X%=INSTR(5,A$,B$)
```

the computer would start at character number 5 of `A$`, and look from that position to find if `B$` was present. This can be useful if you are, for example, looking for a space between a forename and a surname. The program might be misled if there was a space just before the name, so using `INSTR(2,A$,B$)` would skip over this first space and concentrate on looking for the second one. The number `X%` that you can get from this can then be used in `MID$`, `LEFT$` or `RIGHT$` commands to separate out the words. Magic!

Chapter 5

REPEATING YOURSELF

One of the activities for which a computer is particularly well suited is repeating a set of instructions, and every variety of BASIC is equipped with keywords that will cause repetition. GW BASIC is no exception to this rule. We'll start with the simplest of these 'repeater' actions, one which we have already used, GOTO.

GOTO means exactly what you would expect it to mean – go to another line number. Normally a program is carried out by executing the instructions in ascending order of line number. In plain language that means starting at the lowest numbered line, working through the lines in order and ending at the highest numbered line. Using GOTO can break this arrangement, so that a line or a set of lines will be carried out in the 'wrong' order, or carried out over and over again.

Figure 5.1 shows an example of a very simple repetition or 'loop', as we call it. This is a loop in which a different number along with a phrase is printed out

```
10 CLS:N=0
20 PRINT N". BASIC fills your screen."
30 N=N+1
40 GOTO 20
```

Figure 5.1
A simple loop, using GOTO. This one can be broken by pressing the **CTRL BREAK** *keys.*

```
10 CLS
20 FOR COUNTER=1 TO 10
30    PRINT"BASIC rules, O.K."
40 NEXT
```

Figure 5.2
The FOR..NEXT loop, which allows a stated number of repetitions.

each time the computer goes through the actions of the loop. We call this 'each pass through the loop'. Line 10 sets the value of the variable N at 0. This is printed in line 20, along with the phrase, and then line 30 increments the value of N. Line 40 forms the loop, so that the program will cause a very rapid count-up, along with the words 'BASIC fills your screen' to appear on the screen. This is an endless loop, meaning that there is nothing in the program that will stop the loop action, and you'll have to use the Ctrl-Break keys to stop it. This gives you a chance to see how the program will carry on when you type CONT and press **RETURN**.

Now an uncontrolled loop like this is not exactly good to have, and GOTO is a method of creating loops that we prefer not to use except with label names, when we can see where each loop starts. We don't always have a satisfactory alternative in GW, but one possibility is the FOR..NEXT loop. As the name suggests, this makes use of two new instruction words, FOR and NEXT. The instructions that are repeated are the instructions that are placed between FOR and NEXT. Figure 5.2 illustrates a very simple example of the FOR..NEXT loop in action. The line which contains FOR must also include a number variable which is used for counting, and numbers which control the start of the count and its end. In the example, COUNTER is the counter variable, and its limit numbers are 1 and 10. The NEXT is in line 40, and so anything between lines 20 and 40 will be repeated.

As it happens, what lies between these lines is simply the PRINT instruction, and the effect of the program will be to print BASIC rules, O.K. ten times. At the first pass through the loop, the value of COUNTER is set to 1, and the phrase is printed. When the NEXT instruction is encountered, the computer increments the value of COUNTER, from 1 to 2 in this case. It then checks to see if this value exceeds the limit of 10 that has been set. If it doesn't, then line 30 is repeated, and this will continue until the value of COUNTER exceeds 10 – we'll look at that point later. The effect in this example is to cause ten repetitions.

```
10 CLS
20 FOR COUNT=1 TO 10
30    PRINT"Count is";COUNT
40       FOR DELAY=1 TO 2200:NEXT
50    CLS:NEXT
```

Figure 5.3
Nested loops, meaning that one loop is contained inside another. In this example the inner loop serves only as a time delay.

You don't have to confine this action to single loops either. Figure 5.3 shows an example of what we call *nested loops*, meaning that one loop is contained completely inside another one. When loops are nested in this way, we can describe the loops as inner and outer. The outer loop starts in line 20, using variable COUNT which goes from 1 to 10 in value. Line 30 is part of this outer loop, printing the value that the counter variable COUNT has reached. Line 40, however, is another complete loop. This must make use of a different variable name, and it must start and finish again before the end of the outer loop. We have used variable DELAY, and we have put nothing between the FOR part and the NEXT part to be carried out. All that this loop does, then, is to waste time, making sure that there is some measurable time (about one second in this example) between the actions in the main loop. The last action of the main loop is clearing the screen in line 50. The overall effect, then, is to show a count-up on the screen, slowly enough for you to see the changes, and wiping the screen clear each time. In this example we have used NEXT to indicate the end of each loop. We could use NEXT DELAY in line 40 and NEXT COUNT in line 50 if we liked, but this is not essential. It also has the effect of slowing the computer down, though the effect is not important in this program. When you do use NEXT DELAY and NEXT COUNT, you must be absolutely sure that you have put the correct variable names following each NEXT. If you don't, the computer will stop with a NEXT without FOR error – meaning that the NEXT's don't match up with the FOR's in this case. You would also get this message if you had omitted a NEXT.

Even at this stage it's possible to see how useful this FOR..NEXT loop can be, but there's more to come. To start with, the loops that we have looked at so far count upwards, incrementing the number variable. We don't always want this, and we can add the instruction word STEP to the end of the FOR line to alter this change of variable value. We could, for example, use a line like:

```
10 CLS
20 FOR COUNT=10 TO 1 STEP -1
30 PRINT COUNT;" seconds and counting..."
40 FOR DELAY=1 TO 2200:NEXT
50 CLS:NEXT
60 PRINT"Blastoff!"
```

Figure 5.4
Using STEP to produce a different count, in this case a count down.

```
FOR N=1 TO 9 STEP 2
```

which would cause the values of N to change in the sequence 1, 3, 5, 7, 9. When we don't type STEP, the loop will always use increments of +1, but STEP also allows us to use negative increments, i.e. decrements. Figure 5.4 illustrates an outer loop which has a step of –1, so that the count is downwards. COUNT starts with a value of 10, and is decremented on each pass though the loop. Line 40 once again forms a time delay so that the countdown takes place at a civilised speed. This is a particularly useful way of slowing the count down. If we want to speed the rate up, with no delay inner loop, then the easiest way is to use an integer variable such as COUNT% in place of COUNT. If we do this, however, we can't use steps that contain fractions, like .1.

Every now and again, when we are using loops, we find that we need to use the value of COUNT (or whatever variable name we have used) after the loop has finished. It's important to know what this will be, however, and Figure 5.5 brings it home. This contains two loops, one counting up, the other counting down. At the end of each loop, the value of the counter variable, N, is printed. This reveals that the value of N is 6 in line 50, after completing the FOR N = 1 TO 5 loop, and is 0 in line 90 after completing the FOR N = 5 TO 1 STEP -1 loop. If you want to make use of the value of N, or whatever variable name you have selected to use, you will have to remember that it will have changed by one more step at the end of the loop.

One of the most valuable features of the FOR..NEXT loop, however, is the way in which it can be used with number variables instead of just numbers. Figure 5.6 illustrates this in a simple way. The letters A, B and C are assigned as numbers in the usual way in line 20, but they are then used in a FOR..NEXT loop in line 30. The limits are set by A and B, and the step is obtained from an expression,

```
10 CLS
20 FOR N=1 TO 5
30 PRINT N
40 NEXT
50 PRINT"N is now";N
60 FOR N=5 TO 1 STEP -1
70 PRINT N
80 NEXT
90 PRINT"N is now";N
```

Figure 5.5
Illustrating that the counter variable, N in this example, is always changed by one more step after the end of a loop. This can be important if you use the counter later in your program.

```
10 CLS
20 A=2:B=5:C=10
30 FOR N=A TO B STEP B/C
40 PRINT N
50 NEXT
```

Figure 5.6
Each part of a FOR..NEXT loop can contain a number variable or an expression, not just a number.

B/C. The rule is that if you have anything that represents a number or can be worked out to give a number, then you can use it in a loop like this. The only proviso here is that if you want a loop to run fast, as it must if there are to be a large number of passes, then you should try to avoid any calculation of expressions in the loop and keep to straightforward incrementing or decrementing of the number variable, along with the use of an integer variable as the counter.

Loops and Decisions

It's time to see loops being used rather than just demonstrated. A simple application is in totalling numbers. The action that we want is that we enter

```
10 TT=0:CLS
20 PRINT TAB(27)"Totalling Numbers Program"
30 PRINT:PRINT TAB(3)"Enter each number as requested."
40 PRINT TAB(3)"The program will provide the total."
50 BLANK$=STRING$(50,32):FOR N=1 TO 10
60 LOCATE 10,3:PRINT"Number";N;" please ";
70 INPUT YOURS:TT=TT+YOURS
80 PRINT"Total so far is";TT
90 FOR DELAY=1 TO 3000:NEXT
100 LOCATE 10,3:PRINT BLANK$:NEXT
110 LOCATE 12,1:END
```

Figure 5.7
A program that shows a running total for the entry of ten numbers.

numbers and the computer keeps a running total, adding each number to the total of the numbers so far. From what we have done so far, it's easy to see how this could be done if we wanted to use numbers in fixed quantities, like ten numbers in a set. The program of Figure 5.7 does just this.

The program starts by setting a number variable TT to zero. This is the number variable that will be used to hold the total, and it has to start at zero. As it happens, BASIC arranges this automatically at the start of a program, but it's a good habit to ensure that everything that has to start with some value actually does. We can't incidentally, use TO for this variable, because TO is a reserved word, part of the FOR..NEXT set of words. You will get a 'Syntax error' message when the program runs if you have used a 'reserved word' as a variable name.

Lines 20 to 40 issue instructions, and the action starts in line 50. A string called BLANK$ is defined so as to make the presentation of the input neater, and there follows then the start of a FOR..NEXT loop which will repeat the actions of lines 60 to 100 ten times. Line 60 reminds you of how many numbers you have entered by printing the value of N each time, and line 70 allows you to input a number which is then assigned to variable name YOURS. This is then added to the total in the second half of line 70, and line 80 prints the value of this total. After a short delay, the number prompt line is erased selectively by using LOCATE and PRINT BLANK$, and the loop then repeats. At the end of the program, the final total has been printed, with the LOCATE statement used to ensure that when the 'O.k.' prompt is printed it doesn't wipe out part of the total line.

```
10 TOTAL=0:COUNT=0:BLANK$=STRING$(50,32):CLS
20 PRINT TAB(27)"Totalling Numbers Program"
30 PRINT:PRINT"Enter each number as requested.
40 PRINT"The total will be shown - enter 0 to stop."
50 COUNT=COUNT+1:LOCATE 10,3:PRINT"Item";COUNT;" is ";
60 INPUT YOURS: IF YOURS=0 THEN 110
70 TOTAL=TOTAL+YOURS
80 LOCATE 12,3:PRINT"Total so far is";TOTAL
90 LOCATE 10,3:PRINT BLANK$
100 GOTO 50
110 LOCATE 15,1:END
```

Figure 5.8

Another number-totaling program that allows for any number of entries. The GOTO 50 in line 100 forms the loop, and this is broken in line 60 when a zero is entered.

It's all good stuff, but how many times would you want to have just ten numbers? It would be a lot more convenient if we could just stop the action by signaling to the computer in some way, perhaps by entering a value like 0 or 999. A value like this is called a *terminator*, something that is obviously not one of the normal entries that we would use, but just a signal. For a number-totalling program, a terminator of 0 is very convenient, because if it gets added to the total it won't make any difference. To do this, we have to test the number that is input, and change the action of the loop if the input is 0. Figure 5.8 shows one way of doing this. The program is very much as before, but the `FOR..NEXT` loop is not used. Instead, line 60 uses the keyword `IF` to make the test:

```
IF YOURS=0 THEN 110
```

What this amounts to is that if the number which was entered in the first part of line 60 was 0, then the program moves to line 110, which simply closes things down, with the `LOCATE` statement used to avoid erasing the final total. This will stop the loop, and so stop this program.

There is an alternative to the use of `GOTO` or `THEN` like this, however, and Figure 5.9 shows an example of it in action. This uses a `WHILE..WEND` loop, so called because the start of the loop is marked by the word `WHILE` and the end by the word `WEND` *(While END)*. A `WHILE..WEND` loop always start with a test of some condition, and the loop runs for as long as that condition is true. The main thing

```
10 TOTAL=0:COUNT=0:BLANK$=STRING$(50,32):CLS
20 PRINT TAB(27)"Totalling Numbers Program"
30 PRINT:PRINT"Enter each number as requested.
40 PRINT"The total will be shown - enter 0 to stop."
45 YOURS=1:WHILE YOURS<>0
50 COUNT=COUNT+1:LOCATE 10,3:PRINT"Item";COUNT;" is ";
60 INPUT YOURS
70 TOTAL=TOTAL+YOURS
80 LOCATE 12,3:PRINT"Total so far is";TOTAL
90 LOCATE 10,3:PRINT BLANK$
100 WEND
110 LOCATE 15,1:END
```

Figure 5.9

A much better method of forming a loop for an indefinite number of entries. This uses the WHILE..WEND statements to mark the ends of the loop, and the ending condition follows WHILE.

to watch out for here is that if you are forgetful, you can easily create a loop that will never run at all! In this example, a new line 45 has appeared in which variable YOURS has been given a 'dummy' value of 1, and the loop starts. The test that follows WHILE is YOURS<>0, which must be true at this point because YOURS has just been assigned the value of 1. This is the crucial point – it is only too easy to forget that YOURS must be assigned a value before the WHILE statement runs. The value is a dummy in the sense that it is not added to the total, and is replaced by a new input in line 60. This new value, if it not zero, will ensure that the WHILE test is true again on the next loop. When you enter a zero, however, the program jumps to the statement that follows the WEND, that is to line 110. Note, incidentally, that if you press **RETURN** without entering any number, BASIC takes this as a zero, and the loop stops. This is a point to watch if your typing is of the fast 'n 'furious variety rather than the slow 'n 'sure.

The WHILE..WEND loop is one that you should make a lot of use of for many reasons. One is that it does not depend on counting like the FOR..NEXT loop. You can make the condition for ending the loop anything you like, like a string quantity being equal to "END", or the spacebar being pressed. This type of loop is therefore particularly valuable when you don't know in advance how many times you want the loop to repeat. Another valuable feature is that, unlike the GOTO type of loop, you can see where the WHILE..WEND loop starts. A good habit to acquire, in fact, is indenting the lines of a WHILE..WEND loop to make the extent of the loop even more obvious. On the whole, then, you need to have a good reason *not* to use the `WHILE..WEND` loop for anything that is not a purely counted loop. The only point to watch is that you ensure that whatever is tested will allow the loop to run correctly. In addition to the `WHILE..WEND` loop, some versions of BASIC allow you a `DO..WHILE` or `DO..UNTIL` loop.

Decisions, decisions

We can make a number of types of comparisons between number variables or numbers, and these are listed in Figure 5.10. The mathematical signs are used for convenience, and you have to remember which way round the 'greater than' (>and 'less than' (<) signs have to be. It's important to note that the equals sign means *identical to* when it is used in a test like this. If `A` is 3.9999999 and `B` is 4.0000000 then a test such as `IF A = B` will fail – `A` is not identical to `B`, even though it is close enough to be equal to our eyes. The important point here is that the numbers we see on the screen have been rounded, so that `PRINT A` in the example above might give the result 4. The test, however, is made on the

Sign	*Meaning*
=	Exact equality
>	Left-hand quantity greater than right-hand quantity
<	Left-hand quantity less than right-hand quantity
The signs can be combined as follows:	
<>	Quantities not equal
>=	LHS greater than or equal to RHS
<=	LHS less than or equal to RHS

Figure 5.10
The comparisons that can be made in tests for looping, particularly in WHILE loops.

```
10 CLS
20 PRINT"Type y or n"
30 K$=INPUT$(1)
40 IF K$="Y" OR K$="y" THEN 100 ELSE IF K$="N" OR K$="n"
THEN 200
50 PRINT"Your answer ";K$;" is neither Y or N.":PRINT"Please
try again."
60 GOTO 30
70 END
100 PRINT"That was Y for YES":END
200 PRINT"That was N for NO":END
```

Figure 5.11

Testing strings. This also illustrates the use of ELSE to allow another test following a first IF test.

numbers which have not been rounded. Figure 5.11 shows a test on string variables. The instruction is in line 20, you are asked to type the y or n key. Line 30 gets your answer using INPUT$(1) so that you have only to press a key without touching **RETURN**. The key that you press has its value assigned to K$, so that K$ should be y or n, or possibly Y or N. Line 40 then analyses this result. If the key that you pressed was neither 'y' nor 'n', upper-case or lower-case, then the program ignores the THEN 100 and THEN 200 instructions of line 40, and goes on to line 50 and 60. This tells you that you didn't press either y or n, and you must try again.

The tests in line 40 of this example are for identity. Only if K$ is absolutely identical to y or Y will the program jump to line 100, and print the phrase 'That was Y for YES'. Using INPUT$(1) in place of INPUT does not allow you to make such mistakes as typing a space ahead of 'y', or a space following it. If the first test fails, though, then ELSE forces the second test to be tried. This time, the answer is tested for the letter 'n' or 'N', and if this is found, the program jumps to line 200. This line then prints 'That was n for NO', and the program once again ends. It's up to you to form these tests so that they behave in the way that you want! You can use AND and OR to make the tests apply to more than one thing, as has been demonstrated with the IF K$='Y' OR K$='y', for example, to test either form of the 'Y' key. GW BASIC allows you to use the instruction word ELSE, which offers an alternative to the test that is carried out by IF. In the example of Figure 5.11, two tests were combined. You can, however, combine much more than this. You can use lines like:

```
IF X=3 THEN 100 ELSE IF X=4 THEN 200 ELSE IF X=5 THEN
300..
```

and so on.

Looping to a purpose

So far we have been looking at short examples of loops which were designed to show how loops are constructed. It's time now to look at examples of loops in use, and to see how a program which includes an example of how a loop is designed. All loops are intended to carry out a set of actions over and over again. What you have to decide before you try to write the BASIC of a looping program is what actions you want to repeat, and what will make the loop stop. If it is possible to design the loop so that it repeats some definite number of times, this should be done. The reason is that this would allow you to use a `FOR..NEXT` loop, rather than trying to make up a loop with `GOTO`. If a fixed number of repetitions is not possible, then `WHILE..WEND` should be the almost automatic choice. We have looked at some of the arguments already, but another difficulty about `GOTO` loops is that its very easy to make a mistake, and go to the wrong line. The result might be a program that doesn't work. Even worse, the result can be a program that looks as if it works, but doesn't give the correct results.

We'll look, then, at a very simple number-guessing game and how it is designed. Figure 5.12 shows the plan which was used to design the listing is shown in

1. **Pick number at random, 1 to 10. Assign to X%.**
2. **Ask for guessed number, assign to N%**
3. **Increment score% by 2 if guess identical to X%**
4. **Increment score% by 1 if guess 1 or 2 out.**
5. **Display running score.**
6. **Stop after ten guesses.**

Figure 5.12
A plan outline for a number-guessing game.

```
10 CLS:KEY OFF:SCORE%=0:RANDOMIZE (VAL(RIGHT$(TIME$,2)))
20 BLANK$=STRING$(30,32):PRINT TAB(10)"Guess the number"
30 PRINT:PRINT"If you get near, I'll tell you. Number is
between 1 and 10."
40 FOR J%=1 TO 10:LOCATE 5,10:PRINT"Attempt";J%:PRINT
50 X%=INT(RND*10+1)
60 LOCATE 6,10:PRINT BLANK$:LOCATE 6,10:INPUT"Your guess -
";N%
65 LOCATE 7,10:PRINT BLANK$:LOCATE 7,10
70 IF N%=X% THEN PRINT "Spot on. Score
2":SCORE%=SCORE%+2:GOTO 100
80 IF ABS(N%-X%)<3 THEN PRINT"Near - it was";X%". Score
1":SCORE%=SCORE%+1:GOTO 100
90 PRINT"No score."
100 LOCATE 10,9:PRINT"SCORE TOTAL IS";SCORE%
110 FOR TIME=1 TO 2500:NEXT
120 NEXT
130 KEY ON
```

Figure 5.13

The game program listed. It's not exactly a competitor for Game-of-the-Year, but it shows what can be done in a few lines.

Figure 5.13. The description contains no keywords, and in fact it should not, because the use of keywords makes it more difficult to follow. The plan starts with a simple statement of the main operation. The next step is selecting a number at random. This is the first of the steps that will be repeated ten times, and it is followed by 'Input guess'. This is where the user of the program enters the number that is guessed. The next steps are concerned with scoring. If the guess is exactly correct, then two points are scored, and the arrow shows that the next step must be the pause. As an alternative, if the guess is close, one point is added to the score, and again the program moves to the pause stage. If the guess is completely out, then some message will be printed ('No score', perhaps), and once again, the program pauses. The pause will be of about a couple of seconds, and after the pause, the program moves to repeat the loop.

The next item is to fill in some details. This is done on the right hand side of the set of steps of the plan, using brackets to show where several more detailed steps have to be inserted. The points that have been put in here are where the CLS, heading, and instructions steps are placed. We also make notes about messages, and the length of time of the pause. For a simple program like this, that's all we need to start writing the BASIC lines. You don't necessarily have to write numbered lines yet, though. At this stage, it makes more sense to write BASIC for one step at a time, and the order of running the steps is not usually the best order for writing. For example, there isn't much point in writing a heading and instructions until we're sure that the program works. The steps that we should concentrate on first are the selection of a random number, and the scoring steps, because unless these are correct, the rest of the program is of little use.

Start with the random number, then. Since we are dealing with numbers that will all be integers, we can assign an integer variable, and use:

```
X%=INT(RND(1)*10+1)
```

to get a random number as X%. This, remember, will get a random number which lies between 1 and 10. To make sure that the sequence of numbers is different each time the program runs, we will have to use a RANDOMIZE step early in the program before the loop starts. Make a note of it! The testing for equality is easy enough, and we can settle a variable name for the guessed number – N%. There will be a GOTO at the end of this line to lead to the total printing and 'Pause' steps. Testing for near equality can be done by using ABS(N%-X%). ABS will make whatever lies between the brackets into a positive quantity, so if N% happens to be less than X%, the result will be the difference, but with a positive sign. Once again, this step has to be ended with a GOTO to make the 'Pause' step come next. Now there's a last minute thought. It looks odd to have the bottom line of the screen always showing the function-key words while this program is running. We can shut off this display when our program starts by using KEY OFF. At the end of the program, we can restore the 'Key' display by using KEY ON. Now we need only make a few notes at the side of he plan about where on the screen we want the messages to appear, and we're ready to write the final version in Figure 5.13.

Line 10 clears the screen, switches the KEY display off, sets the score variable SC% to zero, and carries out the RANDOMIZE step, using the seconds part of the TIME$ display. This has been used only for the sake of demonstration – it would be easier to use RANDOMIZE TIMER. Line 20 then assigns BLANK$ for wiping out a message, and prints the title. The instructions are contained in line 30. The steps of the loop start with line 40. This locates the cursor and prints the attempt number, so that the user knows how many shots have been used up. The real action starts in line 50, where the X% = INT(RND(1)*10+1) step causes variable X% to take a whole-number value that lies between 1 and 10. You enter your number at line 60, in which the two LOCATE steps and the printing of BLANK$ ensure that this line is wiped clean each time. Line 70 then uses LOCATE twice again to clear a line for the results, and the tests are made in lines 80 and 90. If the number that you picked is identical to the random number, then you get the 'Spot on' message in line 80, two points are added to the score variable SCORE%, and the GOTO 110 skips over the other tests to get to the totaling and 'Pause' stages. The less obvious test is in line 90. If the difference between your guess and the actual number is less than 3 (meaning 1 or 2) then the message in line 90 is printed, the score is bumped up by one point, and you move to the total printing and 'Pause'. If you don't get anywhere near, the program moves to line 90 to announce 'No Score'. The pause is then carried out and then line 130 contains the NEXT that will make the loop repeat. It's very simple, but quite effective. At the end of the loop, KEY ON switches on the display at the foot of the screen.

A lot of the commands that we have looked at in previous chapters take on a lot more meaning when we carry them out inside loops. This is particularly true when the counter variable of the loop can be used as part of the action. Take a look at Figure 5.14 for an example, which makes use of the fact that we can use variable names or expressions in place of numbers in string slicing actions. It all starts innocently enough in line 20 with a request for your name. Whatever you type is assigned to variable NAM$, and in line 30 a bit of mathematical juggling is carried out. How does it work? Suppose you type as your name DONALD. This has six letters, so in line 30, L% is assigned the value 6, and C% is the whole number part of L%/2 (equal to 3), plus 1, making 4. Line 40 then starts a loop of 4 passes. In the first pass you print at TAB(39) because N%=1. What you print is the MID$ of the name using C%-N%+1, which is 4-1+1=4, and N%*2-1, which is also 1. What you print is therefore MID$(NM$,4,1), which is A in this example. On the next run through the loop, N% is 2, C%- N%+1 is 3, and N%*2-1 is also 3. What is printed is MID$(NM$,3,3), which is NAL. The loop goes on in this way,

```
10 CLS
20 INPUT"Your name, please ";NAM$
30 L%=LEN(NAM$):C%=(L%/2)+1
40 FOR N%=1 TO C%
50 PRINT TAB(40-N%)MID$(NAM$,C%-N%+1,N%*2-1)
60 NEXT
```

Figure 5.14
Using expressions in loops and slicing.

```
10 CLS:PRINT
20 PRINT"What's the theme of this book?"
30 PRINT:PRINT"Press any key to find out"
40 K$=INPUT$(1)
50 READ CODE$:L%=LEN(CODE$)
60 FOR J%=1 TO L% STEP 3
70 PRINT CHR$(VAL(MID$(CODE$,J%,3)));
80 NEXT:END
90 DATA 066065083073067032105115032098101116116101114033
```

Figure 5.15
Coding a message with the aid of ASCII number codes.

and the result is that you see on the screen a pyramid of letters formed from your name. It's quite impressive if you have a long name! If your name is short, try making up a longer one. Could you try designing a variation on this which worked in the opposite way, starting with the full name and cutting a letter off each side on each pass through the loop?

We looked briefly in Chapter 4 at the idea of coding messages in ASCII, and reading them from data lines. Figure 5.15 illustrates this use, but with a few twists. Keeping ASCII codes in DATA lines in the form 65,66,32... and so on is just too easy, and it makes the codes a lot more difficult to unravel if they are all put into three-digit form, and then run into one continuous string, as the DATA line of Figure 5.15 illustrates. We can get the characters from this string by picking out three digits at a time, using VAL to convert the string slice to a number, and then CHR$ to convert the number to a character. If the PRINT statement in the loop uses a semicolon to suppress new lines, then the characters will be printed as a phrase, which is what we usually want. The lines up to line 50 are straightforward stuff, and the real action starts when the string CODE$ is read. Its length is found as L%, and the main loop then starts, going from 1 to the length of the string in steps of three. The unravelling of the code is done in line 70, which looks rather fearsome unless you approach it correctly. The correct approach is from the innermost bracket outwards, and this starts us off with MID$(CODE$,J%,3), which extracts three characters from CODE$. Since these three characters make up a number, we can use VAL on this to get the number, and CHR$ gives the character shape for this number code. This type of coding will deter all but really persistent decoders! This example, incidentally, illustrates the use of READ and DATA in a loop. We would normally use READ and DATA only

```
10 CLS:PRINT"Which list do you want?"
20 PRINT:A%=5:WHILE A%>3 OR A%<1
30 INPUT" NUMBER 1 TO 3, PLEASE ";A%:WEND
50 IF A%=1 THEN RESTORE 1000 ELSE IF A%=2 THEN RESTORE 2000
ELSE RESTORE 3000
60 FOR N%=1 TO 4:READ A$:PRINT A$:NEXT
70 END
1000 DATA Austin,Rover,Jaguar,Lotus
2000 DATA BMW, Porsche, Mercedes, Opel
3000 DATA Alfa Romeo, Lancia, Fiat, Ferrari
```

Figure 5.16
Using RESTORE along with READ..DATA to select from different data sets.

for information that we particularly wanted to keep stored in a program like this.

While we are on the subject of READ and DATA, there's another twist to this instruction in the form of RESTORE. RESTORE means that the DATA list will start again from the beginning. If you READ all of the data, and then want to read it all again, you will have to have a RESTORE instruction before the second READ loop. If you didn't, you would get an 'Out of data' error message. RESTORE, however, can do more than this. Take a look at Figure 5.16. This offers a kind of menu choice of headings, but it's done by using RESTORE followed by a line number. When you pick a number, it is used in line 40 to carry out a RESTORE command which has a line number following it. RESTORE 2000, for example, means 'start reading DATA at line 2000'. Each DATA line contains four items, so that when line 50 is carried out, four items will be read from whichever line has been picked. It's a useful way of selecting from a number of lists which will be used each time the program is used. Note also how a WHILE..WEND loop has been used in the number choice – this could have been made quicker by using INPUT$(1) in place of INPUT.

Loops and Arrays

The loop commands of any computer are particularly useful when you have to deal with array variables. The reason is that you can set up a loop, such as FOR N%=1 TO 100, and make the array items use the counter variable N%, as, for example, A(N%), This can make the actions of filling or printing an array very simple pieces of programming. Figure 5.17 illustrates this. Lines 10 to 40 generate an (imaginary) set of twenty examination marks. This is done simply to avoid the hard work of entering the real thing! Line 20 dimensions the integer number array A% to a maximum of twenty items, using the variable name X% to carry this number so that if you want to change to a different number you need change only this assignment of X%$. If we had needed only up to ten items, we could have dispensed with this DIM line, but it's always better to include it even for small arrays, just to remind yourself that you're dealing with an array. The array variable in line 30 is a subscripted number variable, and the 'subscript' is the number that is represented by N%. Each item is obtained by finding a random number between 1 and 100, and is then assigned to A%(N%). Twenty of these 'marks' are assigned in this way, and then lines 60 to 90 print the list. It makes for much neater programming than you would have to use if you needed a separate variable name for each number. Notice the way in which TABs have been used to make the printing neater – try it without TABs if you don't believe me.

Figure 5.18 extends this another step further. This time you are invited to type a name and a mark for each of ten items. When the list is complete, the screen

```
10 CLS:X%=20
20 DIM A%(X%):FOR N%=1 TO X%
30 A%(N%)=RND*100+1
40 NEXT
50 PRINT
60 PRINT TAB(35)"Marks List"
70 PRINT:FOR N%=1 TO X%
80 PRINT"item";N%;TAB(10);" received";TAB(19);A%(N%);TAB(24);"
marks."
90 NEXT
```

Figure 5.17

Using an array or list. Each variable in the list uses the same name of A%, but the subscript number N% separates the list into its constituents.

```
10 CLS:PRINT:X%=10
20 PRINT"Please enter names and marks."
30 DIM NAM$(X%),MARK%(X%):FOR N%=1 TO X%
40 PRINT"Name - ";:INPUT NAM$(N%)
50 PRINT"Mark - ";:INPUT MARK%(N%)
60 NEXT
70 CLS:TOTAL%=0
80 PRINT TAB(35)"Marks List":PRINT
90 FOR N%=1 TO X%
100 PRINT TAB(2)NAM$(N%);TAB(25)MARK%(N%)
110 TOTAL%=TOTAL%+MARK%(N%)
120 NEXT:PRINT
130 PRINT"Average for group is";TOTAL%/X%
```

Figure 5.18

A String array used in parallel with a number array. The advantage here is that the same subscript number refers to a name and the corresponding number from the two arrays.

is cleared and a total variable is set to zero in line 70. The list is then printed neatly, and on each pass through the loop the total is counted up (in line 110) so that the average value can be printed at the end. The important point here is that it's not just numbers that we can keep in this array form. This example uses both a string array (names) and a number array (marks). Remember that in any program like this, the arrays will have to be dimensioned correctly. If you don't know what number to expect when you write the program, you will have to add a line early in the program which reads, for example:

```
INPUT"How many items ";X%
```

in place of the assignment in line 10, so that the user has to specify how many items there will be in the array. The only way that an array can be created without dimensioning it is when the array is created on a disk, and that's something quite different which we shall look at later in Chapters 9 and 10.

```
10 CLS
20 FOR N%=1 TO 3
30 FOR J%=1 TO 2
40 READ N$(N%,J%)
50 NEXT J%,N%
60 FOR N%=1 TO 3
70 PRINT TAB(5)N$(N%,1);TAB(25)N$(N%,2)
80 NEXT
90 DATA Horse,Foal,Cow,Calf,Dog,Puppy
```

Figure 5.19

A two-dimensional matrix, which can be thought of as consisting of rows and columns.

Rows and Columns

You can imagine an array as a list of items, one after the other, but there is a variety of array which allows a different kind of list, called a matrix. A matrix is a list of groups or items, with all the items in a group related. We could think of a matrix as a set of rows and columns, with each group taking up a row, and the items of a group in separate columns. Take a look at Figure 5.19 to see how this works. We use here a variable N$ which has two subscript numbers. The first number is the row number, the second is the column number, and we need two `FOR..NEXT` loops to read data into this matrix. This is carried out in lines 20 to 50. Notice the shortened `NEXT J%,N%` in line 50, which is a way of writing `NEXT J%:NEXT N%`. The items are then printed in columns by the loop in lines 60 to 80. In this loop, the variable `N%` is used as the row number and we use the column numbers 1 and 2. The rows contain animal names, and the columns separate the different names that we use for adult and for young animals respectively.

Figure 5.20 shows a much more ambitious matrix program. This one uses a row number for matrix `A$` which is given by `X%`, assigned here with 50, and so it has to be dimensioned in line 10. The idea is to store sets of names and telephone numbers which are fed in by you in the course of the loop in lines 20 to 60. This is a `WHILE..WEND` loop that will stop if you enter a blank (just press **RETURN** key) for name and number, or if the number of entries has reached the dimensioned limit. Once the matrix has been filled, you can pick an initial letter for a name, and ask the computer to print out the name and number that it has

```
10 CLS:X%=50:DIM A$(X%,2):A$(0,1)="TEST"
20 N%=0:WHILE N%<=X% AND A$(N%,1)<>""
30 N%=N%+1:PRINT"Name ";:INPUT A$(N%,1)
40 PRINT"Tel. No. ";:INPUT A$(N%,2)
50 PRINT:PRINT
60 WEND
70 CLS:PRINT
80 PRINT"List complete"
90 PRINT:PRINT"Pick an initial letter...":PRINT"Use X to end
program."
100 J$="DUMMY":WHILE J$<>"X":Q%=0
110 INPUT "letter..";J$:FOR N%=1 TO X%
120 IF J$=LEFT$(A$(N%,1),1) THEN PRINT "Name is
";A$(N%,1):PRINT"Number is ";A$(N%,2):Q%=1
130 NEXT
140 IF Q%=0 THEN PRINT"Not found":PRINT
150 WEND
160 PRINT"End of program":END
```

Figure 5.20

A name and telephone number matrix program which allows you to search through the matrix to find a name.

located. I've left out tests of inputs (mugtraps) just to keep this example reasonably short, but you would certainly need some sort of mugtraps, even if only to avoid things like entering two letters or a whole name at line 110. The choice here is the entry of a first (capital) letter, and we should really check that this is a capital letter. If a lower-case letter is entered, it can easily be tested for because its ASCII code will be more than 96. We can convert a lower-case letter into an upper-case letter if we subtract 32 from the ASCII code. A step like:

```
J$=CHR$(ASC(J$)-32)
```

will carry out the conversion, or you can use the defined string function illustrated earlier.

The next part of the program deals with picking a name by specifying an initial letter. The important point here is that if we specify 'J', for example, it should not just pick out the first name that starts with J. That way you always get Jim, and never get John! In addition, if there is no name in the list which starts with the letter that you want, you should be told about this. You should also be told how to leave the loop, because this is a another WHILE..WEND type of loop. Line 110 deals with the input, and a choice of 'X' here will end the program. If any other letter has been selected, a loop starts in line 110. Each name is selected in turn by the loop, and the first letter of the name is compared with the letter which was selected. If the two match, then the whole name and telephone number will be printed. At the same time, a variable Q% is set to 1. This variable was made equal to 0 before the loop started, and it is used as a signal that a name has been found. The NEXT in line 130 marks the limit of this loop. When line 140 runs, Q% will be zero if no names have been found. The message will then be printed. If a name has been found then Q% will be 1, and the message is not printed. In either case, the WEND in line 150 forces this selection part of the program to repeat until you type X in response to the INPUT step.

The next thing that you might need to do with sets of names and numbers of this type is to record them. You can do this easily with the disk drive, and that's a subject that we shall look at in the course of Chapters 9 and 10.

Chapter 6

STRUCTURED CHOICES

We have seen how RESTORE, followed by a line number or label name, can be used to make a choice of items that are to be read from a list. Very often, though, we want to present a user with a menu on the screen. A menu is a list of choices, usually of program actions. By picking one of these choices, we can cause a section of the program to be run. One way of making the choice is by numbering the menu items, and typing the number of the one that you want to use. We could use a set of lines such as:

```
IF K =1 THEN GOTO 1000
IF K =2 THEN GOTO 2000
```

and so on. There is a much simpler method, however, which uses a new instruction ON N% GOTO, where N% is a number variable, an integer in this example. You can use any number variable, of course, not just N%, and a very common name here is CHOICE% because this reminds you of what the number is to be used for.

This type of menu selection is useful, but an even more useful method makes use of subroutines. A subroutine is a section of program which can be inserted anywhere that you like in a longer program. A subroutine is inserted by typing the instruction word GOSUB, followed by the label name or line number in which the subroutine starts. When your program comes to this instruction, it will jump to the line that is indicated by the name or number that follows GOSUB, just as if you had used GOTO. Unlike GOTO, however, GOSUB offers an automatic return. The word RETURN is used at the end of the subroutine lines, and it will cause the program to return to the point immediately following the GOSUB statement. Figure 6.1 illustrates this in action. When the program runs, a phrase is assigned

```
10 CLS
20 T$="BASIC Computing."
30 GOSUB 1000
40 T$=STRING$(LEN(T$),"-")
50 GOSUB 1000
60 LOCATE 4,2
70 PRINT"Neat, isn't it?"
80 END
1000 NR%=LEN(T$)
1010 PRINT TAB((80-NR%)/2);T$
1020 RETURN
```

Figure 6.1
Making use of a subroutine which in this example will centre any string assigned to T$.

to the string variable T$. The next line is GOSUB 1000, which means that the program must jump to the routine which starts at the line number 1000. In the subroutine, NR%, the number of characters in T$, is found. The following line then prints T$ centred on the screen. The last line of the subroutine consists only of the word RETURN. As the name suggests, this means that the program must return to a position that immediately follows the GOSUB that started the subroutine. In this first case, that means to the fourth line which carries out another assignment of T$, this time to a string of underlining dashes. Once again, calling GOSUB 1000 in the next line will cause this new value of T$ to be printed centred, and the RETURN this time makes the program return to the following line. With a GOTO, you are stuck with just one destination line number, but the RETURN at the end of a GOSUB makes sure you return to the command which follows the GOSUB. Even if you have a multi-statement line like:

```
T$="MENU":GOSUB centre:PRINT"NOTES"
```

then the subroutine will return correctly, in this case to perform the PRINT action.

One important point in this simple example is the use of END at the end of the main program. A subroutine should be used only by 'calling' it, which means the use of GOSUB. If the subroutine can be run in any other way, then when the RETURN is found, there will be nowhere to return to, and you will get an error message. Subroutines should be placed so that they can never run by normal program action. The best way to ensure this is to place the subroutines following the END statement at the end of the main program. An alternative, not used very much, is to make the first line of a program a GOTO 1000 that leads to the main program, and have all the subroutines placed between this line and the line 1000. See for yourself the effect in the simple example of Figure 6.1 of removing the END statement.

Menus, subroutines and program design

A menu is a list of choices, usually of program actions. By picking one of these choices, we can cause a section of the program to be run. This is a very useful way of keeping a form of central control over what a program does, and so it's not surprising to find that most business programs and other programs for 'serious' applications are based on a menu. A program which is designed around a menu is often described as being 'menu-driven', whether the menu is of the good old-fashioned pick-by-number type or one of the more modern 'icon and mouse' types that always seem to me to take too long to use. We'll start this portion, then, by looking at the display of menus and the way in which choices can be made from them. BASIC allows you a considerable number of options in how you present your menus and make your choices.

One simple way of making the choice is by numbering the menu items, and typing the number of the one that you want to use. Figure 6.2 shows what a typical menu of this type would look like on the screen. The part of the listing

```
                MENU

    1. Make a new list of names
    2. Add names to list
    3. Read names from list
    4. Delete names from list
    5. Select one name
    6. End program

     PLEASE CHOOSE BY NUMBER
```

Figure 6.2
How a typical menu appears on screen.

```
10 CLS:PRINT TAB(38)"MENU":PRINT TAB(38)"____"
20 PRINT:PRINT TAB(2)"1. Daily takings."
30 PRINT TAB(2)"2. Stock situation."
40 PRINT TAB(2)"3. Purchases."
50 PRINT TAB(2)"4. Summary."
60 PRINT TAB(2)"5. End program."
70 PRINT:PRINT TAB(5)"Please select by number 1 to 5"
80 K%=0:WHILE K%<1 OR K%>5:K$=INPUT$(1):K%=VAL(K$):WEND
90 ON K% GOSUB 1000,2000,3000,4000,100
100 PRINT"End of program."
110 END
1000 PRINT"Takings routine here":RETURN
2000 PRINT"Stock routine here.":RETURN
3000 PRINT"Purchase routine here":RETURN
4000 PRINT"Summary routine here":RETURN
```

Figure 6.3

How a menu can be programmed, using ON K% GOSUB to select the routines.

that displayed this menu would then go into a `INKEY$` type of loop, or an `INPUT$` statement, awaiting the pressing of a single-digit number key. This number would be tested for the correct range, with an error message if the range did not suit, and then the choice of routine would be made using the instruction words, `ON VALUE% GOSUB linenumber-list`. This assumes that each choice in the menu corresponds to a separate subroutine, and as you will see, there are very great advantages to be gained from programming in this way. Not least of these advantages is that it prepares you for learning languages like *Pascal*, *C*, *Modula-2* and *ADA* in which you are forced to program in this way.

Looking at the detail of the simple menu system, suppose we want to pick from four items by typing numbers 1 to 4 on the keyboard. In the example of Figure 6.3, the menu displays four fictitious items and an 'End program' choice. In this example, the menu is displayed, and then you are asked to pick from a limited range of numbers that is determined by the figures in the `WHILE..WEND` loop – you could, of course, make your menu routines generally useful by using variables for these numbers. The subroutine for choice contains `INPUT$(1)`, and `VAL` is used to extract a number when a key has been pressed. Choosing a number in the correct range will select one of the subroutines, but an incorrect number has no effect, since it is trapped in the WHILE..WEND loop. Finally, the routines that are called simply print titles and the program ends, since it's the menu system that we want to display, not the subroutines.

Sectional programming

A lot of programs consist of a title, some instructions, and then a menu. Depending on what menu choice you have made, some part of the program is run, and the program ends, or returns to the menu again. The ON choice% GOSUB type of menu selection is ideally suited to this type of programming, and is almost always preferred to the use of ON choice% GOTO. The advantage of using a subroutine for this purpose is that it offers an automatic return to the point immediately following the GOSUB, so that each subroutine now returns to the same place automatically. In general, programming should be based on subroutines, something that we shall plug away at throughout the course of this book, and in this section we shall look at some useful subroutines for program design, and then run through the way in which a program can be designed.

Continuing the theme of subroutines, Figure 6.4 shows an elaboration on a K$=INKEY$ type of subroutine. The trouble with INKEY$ is that it doesn't remind you that it's in use, there's no question mark prompt printed as there is when you use INPUT. As you may have noticed, there's nothing but a blank piece of

```
10 CLS:PRINT"Press any key "
20 GOSUB 1000
30 PRINT"You pressed ";K$
40 END
1000 K$="":WHILE K$="":K$=INKEY$
1010 PRINT"*";:GOSUB 2000
1020 PRINT CHR$(29);CHR$(32);CHR$(29);:GOSUB 2000
1030 WEND:RETURN
2000 FOR N=1 TO 1000:NEXT:RETURN
```

Figure 6.4

An improvement on the use of INKEY$ or INPUT$ for selection r outines. This flashes an asterisk to remind you that the computer is waiting for a key to be pressed.

```
10 CLS:KEY OFF
20 T$="Yout Choice"
30 ST%=2:NR%=4
40 GOSUB 10000
50 LOCATE 12,2:PRINT"You chose option ";CH%
60 KEY ON:END
5000 PS%=PS%-1:RETURN
6000 PS%=PS%+1:RETURN
10000 PRINT TAB((80-LEN(T$))/2);T$
10010 ON KEY(11) GOSUB 5000
10020 ON KEY(14) GOSUB 6000
10030 FOR J%=1 TO NR%
10040 LOCATE ST%+J%-1,5
10050 READ MENU$:PRINT MENU$
10060 NEXT:PS%=ST%
10070 LOCATE PS%,1:PRINT CHR$(175)
10080 FOR J=1 TO 1000:NEXT
10090 LOCATE PS%,1:PRINT CHR$(32)
10100 KEY(11)ON:KEY(14)ON
10110 FOR J=1 TO 1000:NEXT
10120 KEY(11)OFF:KEY(14)OFF
10130 K$=INKEY$
10140 IF K$=CHR$(32) THEN CH%=PS%-ST%+1:RETURN
10150 IF PS%>ST%+NR%-1 THEN PS%=ST%
10160 IF PS%<ST% THEN PS%=ST%+NR%-1
10170 GOTO 10070
10180 DATA Input data,Output Data,Check Data,Alter Data
```

Figure 6.5

A visual selection menu in which you pick the item by moving a pointer with the cursor keys, and confirm with the spacebar. Who needs mice?

screen under the menu. As always, if the program is to be used by you, its maker, and no-one else, this might just be satisfactory, but it's much more pleasing if there is some reminder of what is happening. This is particularly useful if you are likely to leave a program running for a time and then return to it. The subroutine in Figure 6.4 is one that can be added into the menu routine which remedies that problem by causing an asterisk to flash while you are thinking about which key to press. The asterisk is flashed by alternately printing the asterisk and the delete characters:

```
PRINT CHR$(29);CHR$(32);CHR$(29);
```

with a time delay between them. The PRINT CHR$(29) causes the cursor to move one step back, but this does not wipe out the character in this position. To do this, you print a blank using CHR$(32), and then since the cursor will have moved one step right you need to use CHR$(29) again. Do not forget to use the semicolons to keep printing in the same line. To make the rate of flashing reasonably slow, I've put in a delay using a FOR..NEXT loop. Note that the subroutine uses INKEY$, which does not stop and wait for a key to be pressed, so making the loop in the subroutine run until a key is pressed. At the time when a key-press is detected, the asterisk will have been erased, so that the routine does not stop with an asterisk still showing. It's a small point, but one that can save a lot of bother.

While we're on the subject of menus, there's another subroutine, in Figure 6.5, which can make a menu look a lot more interesting. This is a visual menu choice, and its use brings several advantages to your menus. One is that you don't have to have the items of the menu numbered, because you don't choose by number. Instead, a little arrow flashes next to the first item of the menu. This arrow can be shifted by using the cursor keys, the ones which are marked with the vertical up or down arrows. Since the program makes it impossible to shift the arrow beyond the menu items, no sort of testing or mugtrapping of the answer is needed. The choice is passed back to the main routine as a number CH%, which you can then use in a line such as:

```
ON CH% GOSUB 1000, 2000, 3000, 4000, ...
```

Try it for yourself, and see how much better it looks as compared to the traditional menu. It is, incidentally, rather easier to use in my estimation, and certainly easier to program, than the menus using the mouse which are featured in some other versions of BASIC.

The subroutine needs to have some values passed to it. The title is passed as T$, and two integer numbers are needed also. One of these is ST%, which is the line at which the first item of the menu will appear.The other is NR%, which is the number of items on the menu. The actual menu items are placed in a DATA line which can be anywhere in the program. If you have more than one menu, you can use RESTORE to get the correct set of data items. Once these quantities have been assigned, the subroutine can be called. In the example, the numbers have been set up to start on line 2 and use four items only.

The subroutine starts in line 10000 to 10040 by printing the title, centred, and then activating the cursor up and down keys. You will find that the cursor keys do not give ASCII codes, so that special methods of reading them are needed. The method that is used is of generating an interrupt. This means that if a designated key is pressed, the action of the computer, whatever it happens to be at the time, will be interrupted and a subroutine run. It's up to you to say what subroutine this should be, and in lines 10010–10020 we designate that key(11) should run the subroutine at 5000, and key(14) should run the key at 6000. The key whose code number is 11 is the cursor up (⇑) key, and the key with code 14 is the cursor down (⇓)key. Numbers 12 and 13 are used for cursor left and right, and numbers 1 to 10 are the function keys, so that you can cause a subroutine to run by pressing one of these keys. Simply stating the subroutines for specified keys, however, does not in itself make the keys respond – for that you need on and off statements so that you can control the parts of the program in which these keys are active. Having specified these keys and their subroutines, we then start reading the menu items and printing them. Variable ST% is used to make sure that the items are placed on the correct lines. The LOCATE command makes sure that the items are all tabbed to column number 5. At the end of line 10060, using PS%=ST% passes the value of ST% (4 in this example) to another variable PS% which will be used to control the position of the arrowhead. Line 10070 then starts a loop which will print the arrowhead, wait, delete the arrow and then look for a key being pressed while it waits. During this time, the keys 11 and 14 are switched on by the statement in line 10100, so that if either cursor key is pressed in this interval, one of the subroutines at 5000 or 6000 will be run. The INKEY$ statement then looks for the spacebar being pressed, and if it is then the program assigns CH% and returns. The movement of the cursor, expressed as PS%, is then checked to make sure that it cannot be above or below the menu items.

The idea in the CH% calculation is that ST% is the number of the first screen line which contains a menu item, and PS% is the one that the arrow points to. If the arrow is still on the first line, PS%-ST%+1 is 1–1+1=1, if the arrow is on the second line, then PS%-ST%+1 is 2–1+1=2 and so on. If you only use the menu subroutine once, then you can substitute numbers in place of ST% and NR%. The key detection for keys 11 and 14 is on only in the interval during which the arrow is deleted. This avoids leaving an arrowhead behind when a key is pressed, but if you want greater key sensitivity, you could use the key on statements at the start of the subroutine and cancel at the end. The problem of deleting an unwanted arrow would then have to be tackled by using a LOCATE and PRINT CHR$(32) statement in each of the arrow subroutines at 5000 and 6000 before the value of PS% was changed, Lines 10150 and 10160 then test the value of PS%. If this has gone out of limits, then it is returned to the opposite limit. If PS%

would place the arrow above the top menu item, it's placed at the bottom item. If the value of PS% would put the arrow below the bottom item, then it it returned to the top. This sort of action is called *wraparound*. Finally, line 10180 is the GOTO which completes the loop. The loop is broken only when the spacebar is pressed. You could, of course, alter this so that the **ESC** or **TAB** or any other key operated this action. Now try it out in your own programs!

Drive it yourself

You can get a lot of useful actions and enjoyment from your PC when you use it to enter programs from disks that you have bought. You can obtain even more enjoyment from typing in programs that you have seen printed in magazines which carry out some actions that will be useful to you. Even more rewarding is modifying one of these programs so that it behaves in a rather different way, making it do what suits you. The pinnacle of satisfaction, as far as computing is concerned, however, is achieved when you design your own programs. These don't have to be masterpieces. Just to have decided what you want, written it as a program, entered it and made it work is enough. It's 100% your own work, and you'll enjoy it all the more for that. After all, buying a computer and not programming it yourself is like buying a Ferrari and getting someone else to drive it for you – while you pump up the tyres now and again and fill up the tank quite often.

Now I shall assume that it's likely that you will have serious intentions of writing programs. By serious, I mean that you want your programs to serve some useful purpose such as keeping tabs on a stamp collection, a record collection, a set of notes on food preparation or the technical details of vintage steam locomotives. Programs of this type are called 'database' programs, because they need a lot of data items to be typed in and recorded. On the other hand, you might be interested in the presentation of data on the screen, particularly for business or educational applications. These are more specialised topics, and what we are going to look at in this section is the database type of program, because it's designed in a way that can be used for all types of programs.

Two points are important here. One is that experience counts in this design business. If you make your first efforts at design as simple as possible, you'll learn much more from them. That's because you're more likely to succeed with a simple program first time round. You'll learn more from designing a simple program that works after a bit of thought and modification, than from an elaborate program that never seems to do what it should. The second point is that program design has to start with the computer switched off, preferably in another room! The reason is that program design needs planning, and you can't plan properly when you have temptation in the shape of a keyboard in front of you. Get away from it!

Put it on paper

Program design starts, always, with a pad of paper. For myself, I use a 'student's pad' of A4 which is punched so that I can put sheets into a file. This way, I can keep the sheets tidy, and add to them as I need. I can also throw away any sheets I don't need, which is just as important. Even a very simple program is probably going to need more than one sheet of paper for its design. If you then go in for more elaborate programs, you may easily find yourself with a couple of dozen sheets of planning and of listing before you get to the keyboard. These sheets are important because not only do they form the basis of your listing, and help to trace where a fault may have occurred, they also act as the basis of your documentation. Never assume that your program will not need some sort of manual. Even if only you ever use it, there will come a day when you can't quite remember what you had to enter at some stage, or in what order some quantities were printed out. A lot of commercial programs use HELP pages, but paper documentation is much more satisfactory. It doesn't need any memory or disk space, and you can look at it even before you start using the program. If you keep your design notes in an orderly state they will form the basis of such a guide, even if it amounts only to a sheet or two. Another point about preparing such documentation is that it may assist you to see what features might usefully be added to the program. I must stress the word usefully. Too many commercial (and some non-commercial) programs are grossly overloaded with 'features' of questionable utility, all of which combine to make the programs run slower, take up more disk and memory space, and make the manual twice as large as it need be. Worse still, on such programs it's often very difficult to find how to do the comparatively simple things you want to do because there is so much to wade through. Start with a simple program, and add only what you find to be necessary and useful.

Start, then, by writing down what you expect the program to do. You might think that you don't need to do this, because you know what you want, but you'd be surprised. There's an old saying about not being able to see the wood for the trees, and it applies very forcefully to designing programs. If you don't write down what you expect a program to do, it's odds on that the program will never do it! The reason is that you get so involved in details when you starting writing the lines of BASIC that it's astonishingly easy to forget what it's all for. If you write it down, you'll have a goal to aim for, and that's as important in program design as it is in life. Don't just dash down a few words. Take some time about it, and consider what you want the program to be able to do. If you don't know, you can't program it! What is even more important is that this action of writing down what you expect a program to do gives you a chance to design a properly structured program. Structured in this sense means that the program is put together in a way that is a logical sequence, so that it is easy to add to, change, or re-design.

If you learn to program in this way, your programs will be easy to understand, take less time to get working, and will be easy to extend so that they do more than you intended at first. In particular, your structure should make use of the building-bricks of computing, input, computation and display. This means that your outline plan should consist of these elements – what you need to add is just what you want input, worked with and displayed, and what order of actions will do what you require. All of this is made easier if you design using a core and subroutines. If you get the program working using the simplest and most direct methods, you can easily elaborate it later. Tired of the type-a-digit menu choice? Replace the subroutine by the visual one from Figure 6.5 and you can concentrate on this, knowing that what you are doing should not interfere with the running of the rest of the program. Once again, good documentation is needed, because if you are to be certain that a new subroutine in BASIC will not interfere with the smooth running of the rest of the program, you have to know that the variable names you use are not ones that are used with different values elsewhere. Other programming languages are greatly superior to BASIC in this respect.

As an example to follow through, take a look at Figure 6.6. This shows a program outline plan for a simple indexing program. The aim is to be able to type in words and page numbers, edit out any mistakes, and then display or print the list, sorted into alphabetical order. I know that this can be done in about five lines using an MS-DOS batch file, but that's not relevant here. The program plan shows what I expect of the first attempt at this program. It must allow me to enter words, with suitable prompting, and page numbers. It should keep a tally of the number of words, and prevent the array from becoming over-filled. It must then allow me to edit each word or number in case of mistakes. The lists should then be sorted into alphabetical order, and finally presented either on the screen or to the printer. Now this is about as much detail as we need, unless we want to make the program more elaborate. For a first effort, this is quite enough. Very few programs emerge like an insect perfect from a chrysalis, and most are evolved from simple beginnings, even if these beginnings were

```
START
    REPEAT
        INPUT item (exit if blank)
    LOOP BACK
    REPEAT
        EDIT list
    UNTIL DONE
    SORT list
    PRINT list
END
```

Figure 6.6

An outline plan for a word/page number indexing program. This is the start of a program development.

another program, or a subroutine published in a magazine. How do we start the design from this point on?

The answer is to design the program in the way that an artist paints a picture or an architect designs a house. That means designing the outlines first, and the details later. The outlines of this program are the steps that make up the sequence of actions. We shall, for example, want to have a title displayed. Give the user time to read this, and then show instructions. At this stage, you can put instructions completely out of your mind, because the essential task at present is to get the program doing what it's supposed to do, even if in a very imperfect form. There's little doubt that we shall want to do things like assign variable names, dimension arrays, and other such preparation. All of this forms an 'initialiastion section', which is not part of the actual program itself. We then need to enter the words and page numbers, which is the essential input stage of the program. After this has been done, the user might want to edit the lists, another aspect of data input. After editing, the lists can be sorted, which is the computing portion, and then displayed, giving the output. Note that, as in so many programs of this type, the input and output take up much more of the program than the computing itself. In a more elaborate effort, we might want to keep the items stored on a disk, either before or after sorting, but we haven't come to disk filing yet. No matter, with a program designed in this way, we can easily add disk storage afterwards.

Laying foundations

Now at last, we can start writing a chunk of program. This will just be a foundation, though. What you must avoid at all costs is filling pages with BASIC lines at this stage. As any builder will tell you, the foundation counts for a lot. Get it right, and you have decided how good the rest of the structure will be. Figure 6.7 shows what you should aim for at this stage. There are only eleven lines of 'program' here, and that's as much as you want. This is a foundation, remember, not the Empire State Building. It's also a program that is being developed, so several of the lines are simply REM lines that will be removed later in the development of the program. REMs are useful, but they make an interpreted program in GW BASIC take up more space in memory, and run slightly slower. I always like to keep one copy of a program with the REMs in place, and another 'working' copy which has no REMs. That way I have a fast and efficient program for everyday use, and a fully-detailed version that I can use if I want to make changes. Let's get back to the program itself. As you can see, it follows the plan of Figure 6.6 exactly. Take a good long look at this eleven-line piece of program, because it's important. The use of the subroutines will mean that we can check this program easily – there isn't much to go wrong with it. We can now decide in what order we are going to write the subroutines. The wrong order, in practically every example, is the order in which they appear. Always write any title and instructions last, because they are the least important to you at this stage. In any case, if you write them too early, it's odds on that you will have some bright ideas about improving the program soon enough, and you will have

```
10 REM initialising actions
20 MX=5:REM for first testing
30 REM input of words and numbers.
40 GOSUB 1000
50 REM editing
60 GOSUB 2000
70 REM sort
80 GOSUB 3000
90 REM display
100 GOSUB 4000
110 END
```

Figure 6.7
The core program. This follows the outline of Figure 6.6, and leaves the details to the subroutines.

to write the instructions all over again. If you leave these lines unwritten then nothing will be executed, and then you can type in a GOSUB to some line number later and type in your instructions. This saves a lot of time when you are testing the program, because you don't have the delay of printing the title and instructions each time you run it.

The next step is to get to the keyboard (at last, at last) and enter this core program, save it, and then keep adding to the core. If you have the core saved, then you can load this in, add one of the subroutines, and then test. When you are satisfied that it works, you can record the whole lot as another disk file. Next time you want to add a subroutine, you start with this version, and so on. This way, you keep files of a steadily-growing program, with each stage tested and known to work. Again, this is important. Very often, testing takes much longer than you expect, longer than planning or typing, and it can be a very tedious job when you have a long program to work with. By testing each subroutine as you go, you know that you can have confidence in the earlier parts of the program, and you can concentrate on errors in the new sections.

Subroutine routine

The next thing we have to do is to design the subroutines. In fact, you don't have to learn anything new to do this. Each subroutine is designed in exactly the same way as we designed the core program. That means we have to write down what we expect it to do, and then arrange the steps that will carry out the action. If there's anything that seems to need more thought, we can relegate it to yet another subroutine to be dealt with later. As an example, take a look at Figure 6.8. This is a plan for the word/number input subroutine, which also includes information that we shall need for the setting-up steps. The plan starts by setting an item number at 0, then follows a loop in which the item number is incremented, the name and number are input, with the item number is printed so that you can keep a check on what has been done. The program then checks for the limits – the loop will have to be left if the word END has been used as a name or if the maximum number mx% of entries has been used. All of this hinges on a plan to use arrays to hold name and number. At this point, we might think hard about whether we want to use one array to hold both, or separate arrays. We often want to print an index in a form like byte, 38, using a comma to separate the two. If we want to do this, then we have to remember that we certainly can't type the comma if we choose to keep both name and number in one array. This is because the comma is taken to mean that more than one item is being entered. By using separate arrays, we can type the input using a comma,

```
START
ITEM NO 1
    REPEAT
        PRINT item number
        INPUT name, number (same line)
        INCREMENT item number
        CHECK: at end?
        OUT IF END
    ELSE LOOP BACK
RETURN
```

Figure 6.8
A plan for the word/number subroutine. Each subroutine can be planned in this way until you reach items that are simple enough to write straight away.

which seems more natural. The other point is that we might eventually want to merge items in which the same name appears with different page numbers. For example, if we have the items:

```
Memory, 22
Memory 58
```

then it's likely we'll want to combine these in the form:

```
Memory, 22, 58
```

and this is not so easy if the name and the number are contained in one array item. On balance, then, two arrays seem to be indicated, as we can use NAM$ and NUMBER$ for them. Why use a string array to hold a number? Simply because we can do more with strings, and since we aren't going to perform any arithmetic with the number there doesn't seem to be much point in keeping it as a number array. Knowing all this, then, we can write the initialising subroutine, as shown

```
200 MX%=5:N%=0:DIM NAM$(MX%+1),NUMBER$(MX%+1)
210 MES$="End of Entry"
220 RETURN
```

Figure 6.9
The initialising routine for the indexing program.

in Figure 6.9. This sets (temporarily) mx% to 5, allowing us to test with five items only, n% at 0, and dimensioning both NAM$ and NUMBER$ to MX%+1. The reason to dimensioning to one more than the maximum is to allow for N% to be incremented in its subroutine so as to test for the maximum being exceeded. The message MES$ is for placing at the end of the entry subroutine.

Entry subroutine

Figure 6.10 shows a first attempt at a suitable entry subroutine which is simple but effective. The initialisation subroutine at 200 has set the counter variable N% to 0, so a dummy entry is created as NAM$(0), and assigned with "TEST". As usual, this is the dummy entry that permits the WHILE..WEND loop to run. The entry loop then starts in the next line with the item number being incremented. This is the best place to increment the number, because it means that all the input and testing will be carried out with this same item number. The item number is printed, and the INPUT statement gets the inputs to the array. The next line then tests for the last entry number having been reached, and prints a suitable message if it has, then leaves the loop. This is done by making the new NAM$ item a blank, since this is what is tested for. You cannot INPUT as blank by pressing **RETURN** by itself, since this causes a 'Redo from start' message. Remember that you can temporarily take this or any other routine out of service by putting in the word REM just ahead of its GOSUB call. This also can be useful for testing. The routine appears to do just about what we need when we test it, and that's another important point. The testing must check for three things in

```
1000 NAM$(N%)="TEST"
1010 WHILE NAM$(N%)<>"":N%=N%+1
1020 PRINT TAB(5)"Item";N%": ";
1030 INPUT NAM$(N%),NUMBER$(N%)
1040 IF N%=MX% OR NAM$(N%)="END" THEN PRINT MES$:GOSUB
10000:N%=N%+1:NAM$(N%)=""
1050 WEND:RETURN
```

Figure 6.10

A simple entry subroutine. This is not up to the standards of an editing program, but it doesn't need to be. You can replace it by a more elaborate routine when needed.

```
1000 REM for testing only
1010 RESTORE:FOR J%=1 TO 5
1020 READ NAM$(J%),NUMBER(J%):NEXT
1030 RETURN
1040 DATA Memory,22,Catalogue,35,Zero,47
1050 DATA Abacus,62,ROM,64
```

Figure 6.11
Using READ..DATA lines for input when a program is tested at first. This avoids the tedious repetition of inputs if the program stops with an error.

particular. One is that the entries are as you would expect, another is that the program ends as you expect (an END entry or reaching maximum entry number). The other thing is that no 'silly' entry causes problems. In this case, ending the routine before the maximum number has been input is not straightforward, because you have to type END, press **RETURN**, then a comma, and then any number, then **RETURN** again. This is because of the use of INPUT name$, number$. We can live with this for the moment, and tidy it up later, because the essential thing is to get a working overall scheme. If END is a word that you might want to have in an index you will need to pick something else like X for termination.

Another point is that manual entry of words and numbers like this is not a particularly bright idea when you are testing, because it can cause a lot of work at the keyboard. In the early stages, its better to write a separate simple READ..DATA routine for this purpose, and throw it away when you are sure that every part of the program apart fro manual entry is functioning. Figure 6.11 shows the kind of thing that can be used.

The edit subroutine

We can leave sorting and display for the moment, because we already know how to tackle these points, and we'll turn now to the editing routine. The essentials here are to display items, amend them as needed, and ensure that they are corrected in the list. Now we might in a later version be able to write a dazzling on-screen selection type of editor, perhaps in a V3.0 of this program, but for the moment something simple that works is more important. One of the main reasons for using BASIC is that it's nearly always possible to get something going

```
2000 CLS:PRINT TAB(5);:INPUT"Type item number (0 to skip)"
;N%
2010 WHILE N%<0 OR N%>MX%
2020 PRINT TAB(5)"Unacceptable number- range is 1 to";MX%"."
2030 PRINT TAB(5)"Please try again.":GOSUB 10000:GOSUB
2000:WEND
2035 IF N%=0 THEN GOTO 2060
2040 PRINT TAB(5)"Item"N%": is ";NAM$(N%)","NUMBER$(N%)
2050 PRINT TAB(5);:INPUT"Your changes: ";NAM$(N%),NUMBER$(N%)
2060 RETURN
```

Figure 6.12

The editing subroutine. This again is a very simple version that requires you to retype the entry completely.

fairly quickly to cope with your needs, and put in subtle subroutines later on. What we need at the moment is something reasonably simple, but capable of letting us see what we want and correcting the mistakes.

The new lines of code are shown in Figure 6.12, and are the minimum that will serve. The correction is of a very simple type – just displaying the existing item and then making another input. If your typing is precise, you might have so few corrections to make that this system is perfectly adequate – remember that there is no point in adding embellishments for their own sake or, worse still, to show how good your grasp of BASIC is. For this sort of work, typing mistakes should be few, because indexing is a calm unhurried type of business – but please don't report me to the Society of Indexers.

The next step is display and printing. Display on the screen is straightforward, because it has been done already in the course of editing. You have to decide at this point whether to use a subroutine to serve both purposes, or to write a new one for final display. Since we want to allow the possibility of printed (hard-copy) output as well as screen, we might as well make this a new routine. The choice of printer or screen will have to be made before the data is printed. Figure 6.13 shows this part of the program. A novelty in this routine is that the choice of screen or printer is done by allocating the device number as `prn%`), using the numbers of 2 for the screen and 1 for a printer. This gets around the difficulty of having to use `PRINT` for screen and `LPRINT` for paper. By using:

```
4000 CLS:PRINT TAB(5)"(P)rinter or (S)creen?"
4005 OPEN "scrn:" FOR OUTPUT AS #2
4006 OPEN "lptl:" FOR OUTPUT AS #1
4010 PRN%=0:WHILE PRN%=0
4020 K$=INPUT$(1)
4030 PRN%=INSTR("PSps",K$):WEND
4035 IF PRN%/2=PRN%\2 THEN PRN%=2 ELSE PRN%=1
4040 CLS:FOR N%=1 TO MX%
4050 PRINT #PRN%,NAM$(N%) "," NUMBER$(N%)
4060 IF ASC(K$) AND 112=112 THEN GOTO 4080
4070 IF N%/23=N%\23 THEN GOSUB 4100
4080 NEXT
4090 RETURN
```

Figure 6.13

The display subroutine, which offers the choice of printer or screen. This is done by using a stream number variable which can be assigned with a number for printer or screen.

```
OPEN "scrn:" FOR OUTPUT AS #2
```

we ensure that a `PRINT #2`, statement like `PRINT #2, "TEST"` will be sent to the screen, just like `PRINT "TEST"`. By using the line:

```
OPEN "lptl:" FOR OUTPUT AS #1
```

we make any `PRINT #1`, statement deliver characters to the printer. Note the comma following the hash – you can't omit this. Here we can have a statement:

```
PRINT # prn%, text$
```

which will go to screen or to printer depending on the value of the variable `prn%`. When the message about using screen or printer appears, a `WHILE..WEND` loop in lines 4010 to 4030 gets your reply and tests it with `INSTR("PSps",k$)`. This ensures that if you have not typed either of the letters, upper-case or lower-case, the loop keeps running until you do. When a satisfactory result is obtained then, because the answers are in the order `"PSps"`, then `INSTR` will return 1 or 3 for `P/p` and 2 or 4 for `S/s`, but `0` for any other answer. A crafty test checks for the number being even or odd (`prn%/2` will contain a fraction if `prn%` is odd, and this can't be identical to `prn%\2`, the integer division). If `prn%` is odd, then it has 2 assigned to it, 1 otherwise, so forming the correct numbers for the `print # prn%` statement. Don't use the `P` option unless you have a printer connected and on line.

If the screen option is chosen, you will want to avoid having the data scrolling past you with no time to watch. The screen output is therefore paged. This is done using the test:

```
if n/23=n\23 then GOSUB 4100
```

which uses the two different division operators once again. The result of `n\23` will always be an integer like 0, 1, 2, 3, and so on, but `n/23` will contain a fraction except for values of `n` of 23, 46, 69 and so on. This test will therefore send the program to the 'pagit' subroutine on each 23 lines. The subroutine prints a messages and waits for a key to be pressed. When this is done, the screen is cleared and the next page of 23 lines is printed. You might want to place a `KEY OFF` statement into the initialising step and a `KEY ON` at the end of the program to create more screen space.

Now all that is left is to put in the sort routine, and once again that's something that we have covered before. Once again, on the basis that you keep it simple until you are sure of what you are doing, we'll use the straightforward string sort. Figure 6.14 shows the final listing for this part of the routine. The only change from the earlier example of this type of sort are the addition of another `SWAP` for sorting the `number$` array along with `NAM$`. There is, however, no conversion to upper-case so that names are sorted into the correct order no matter whether they are entered in lower- or in upper-case. This is important,

```
3000 PRINT TAB(5)"Sorting .....please wait."
3010 Y%=1:WHILE Y%<MX%:Y%=2*Y%:WEND
3020 Y%=(Y%-1)/2:IF Y%=0 THEN RETURN
3030 JT%=MX%-Y%:FOR J%=1 TO JT%:K%=J%
3040 Z%=K%+Y%
3050 IF NAM$(Z%)<=NAM$(K%)THEN SWAP NAM$(Z%),NAM$(K%):SWAP
NUMBER$(Z%),NUMBER$(K%):K%=K%-Y%:IF K%>0 THEN GOTO 3040
3060 NEXT:GOTO 3020
```

Figure 6.14
The sorting routine, using a straightforward Shell-Metzner sort.

because if ASCII code order is taken, then a word in capitals will be placed ahead of a word in lower-case. For example, if you had the words Zebra and abacus, then the order of an ASCII sort would be Zebra then abacus, placing the upper-case always before the lower-case. A BASIC that can use UCASE, like Turbo BASIC, is at a great advantage here. For GW users, you either have to be careful about the words you use, or you have to write a subroutine that will change case. Since this greatly slows the sort, it's not something to use unless you really have to, and unless you are entering words that contain a mixture of upper and lower-case you don't really need it.

All the testing so far will have been done with the aid of READ..DATA lines, and these will be kept until we can be absolutely sure that the program works perfectly. Once that has been accomplished, we can delete these lines and put in the initialization that we need in order to make this a useful program. In the initialisation, we can use an array of 300 entries, enough for the indexing of a small book. Obviously, if your needs require more than this, you can extend the dimensioning to suit yourself, but for large numbers of entries, there are other methods open to you, and in particular, you would probably want to keep the entries, both before and after sorting, on a disk file. Figure 6.15 shows the final product so far, with some tidying up and with title and instructions. Now you have a working program, you can start to embellish it as you please.

In all of this work, you may be surprised to see no elaborate flowcharts or other planning aids. The reason is that when you plan to make use of standard subroutines, the use of flowcharts is unnecessary. Providing that you draw up a plan of what the program will do and in what sequence, you can build the program in stages as I have demonstrated, knowing that you can rely on each stage which has been used in other programs, and testing each stage, old or new, as you go. This is one very great benefit of programming in this core and subroutine form, and another is the ease with which you can alter the program to suit yourself. There's a lot, in fact, that you can do to make this program into something more elaborate, or perhaps better suited for your purposes. The reason that I have used it as an example is to show what you can design for yourself at this stage. Take this as a sort of BASIC 'construction set' to re-build any way you like. It will give you some idea of the sense of achievement that you can get from mastering BASIC. As your experience grows, you will then be able to design programs that are very much longer and more elaborate than this one by a long way.

Figure 6.15
The final version of the program, along with title and instructions.

```
10 REM initialising actions
20 GOSUB 200:REM alter for first testing
30 REM input of words and numbers.
40 GOSUB 1000
50 REM editing
60 GOSUB 2000
70 REM sort
80 GOSUB 3000
90 REM display
100 GOSUB 4000
110 END
200 MX%=5:N%=0:DIM NAM$(MX%+1),NUMBER$(MX%+1)
210 MES$="End of Entry"
220 RETURN
1000 NAM$(N%)="TEST"
1010 WHILE NAM$(N%)<>"":N%=N%+1
1020 PRINT TAB(5)"Item";N%": ";
1030 INPUT NAM$(N%),NUMBER$(N%)
1040 IF N%=MX% OR NAM$(N%)="END" THEN PRINT MES$:GOSUB
10000:N%=N%+1:NAM$(N%)=""
1050 WEND:RETURN
2000 CLS:PRINT TAB(5);:INPUT"Type item No (0 to skip)" ;N%
2010 WHILE N%<0 OR N%>MX%
2020 PRINT TAB(5)"Unacceptable number - range is 1 to";MX%"."
2030 PRINT TAB(5)"Please try again.":GOSUB 10000:GOSUB
2000:WEND
2035 IF N%=0 THEN GOTO 2060
2040 PRINT TAB(5)"Item"N%": is ";NAM$(N%)","NUMBER$(N%)
2050 PRINT TAB(5);:INPUT"Your changes: ";NAM$(N%),NUMBER$(N%)
2060 RETURN
3000 PRINT TAB(5)"Sorting .....please wait."
3010 Y%=1:WHILE Y%<MX%:Y%=2*Y%:WEND
3020 Y%=(Y%-1)/2:IF Y%=0 THEN RETURN
3030 JT%=MX%-Y%:FOR J%=1 TO JT%:K%=J%
3040 Z%=K%+Y%
3050 IF NAM$(Z%)<=NAM$(K%)THEN SWAP NAM$(Z%),NAM$(K%):SWAP
NUMBER$(Z%),NUMBER$(K%):K%=K%-Y%:IF K%>0 THEN GOTO 3040
3060 NEXT:GOTO 3020
```

```
4000 CLS:PRINT TAB(5)"(P)rinter or (S)creen?"
4005 OPEN "scrn:" FOR OUTPUT AS #2
4006 OPEN "lpt1:" FOR OUTPUT AS #1
4010 PRN%=0:WHILE PRN%=0
4020 K$=INPUT$(1)
4030 PRN%=INSTR("PSps",K$):WEND
4035 IF PRN%/2=PRN%\2 THEN PRN%=2 ELSE PRN%=1
4040 CLS:FOR N%=1 TO MX%
4050 PRINT #PRN%,NAM$(N%) "," NUMBER$(N%)
4060 IF ASC(K$) AND 112=112 THEN GOTO 4080
4070 IF N%/23=N%\23 THEN GOSUB 4100
4080 NEXT
4090 RETURN
4100 PRINT TAB(5)"press any key for next page"
4110 G$=INPUT$(1):CLS:RETURN
10000 FOR X=1 TO 2000:NEXT:RETURN
```

Figure 6.15 *Continued.*

Chapter 7

SPECIAL EFFECTS AND GEOMETRICAL SHAPES

Any modern computer is expected to be able to produce dazzling displays of colour and other special effects. The PC computer is no exception, but precisely what you can achieve depends rather a lot on the version of BASIC that you are using, so in this chapter, we'll start to look at some of the effects that are possible. To start with, we have to know some of the terms that are used, and the first of these is Graphics. Graphics means pictures that can be drawn on the screen, and all modern computer languages have instructions that allow you to draw such patterns. Some shapes can be produced on the screen along with text by using `PRINT CHR$()` statements, such as `PRINT CHR$(185)`. These ready-made shapes are probably illustrated in your PC manual. You can make up strings that consist of these characters and then print each string as shown in Figure 7.1. This string consists of four characters with two printed on each line, and it can be printed as shown here on the left hand edge of the screen.

```
10 CLS
20 X$=CHR$(204)+CHR$(185)+CHR$(10)+CHR$(200)+CHR$(188)
30 PRINT X$
```

Figure 7.1

Printing graphics strings. These are simple enough to print at the left-hand side, but need to be printed line by line if you want to TAB them to a different position.

You cannot, however, use TAB or LOCATE to print this shape anywhere else in a line. If you do, you will find that only the top half is correctly tabbed. You might think that you could replace CHR$(10) by SPACE$(78) so as to ensure shifting the lower part of the symbol, but for some curious reason, when SPACE$(78) is included in the string, the TAB and LOCATE functions no longer work, and the symbol always appears at the left-hand edge! Since this rather limits the utility of graphics strings of this type, we'll leave it at that.

When it is switched on, your computer defaults to a 'text screen'. In other words, it automatically sets up the screen so as to print words and numbers, plus the limited range of graphics symbols. You cannot use any of the large number of graphics drawing commands on such a screen. You can get round this by switching to a different screen layout, one which allows fewer characters per line, but which displays the graphics characters fully. This is done by typing SCREEN 1 for low-resolution (coarse textured) images, or SCREEN 2 for high-resolution (fine textured) images. If you are using a monochrome monitor, you might as well always work with SCREEN 2, since this allows only two colours (background and foreground, normally black and white), but if you want to create patterns in up to four colours you will need to use SCREEN 1. Using SCREEN 1 also sets to 40 characters per line, which makes text appear very large. From now on, then, each graphics program will use SCREEN 1 or SCREEN 2 in place of the 'text screen', which is SCREEN 0. If you want to switch back to the text screen, you need only type SCREEN 0 (then **RETURN**), or press the **F10** key (though this does not return you to 80 characters per line if you have been using SCREEN 1, and you need WIDTH 80 as well). A SCREEN command will have the effect of clearing the screen as well as changing it, so CLS isn't needed after a SCREEN 1 or SCREEN 2.

Vivid impressions

If you are using a colour monitor, you can, of course, display both text and graphics in colour. If you are using a monochrome monitor, then the colours will appear only as shades of black or white. The colour statement uses the word COLOR (US spelling, remember), which can be followed by up to three numbers, each number specifying a colour. For a text screen, SCREEN 1, the order of numbers is foreground, background, border, and the meaning of the numbers is shown in Figure 7.2. As an illustration, make sure you are using SCREEN 0 and try:

```
COLOR 13,5,1:CLS
```

For SCREEN 0, you can set both foreground and background colours with the COLOR statement in the form `COLOR fore%,back%`, using the following numbers:

Number	*Colour*
0	Black
1	Blue
2	Green
3	Cyan
4	Red
5	Magenta
6	Brown
7	White
8	Green
9	Light Blue
10	Light Green
11	Light Cyan
12	Light Red
13	Light Magenta
14	Yellow
15	Bright white

Figure 7.2
The numbers that are used to code the screen colours. For monochrome monitors, the colours translate to shades of grey but, unfortunately, with no simple relationship between the number and the shade.

– which will make the foreground colour light magenta, the background dark magenta, and the border dark blue. This really is useful only on a colour monitor, because the contrasts are not so useful on a monochrome one. Note that if you omit the cls then you will not see the background colour appear except where a character appears. You can use a `COLOR` statement with the text screen (`SCREEN 0`) as shown above, or with the low-resolution graphics screen (`SCREEN 1`) in a different way, but not with the high-resolution screen `SCREEN 2` which is limited to black and white. In addition, there are some additional factors about the `COLOR` statement. You can add 16 to your choice of foreground colour number to make the characters flash – try `COLOR 23,0,0`. If, after placing some characters on the screen you change back with `COLOR 7,0,0`, the flashing will continue for

```
10 SCREEN 0:COLOR 0,4,5:CLS:KEY OFF
20 FOR N%=0 TO 15
30 COLOR N%,4,5
40 PRINT CHR$(N%+65);
50 NEXT
```

Figure 7.3

A program which illustrates the colour numbers for SCREEN 0. This gives quite different results for SCREEN 1, as explained in the text.

the characters that were made to flash until the screen is cleared or scrolled away. You are also limited to using colours 0 to 7 for background, and if you omit a border number then the border will remain unchanged.

With that in mind, take a look at the program of Figure 7.3. It starts by calling up the text screen, using `SCREEN 0`. This is then followed by a `COLOR` statement, and `CLS` to ensure the the screen background is established. The next part is a loop, which uses numbers 0 to 15. These are the colour numbers, and they are used in line 30 to set the foreground colour on each pass through the loop. In line 40, we print characters. Because we have used `PRINT CHR$(N%+65)`, these will be the letters of the alphabet, because ASCII code 65 is the code for 'A'. What you will find unexpected is the different colour of each letter! Run this, and just look at it.

Now try altering the screen statement to `SCREEN 1`. Obviously, the medium-resolution graphics screen does not behave like the text screen, because this time you see the background changing while the characters remain in the same colour. Only two numbers need to follow `COLOR` when `SCREEN 1` is being used. Of these, the first is a background colour this time, and the second is a palette number. This is a more complicated principle, though it will be familiar to many users of smaller computers in the past. The `SCREEN 1` type of display allows the use of four colours, numbered 0 to 3. These numbers, however, are not the colour number of the table in Figure 7.2, simply reference numbers. The colour number 0 means the background, and the numbers 1 to 3 are the three foreground colours. By using `COLOR`, you can specify which of the colour numbers in Figure 7.2 you want to use as the background colour, and what colours can be used for the other three. Your choice here is not unlimited, 0 or 1 only as shown in Figure 7.4. For example, by using `COLOR 2,1` you select Green (2) as background, number 0, along with cyan (1), Magenta (2) and white (3). These numbers 0 to 3 will be used in the statements for drawing lines that we shall look at later.

For SCREEN 1 the COLOR statement selects the background colour and the palette number. The Background number is selected from the list above, and the palette number selects three foreground numbers as follows:

COLOR number	*Palette 0*	*Palette 1*
1	Green	Cyan
2	Red	Magenta
3	Brown	White

– so that the use of numbers 1, 2 or 3 in graphics statements that use colour will use one of the three colours in the palette specified in the COLOR statement.

Figure 7.4
The COLOR choice for SCREEN 1.

PSET graphics

BASIC offers one way of producing graphics that is based on specifying whether a specified point on the screen should be in background or foreground colour. These points are 'high-resolution' in the sense that they use very small blocks, or, to give them their proper name, pixels. The pixels of the `SCREEN 2` are, in fact, the smallest units that we can place on to the graphics screen. We can place up to 640 pixels across the screen, and up to 200 down the screen, a total of 128000 pixels. Using `SCREEN 2`, BASIC allows you only to specify each of these pixels as black or white. When you use `SCREEN 1`, you can place up to 320 pixels across the screen and up to 200 down, a total of 64000 pixels.

The key instructions now are `PSET` and `PRESET`. `PSET` has to be followed by two numbers within brackets, and its effect is to make a pixel appear in a selected place. By adding another number, outside the brackets, we can also select a colour. If this colour code is omitted for a `SCREEN 1` statement, the pixel will appear in foreground colour 3 from the palette that was selected by the `COLOR` command earlier in the program. For `SCREEN 2`, the colour is always white. The

```
10 SCREEN 2:CLS
20 FOR N%=0 TO 630 STEP 15
30 PSET(N%,100)
40 NEXT
50 FOR N%=0 TO 630 STEP 2
60 PSET(N%,120)
70 NEXT
```

Figure 7.5
Pixel size illustrated for SCREEN 2, using PSET.

position of the pixel is specified by two numbers. The first of these, called the X co-ordinate, is the number of units across from the left hand side of the screen. The screen is divided (in our imagination) into 320 or 640 units across, depending on SCREEN number, and 200 down. We can use numbers 0 to 319(or 0 to 639) to control the position across the screen, the X-position. We can use numbers of 0 to 199 to control the position down the screen, the Y-position. X=0 means the left hand side, and Y=0 means the top of the screen. These are very tiny pixels, as you can see from the program in Figure 7.5. This sets SCREEN 2, so that no colours are used. In line 20 a loop starts which will print pixels in a line across the screen. By choosing 100 as the Y-number, we will make this line appear about half way down the screen. Using N% for the X-number allows us to PSET a number of positions, 15 units apart. The distance apart is measured from the left hand side of each pixel. Lines 50 to 70 show the effect of using STEP 2. The pixels appear almost joined, and the line of pixels takes slightly longer to draw, though in both cases the drawing is very fast.

The effect of PRESET is, as you might guess, to 'reset' the pixel, change it to background colour so that it disappears. This is used mainly to make pixels appear to move, and we'll look at that point later on. It's time for another example. The main use of PSET and PRESET is in drawing graphs, so that's what we'll illustrate. Figure 7.6 shows a graph drawing program. This draws several graphs at the same time, using different colours. Because the pixels of the high-resolution screen are so small, however, it's not easy to see the dots, and since all the dots are in the same colour, you can't easily distinguish the graphs. Line 20 starts the loop which makes use of all the permitted values of X%. The graph shapes are achieved by using the SIN function, with one used as it is, one squared, and one cubed. The multiplying factors are put in to make the shape fill a reasonable amount of the screen in the Y direction. The sine or cube of

```
10 KEY OFF:SCREEN 2:CLS
20 FOR X%=0 TO 635
30 PSET(X%,100+SIN(.1*X%)*90)
40 PSET(X%,100+SIN(.1*X%)^2*90)
50 PSET(X%,100+SIN(.1*X%)^3*90)
60 NEXT
```

Figure 7.6
Graph drawing using PSET with SCREEN 2.

the sine of an angle cannot have a value less than –1 or more than +1, so we have to 'amplify' it a bit by multiplying by 90. The square cannot have a value of more than +1 or less than 0. The value of X has to be multiplied by .1 to make the range of angles suitable. BASIC does not use angles in units of degrees. Instead, it uses a more natural unit, the radian which is about 57 degrees.

The separation of the graphs is easier if you plot in three colours, using SCREEN 1, as shown in Figure 7.7. The range of X numbers has had to be altered, and the use of COLOR 0,1 specifies a black background and colours cyan, magenta and white for the numbers 1, 2, and 3 respectively in palette 1. These numbers are added to the PSET statements, following a comma and even on a monochrome monitor you can see that it is easier to separate the three different graph shapes.

Sometimes, instead of specifying the exact position on the screen by means of X and Y numbers, you just want to specify a shift, or 'displacement' of a number of pixels. You can do this by using STEP (a,b), meaning that quantity 'a' will be

```
10 KEY OFF:SCREEN 1:COLOR 0,1:CLS
20 FOR X%=0 TO 319
30 PSET (X%,100+SIN(.1*X%)*90),1
40 PSET (X%,100+SIN(.1*X%)^2*90),2
50 PSET (X%,100+SIN(.1*X%)^3*90),3
60 NEXT
```

Figure 7.7
Using SCREEN 2 for a graph drawing program so that the three graphs appear in different colours. The separation is reasonable even with monochrome, and the increased pixel size is not disturbing.

added to the X value and quantity 'b' added to the Y value. Any of the instructions that make use of X and Y (usually in the form of X% and Y%) can use STEP in this way.

Lines, boxes, circles, and paints!

PSET and PRESET have their uses, when you may want to use a few pixels. It would be hard work, however, to design a program which used PSET and PRESET to draw lines. Fortunately, BASIC allows you to draw lines, boxes, and circles without having to resort to any special effort. This is because of the use of the LINE and CIRCLE commands.

The LINE command, used at full power, can be quite a lot to take in, so we'll start very simply. Try the program in Figure 7.8. This draws a diagonal line, using the medium sized pixels that you should have become used to by now in SCREEN 1. The last statement has been made a closed loop to prevent the cursor and the O.K. prompt from spoiling the appearance of the drawing. You will need to use **CTRL-BREAK** to get back to editing after this has run. The LINE command is followed by two sets of numbers. The first pair, in brackets, are the X and Y numbers for the starting point of the line. By using X=10 and Y=10, we have chosen a position very near the left hand side and the top of the screen. After the second bracket, there must be a 'dash' sign (-). This is followed by the finishing point of the line, in another set of brackets. This uses numbers X=240 and Y=180 to ensure that this point is near the bottom of the screen and at the right hand side. The result – a diagonal line from top left to bottom right. How about drawing for yourself a line from top right to bottom left? Try also using SCREEN 1 with the colour number 11 and its comma omitted. You'll see that the line slopes more sharply because we are using less than half of the possible range of X values.

```
10 SCREEN 1:CLS
20 LINE (10,10)-(240,180),15
30 GOTO 30
```

Figure 7.8

Using the LINE statement to draw a diagonal line with colour number 15. The closed loop prevents the Ok and cursor from appearing.

```
10 SCREEN 2:CLS
20 LINE(10,10)-(600,180)
30 LINE -(10,150)
```

Figure 7.9
Adding one line to the end of another, using a LINE statement with no starting coordinate numbers.

Now take a deep breath, because there are a lot of extras that can be tacked on to this command. Special offer number one is that once you have drawn one line, you can make the `LINE` commands simpler. Suppose that you want to draw another line which starts where the first one left off. You don't have to type the starting position all over again, simply omit the first bracket. Figure 7.9 shows what is needed, with line 30 containing `LINE -(10,150)` causing another line to join on to the end of the first one. This extension to `LINE` is particularly useful if you want to draw squares – and for random patterns it's essential. Just try Figure 7.10, which draws a starter line, and then uses a loop in which random numbers are used to place the finishing point of the next lines. You'll see, incidentally, just how fast BASIC draws these lines when you run this one. You could exhibit these at the Hayward Gallery and make your fortune, incidentally, if they weren't so well drawn.

The next one is quite an astonishment. Try the program in Figure 7.11, in which the letter B has been added after the rest of the LINE command. The effect is to draw a box – hence the letter 'B'. When you want to draw a box in this way, you must either use the colour number, or the correct number of commas, then the B. You cannot place the B immediately following the last bracket, because

```
10 SCREEN 1:COLOR 1,1:CLS
20 LINE(20,20)-(150,150),9
30 FOR N%=1 TO 50
40 X%=RND*255:Y%=RND*199
50 LINE-(X%,Y%),9
60 NEXT
```

Figure 7.10
A random-line program for aspiring abstract artists.

```
10 SCREEN 1:COLOR 0,1:CLS
20 LINE (30,30)-(210,140),1,B
```

Figure 7.11

Using the B sub-command in LINE to create a box. The first coordinate pair is the top left hand corner, the other is the bottom right hand corner.

```
10 SCREEN 1:COLOR 0,1:CLS
20 FOR N%=1 TO 10
30 X%=RND*255:Y%=RND*199
40 X1%=RND*255:Y1%=RND*199
50 LINE(X%,Y%)-(X1%,Y1%),N% MOD 4,B
60 NEXT
```

Figure 7.12

Random boxes for students of abstract sculpture.

this will not be taken as a box command when it is in the place where the computer expects to find a colour command. The two points in the `LINE` command form the opposite corners of the box, so you will always get neatly rectangular boxes when you use this command,. If any of the sides looks bent, it's time to get your monitor serviced! Figure 7.12 shows something of the speed of this command. It chooses two sets of X and Y numbers at random, and then draws a box in a random colour. The colour has been selected by using `N% MOD 4`, the remainder after `N%` has been divided by four, and this will, of course, make some boxes be drawn in colour 0, which is black. A better method would be to use `1+(N% MOD 3)` to eliminate the possibility of this number coming out at 0.

No, we haven't finished, because there is one more twist to `LINE`. Take a look at the simple program in Figure 7.13. This draws two boxes, using `LINE` in the way that you have seen earlier, but with 'F' added to the 'B'. You don't need any commas or other dividers here, just the 'F' at the end. Now the effect of the 'F' is to fill the rectangle with colour. The colour that is used is the colour that you have specified in the `LINE` command, which will be the palette colour 1 to 3 as specified by the `COLOR` statement. You'll see from the example that more than one box can be drawn and filled in this way.

```
10 SCREEN 1:COLOR 0,0:CLS
20 LINE(10,10)-(100,100),2,BF
30 LINE(150,20)-(250,190),3,BF
```

Figure 7.13
Filling a closed box with colour, using the F subcommand following B.

Better circles

Drawing straight lines and boxes is useful, but being able to draw circles greatly extends our artistic range. BASIC as you might expect by now, have a very useful CIRCLE instruction. As usual, we'll keep it simple for starters. CIRCLE has to be followed by a pair of co-ordinate numbers, in brackets, and then by another number outside the brackets. As usual, commas separate the numbers. The co-ordinate numbers are of the centre of the circle. The number that follows the brackets is the radius of the circle. In case you've forgotten, that's the distance from the centre to the outside. It's measured in screen units, these 320/640 by 199 units that we work in all the time, depending on SCREEN number. If you want to show the whole of a circle on the screen, the largest number that you can use for the radius is 99, assuming that the centre of the circle is the centre of the screen. Following the radius number we can, if we are using SCREEN 1, have another number, the colour number for the circle.

After that introduction, take a look at Figure 7.14. Line 10 sets up the familiar SCREEN 1 conditions, and the loop that starts in line 20 causes a set of circles to be drawn. You may find that they don't look very circular. This is something that depends very much on how well adjusted your monitor is. On my monitor, the circles were no more than a millimetre out, which compares well to a certain

```
10 SCREEN 1
20 FOR N%=10 TO 80 STEP 20
30 CIRCLE(127,96),N%,1
40 NEXT
```

Figure 7.14
The CIRCLE statement, which produces circles of excellent shape, unlike some versions of BASIC.

```
10 SCREEN 1:COLOR 0,0
20 CIRCLE(127,96),80,1,0,3.14
```

Figure 7.15
Drawing partial circles (arcs) with an extended CIRCLE statement. Angles have to be specified in radians.

other variety of BASIC that produced very squashed circles. We're not finished with circles, though. What you know of BASIC so far might lead you to believe that there could just be more to this `CIRCLE` command. There is. Try Figure 7.15, which shows how you can draw part-circles. The key to this is the provision of start and stop numbers. The number 0 is taken as the 3 o'clock position on

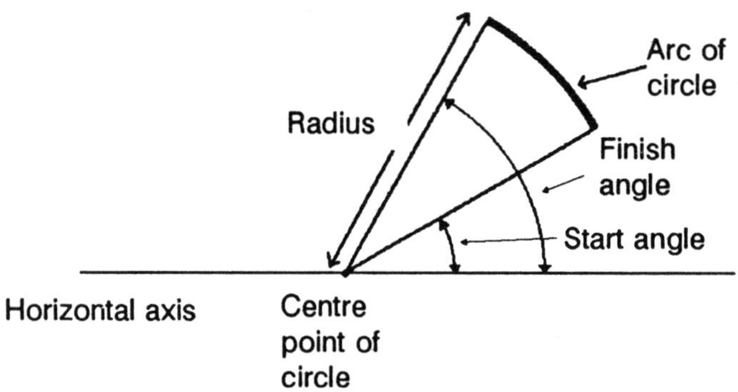

1. **Draw out the part-circle you want, as illustrated.**
2. **Measure start & finish angles, starting from horizontal axis to right of centre.**
3. **Convert angles to radians. Measure radius and convert to pixel units.**
4. **Place into `CIRCLE` command.**

Notes: Length of arc = radius × (finish angle − start angle)

Angles measured in radians.
Angles can range up to 360°, depending where start and finish are placed.

Figure 7.16
How to go about designing part-circles, and how to cope with angles in radians.

the screen, and the circle is drawn, going anti-clockwise from this position. The end-point is specified by the second number. I have made this 3.14, which is the value of PI. Using this number gives a semicircle, and for other parts of a circle, just use the appropriate fraction. Figure 7.16 shows how you can design your part-circles for yourself, and convert from degrees to the radian units that are needed in this command.

Don't square it, squash it!

BASIC also allows you to draw shapes which are ellipses, squashed circles. The re-shaping of a circle is done by adding yet another number to the circle instruction. If this number is 1, then we simply get a circle. If this extra number is less than 1, however, we get an ellipse which is wider than it is high. If the extra number is greater than one, the ellipse is higher than it is wide. We can even make ellipses which are stretched out so much that they look like straight lines! We can also correct the shape of circles that look elliptical because of the monitor. This gives you unparalleled power to create all sorts of curved shapes. One of the features of the `CIRCLE` command is that it allows the use of numbers which take the cursor beyond the screen area, so that what you see on the screen is only part of a drawing.

Take a look at Figure 7.17. Lines 10 to 60 are used to illustrate the ellipses that we can create. The range of the number that we can use, following the radius number (don't forget the comma) is 0 to 255, but the range that I have illustrated here is the most useful part. The only problem with this command is that it comes after the "start and finish" commands which we use to draw a part-circle.

```
10 SCREEN 1:COLOR 0,0
20 FOR E=1 TO .1 STEP -.1
30 CIRCLE(128,96),100,1,,,E:NEXT
40 FOR N=1 TO 3000:NEXT:CLS
50 FOR E=1 TO 3 STEP .2
60 CIRCLE(128,96),80,1,,,E:NEXT
```

Figure 7.17

Creating elliptical shapes by adding yet another number in the CIRCLE statement. Note that where quantities are missed out, such as the part-circle numbers in this example, the commas must be inserted.

```
10 SCREEN 1:COLOR 0,0
20 CIRCLE(127,96),88,1
30 CIRCLE(127,96),30,1
40 PAINT(127,50),1
```

Figure 7.18
Using the PAINT statement to fill a closed space with colour.

If you want a complete ellipse, you won't want to use these numbers. We can get round this, as the program indicates, by omitting the start and finish numbers, but putting in their commas. It makes the command look rather odd, but it works! Notice how the circles are drawn starting from the two horizontal ends.

Meantime, there's another command to look at. Figure 7.18 demonstrate another amazing feature of this BASIC, the PAINT instruction. This will fill a space with colour, providing that you have enclosed the space with lines. Lines 20 and 30 draw two circles, one within the other. The PAINT instruction in line 40 then fills with colour the space between the circles. PAINT needs the usual pair of co-ordinate numbers following it, in brackets. You have to choose these numbers so that they will act as a starting point for the painting operation. They must, therefore be somewhere inside the area that you want to paint. You may get odd things happening if you select a point on the edge of the area that you want to paint. You will certainly not get what you want if you pick a point which is outside the area you want to paint! Following the starting point, we've used one other number. This is the number of the colour that we want to use for painting. We don't have much choice about this colour, it has to be the same as the colour we have used as a boundary. Both of the circles are drawn in green, the first number in palette 0, so we have to paint in this colour. If you ignore this, you may find that the colour spills all over the screen. Trouble will also be inevitable if there is a gap in your boundary that will allow the paint to leak out.

POINT the way!

There's another command which fits along with PSET and PRESET, and which gives me a chance to show you PRESET in action. The command is POINT, and it's a way of reporting what's going on. POINT gives you the colour of a pixel. It has to be followed by the usual X and Y location numbers, and you can find

```
10 SCREEN 1:COLOR 0,0:CLS
20 FOR Y%=0 TO 199:PSET (10,Y%),1:NEXT
30 FOR Y%=0 TO 199:PSET(254,Y%),1:NEXT
40 K%=1:X%=11:Y%=1
50 WHILE Y%<199
60 PSET(X%,Y%),2
70 IF POINT(X%+K%,Y%)<>0 THEN K%=-K%:Y%=Y%+1
80 PRESET(X%,Y%)
90 X%=X%+K%
100 IF Y%=199 THEN END
110 WEND
```

Figure 7.19
Using POINT to detect a boundary.

what it does by using something like PRINT POINT(X,Y) or A=POINT(X,Y). What is printed or assigned to A by these commands will be a number between 0 and 15. It is the colour number for the pixel, so that you can tell whether the pixel is at background or at foreground colour.

Now that description makes it sound quite simple, but it's not quite so simple as it seems, as the program in Figure 7.19 will illustrate. The program sets a black background, and draws a vertical line down each side. A dot is placed at the top left hand side, and it moves across the screen. This is done by using PSET(X%,Y%),2. The future position of the dot is tested by using POINT, and if this point is background, the point is PRESET, the value of X% is increased, and the new point is PSET. When the wall is found from POINT, then the variable K% is made negative, so that X%+K% will have the effect of subtracting 1 instead of adding 1. This causes the point to move left rather than right. At the same time, Y%=Y%+1 has the effect of moving the point one step down. The POINT function test to find if the next position will be background, and if it is not, you have reached the wall. The PRESET(X%,Y%) will erase the previous dot position so that the movement of the dot does not leave a line behind it.

In this example, of course, there was no need to use POINT, because we knew exactly where the walls were. In maze games, however, the walls are drawn at random, and you can't put their X and Y numbers so easily into a POINT command. It's then that POINT really comes into its own. Another reason for using POINT is that if you have two objects moving on the screen, it's easier to detect any kind of collision (object to object or object to background) with POINT. Just one

POINT test will detect any type of collision, but if you were testing values of X% and Y%, you might have to use a lot of tests.

Computer drawing

The ability for drawing lines and circles is just the start of the BASIC computer's amazing graphics capabilities. We're going to look at another way of drawing now, one which uses the instruction word DRAW. DRAW has to be followed by a string variable name, like DRAW A$ or DRAW GR$, and it's what you put into this string variable that decides what is drawn. Figure 7.20 shows a list of the letters that can be used. What you have to do is to chart your drawing in terms of a starting point, then as up, down, left, right, or diagonal movements. The amount of each movement can be small, just one pixel, so that it's possible to make very detailed patterns in this way when you use SCREEN 2, and SCREEN 1 is quite effective also. You can also move to a new starting point without drawing a line.

Letter	*Effect*
U	Upward movement
D	Downward movement
L	Move to left
R	Move to right
M	Move to point whose x ,y coordinates follow

The following letters can precede any movement letter

B	Blank, leave no trace
N	Move but return to start after movement

The following set effects rather than movement

A	Set angle in multiple of 90 degrees.
TA	Turn angle, followed by angle in degrees, range ±360°
C	Colour (followed by colour number 0 to 15)
S	Set scale factor 1–255 (4 is normal scale)

Figure 7.20
The letter subcommands for the DRAW statement.

```
10 SCREEN 2:CLS
20 GR$="bm20,180;u100r20d100r20u100r20d100"
30 DRAW GR$
```

Figure 7.21
A simple DRAW string illustrated.

The very considerable advantage of using DRAW is that a complete pattern can be put on to the screen by just one simple instruction like DRAW G$.

Now to the nitty-gritty. Figure 7.21 illustrates just how we go about creating a drawing in this way. Line 10 is familiar stuff – using SCREEN 2 just for a change – but line 20 is new. In this line, a string is defined. It's a funny-looking sort of string which consists of command letters and numbers. The command letters are the letters of the draw commands, and the numbers are the units of screen size. As you know by now, these are 0 to 639 in the X direction, and 0 to 199 in the Y direction for SCREEN 2. The string starts with BM. 'B' means 'blank' and it's used to ensure that no line is drawn, and 'M' means move. The letter 'M' has to be followed by two numbers, which are the X and Y numbers for the place where you want the drawing to start. I have chosen a point near the bottom left hand side of the screen. Following the BM step, you might need to indicate what colour you want for your drawing, but this is not necessary for a SCREEN 2 production (it would be done by using the letter 'C', followed by the colour number). The next parts are movements – 100 up, 20 right, 100 down, 20 right and so on. The string ends with a quote mark as usual.

Now all that we have to do to draw this in line 30 is the command DRAW GR$. It's delightfully simple, but a very fast and powerful way of creating a drawing. It's particularly easy to make repetitive drawings in this way, because we can

```
10 SCREEN 1:COLOR 0,1:CLS
20 SB$="u100r20d100r20"
30 XS$="":FOR N%=1 TO 5:XS$=XS$+SB$:NEXT
40 GR$="bm20,180;c2xxs$;"
50 DRAW GR$
```

Figure 7.22
Using a sub-string within a DRAW string.

include a sort of subroutine. This is called a 'sub-string', and Figure 7.22 shows how it is used. What it amounts to is that you can define a string which is part of a pattern, then 'execute' this sub-string inside the main string. In this case, I have illustrated only the sub-string being used. The calling command is X (eXecute), and it must be followed by the string name and then a semicolon. If you miss out the semicolon, you will get an error message, but the error will be reported in line 50, where the DRAW GR$ instructions is. This can be confusing, because the error is not actually in this line, it's just that it's been found when this line was run. In this example, I have used SB$ to contain a simple up, across, down, across, set of instructions. The loop in line 30 then packs five of these patterns into a longer string, and line 40 calls for this string to be called as a sub-string of GR$. The result is five sets of the pattern on the screen.

Now for a much more elaborate drawing, in Figure 7.23, that makes use of all of the commands so far. Line 20 as usual sets up the screen conditions, and lines 30 to 50 then define the strings. M$ is the main string, and it starts with BM40,20. Two sub-strings are used. In this example, C$ is the chimney, and D$ is the dome. Using XC$ and XD$ in the main string therefore draws these details in the correct places. If you aren't pleased with these places, it's easy to move position. All you have to do is to alter the place where the sub-string is called. Incidentally, I typed this with the **CAPS LOCK** pressed, because in the graphics strings, a capital 'L' is less likely to be confused with a "1" than a small 'l'. You can use either, because the machine is not confused by the difference between 'L' and 'l'.

```
10 REM More substrings.
20 SCREEN 1:COLOR 0,0:CLS
30
M$="BM40,20;C1D10R10D60L10U5D20U5R200U60L10U10;XC$;D10L60;XD$;
L50U20L60"
40 C$="U2LU2LU2LU2L2U2L5U2R30D2L5D2L2D2LD2LD2LD2L"
50 D$="U5LU5LU2LU3L2U2L4U3L4UL2DL4D3L4D2L2D3LD2LD5LD5"
60 DRAW M$
70 FOR X%=100 TO 200 STEP 50
80 CIRCLE(X%,100),20,1:NEXT
90 LINE(100,110)-(200,110),1
```

Figure 7.23

A more elaborate drawing which demonstrates the speed and simplicity of this method.

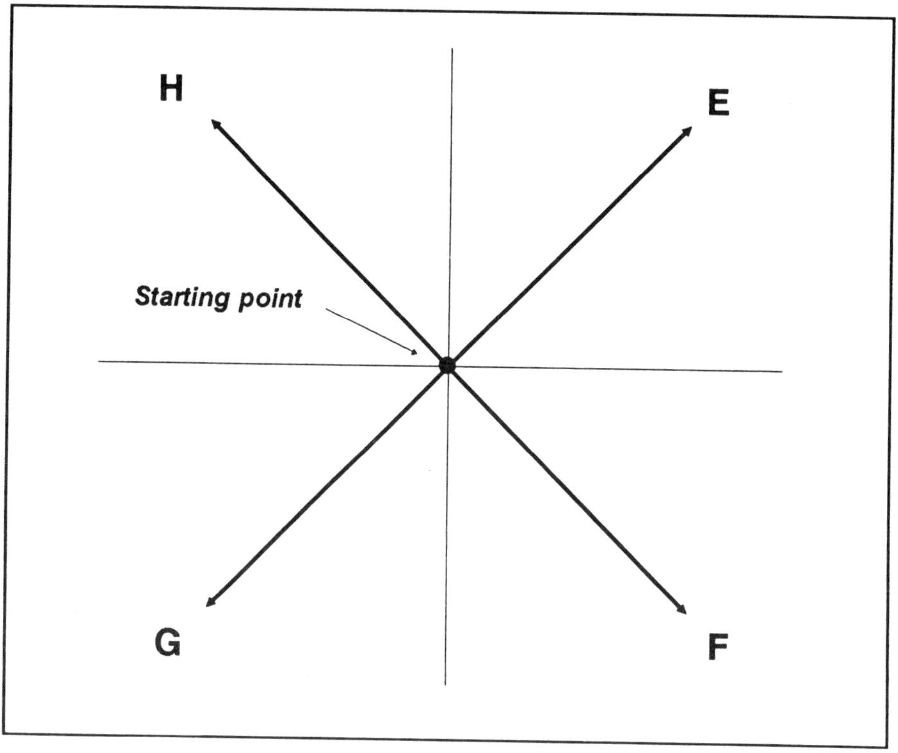

Figure 7.24
The diagonal direction letter subcommands of DRAW.

I have used semicolons after `BM40,20p`, and before and after each sub-string. The semicolon must be used after the string ($) sign, but it doesn't have to be used in the other positions. I have put in the extra semicolons just to make it easier to read the items in the string by marking out the positions of the sub-strings. The main body of the drawing is then carried out at an astonishing speed by `DRAW M$` in line 60. The next point in this example is that you can mix the familiar `LINE` and `CIRCLE` commands along with the `DRAW!`. The circle commands are used for drawing the driving wheels, because there is nothing in a `DRAW` string that can do this. The `LINE` could have been replaced by a `DRAW`, but it's easier to use `LINE` in this case, because it needs only one instruction.

Now for some more `DRAW` magic. As well as the up, down left and right commands, there are letters which indicate diagonal directions. These are illustrated in Figure 7.24, and a program which uses them is shown in Figure 7.25. This uses a string which draws a diamond pattern, and then chooses ten randomly selected

```
10 SCREEN 1:COLOR 0,0:CLS
20 DM$="G10H10E10F10"
30 FOR N%=1 TO 10
40 P%=INT(RND*220+20):Q%=INT(RND*150+20)
50 PSET(P%,Q%):DRAW DM$
60 NEXT
```

Figure 7.25
A diamond pattern to illustrate the use of diagonal drawing.

places on the screen. Now you have to be careful here as to how you get to these places. Using LOCATE works only for the instructions of the text screen, like PRINT, but does not move the DRAW position. The command that you have to use is PSET (or PRESET). By picking P% and Q% values at random, followed by PSET (P%,Q%), the invisible graphics cursor is in the correct place to draw the diamond pattern. You might think that you could use BM P%,Q% for this, but you can't. You are not allowed to use variable names inside a graphics string, except in ways that we'll come to later. The BM command is not one of the commands that can make use of variables.

Artistic creations

The DRAW command is a very useful way of making straight line drawings with less effort than is needed by LINE. You can use the LINE commands as well, and all the varieties of CIRCLE, along with box fill and PAINT to create any shape you want. What we have to look at now is how to plan these shapes. Trying to make a program that creates shapes on the screen is difficult enough, without planning it's almost impossible! The planning must start, as always, with a piece of graph paper.

You will have to start with a sheet of A4 graph paper. They should be A4 size and scaled in centimetres and millimetres. In addition, you will need a pad of tracing paper from the same suppliers. These items are not cheap, but they will last you for a long time. The principle is to mark out on the graph paper the co-ordinate numbers for your graphics screen, place the tracing paper over the graph paper, and then to make drawings on to the tracing paper. Because the tracing paper is transparent, you can see through it to the grid of co-ordinates underneath, and you can read off the values. Strictly speaking, you should use scales of 0 to 319 or 639 and 0 to 199, but its unusual to have to draw right to the edges of the screen, and using 10 to 310/630 and 10 to 190 is much more convenient – it fits the paper better! You count each square on the graph paper as having sides of ten pixels, and diagonals also of ten pixels. That point about the diagonals is very important, because it saves a lot of awkward calculations or measurements. You draw your patterns on the paper, remembering that you can use up, down, left and right. When it comes to diagonals, remember that these must be 45 degree diagonals. This makes some shapes look distorted, and if the distortion is unacceptable, then you will have to use `LINE` instructions for these parts. When you make the drawing, you will make life a lot easier if you keep to simple dimensions, like multiples of five and ten. It is a lot more difficult to follow a pattern that goes `U13L27D17R29` and so on! Working with the tracing paper over the graph paper makes it much easier to see what you are doing, and check your measurements.

The next step, once the drawing is to your satisfaction, is to obtain any distances and co-ordinates that you need. If you are using `LINE` and `CIRCLE`, you will need to read the X and Y co-ordinates of points such as the start and end of a line or the centre of a circle. These are easily read from the graph paper underneath the tracing paper. `DRAW` graphics are just as easy – you simply count sides of squares or complete diagonals as ten pixels each, and then write the numbers against the lines. It helps if you write the letters like `U,D,G,H` and so on as well. You can then program directly from this. Programming is made easier if you program a section at a time, and join the strings up for final drawing.

Shrink, grow, and turn

The possibilities for creating drawings with the `DRAW` instruction are made even greater by the options of altering both the size and the angle of patterns. These actions are carried out by using the letters `S` (for scale) and `A` (for angle) within the `DRAW` string. We can also add these instruction letters to a string, and we can put numbers in along with them by using `STR$(number)`. BASIC allows another way of putting variables into these `DRAW` strings. If you have a variable, such as `J%`, which carries a value, then you can put something like `S=J%;` into the string. The semicolon is essential and you will get an error message if you omit it. The effects which can be produced with this scale command are spectacular – most other machines could do these actions only with a lot of very complicated programming.

```
10 SCREEN 1:COLOR 0,0:CLS
20 G$="U50R50D50L50"
30 DRAW"BM128,96"+G$
40 FOR N=1 TO 3000:NEXT
50 FOR J%=1 TO 60:CLS
60 DRAW"BM128,96S"+STR$(J%)+G$
70 FOR Z=1 TO 2000:NEXT
80 NEXT
```

Figure 7.26

The use of the scaling subcommand which allows you to shrink or expand your drawings. This allows you, for example, to display a drawing on the whole screen, then to shrink it to one corner.

Try the program of Figure 7.26 now. This, up to line 30, is a simple piece of programming that draws a box. After the delay in line 40, though, things start to happen. The fancy business starts in line 50, with the loop that uses variable J%. The range of the counter J% is 1 to 60, and you can use up to 255. This figure of 255 is the whole of the permitted range for the scale instruction, which uses the letter 'S'. The scale which will be used for drawing is one eighth of the number which follows 'S'. For example, if you use S2, then the drawing is 2/8, which is ¼ size. Using S16 would make the drawing 16/8, which is double size. This letter 'S' has been put into the DRAW instruction in line 60, so that the pattern is drawn with a different scale number each time. Watch these scale effects carefully. They are very easy to use, but the effects may not be exactly what you want. One point is that the start which is given by the BM part of the command is one edge of the square. The square will always start at this edge and grow from that point. The other problem occurs if the pattern 'grows' too much, because this can take some of the boundaries beyond the screen edges. Some careful planning, with graph paper and tracing paper, is needed when you start to work with these 'Incredible Hulk' graphics!

Take a quick look now at a small change which makes a big difference. The program is in Figure 7.27, and starts with items that should be familiar territory for you now. Line 20 is a short and simple string for a shape. Notice that this shape has no defined starting point, and it starts with a blank move upwards. The reason, as you'll see later is so that the starting point is the centre of the shape. When we expand the shape, the expansion is always around the starting point. If this now is the centre, then the centre of the shape stays put. In the previous example, because the starting point was at a corner, then the shape expanded from that corner outwards. Line 30 then draws this shape, but with a

```
10 SCREEN 1:COLOR 0,0:CLS
20 G$="BU5L10F5G5R20H5E5L10"
30 DRAW"BM140,80"+G$:FOR N=1 TO 2000:NEXT
40 FOR J%=1 TO 60:CLS
50 DRAW"BM140,80s"+STR$(J%)+G$
60 FOR Z=1 TO 1000:NEXT
70 NEXT
```

Figure 7.27
A scale-changing program adapted so that the centre of the shape remains in the same point.

starting point added at 140,80. Notice how this is done, using the + sign to join the strings.

Angle antics

The use of the command letter S to make the drawing take different scales is a splendid feature of this BASIC, but there is another command letter that we can use. This time it's A, and its effect is to alter the angle at which a shape is seen. With A0, the shape is shown just as it has been drawn. With A1, the shape is turned through 90 degrees anticlockwise. Using A2 make the shape turn through 180 degrees, and A3 makes it turn through 270 degrees. The number which is used with A must not exceed 3, otherwise the program will stop with the `Illegal function call` error message. Figure 7.28 shows an example of this command

```
10 SCREEN 1:COLOR 0,0:CLS
20 G$="BU5L10D10R20H5E5L10"
30 DRAW"BM140,80S8A0"+G$:FOR N=1 TO 2000:NEXT:CLS
40 FOR J%=0 TO 3
50 DRAW"BM140,80a"+STR$(J%)+G$
60 FOR Z=1 TO 1000:NEXT:CLS:NEXT
```

Figure 7.28
The angle subcommand letter A will allow a shape to be rotated by multiples of 90 degrees.

in action. The shape is drawn, using S8A0 to make sure that its size and angle will be unaffected by any previous program that was running. It is then rotated by using values of J% ranging from 0 to 3, with the value put into the graphics string in the same way as before, using STR$.

Multiple shapes

Now take a look at Figure 7.29. This illustrates how a number of shapes can be joined up easily. The key to this is the use of the + or – signs along with M or BM. Adding the sign + to a BM or M instruction will cause a movement of as many spaces as you specify. This is an important difference. BM 10,10, for example, means *move to position X+ 10, Y+ 10.* If we use BM +10,+10, we mean a move of ten places left and ten places up from where the last piece of drawing finished. Note the contradiction here. You would normally expect BM+10 to mean that the X position number was increased by 10, so causing movement to the right. It works exactly the opposite way round, and so does the Y-position number. Similarly, BM-10,-10 would mean a move of ten places right and ten places down. The tricky bit here is adding the + or – signs to the string, and line 50 shows two ways of doing this. The + sign which is enclosed by quotes is the one that is put into the string, the others are there only to provide the joining action. The method that uses STR$(20) is more useful when the quantity that is being added is a variable value. The method that uses ,5 is more suitable when the value is a fixed and known number. All that doesn't exhaust the graphics possibilities of BASIC, because we haven't looked at PUT and GET for recording and replaying graphics patterns in the form of arrays, nor at the principle of making 'invisible' drawings that can be put on to the screen with a single command.

```
10 SCREEN 1:COLOR 0,0:CLS
20 DRAW"BM10,80"
30 G$="BU5L10F5G5R20H5E5L10"
40 FOR X%=1 TO 8
50 DRAW"BM"+"+"+STR$(20)+",5"+G$
60 FOR N=1 TO 2000:NEXT
70 NEXT
```

Figure 7.29
Shifting shapes with the + or – subcommands.

Chapter 8

SOUNDS UNLIMITED

The ability to produce sound is an essential feature of all modern computers. The sound of the PC computer comes from the loudspeaker that is built into it, and this has its own volume control so you have more control over the volume of this sound than is possible with a lot of other computers. In addition GW BASIC allows you a number of different ways of creating sound effects, depending on whether you want just a reminder, or a melody, or a noise.

What we call sound is the result of rapid changes of the pressure of the air round our ears. Everything that generates a sound does so by altering the air pressure, and Figure 8.1 shows how the skin of a drum does this. All other musical instruments also rely on the principle of something which vibrates, and pushes the air around. Air pressure, however, is invisible, and we don't notice these pressure changes unless they are fairly fast, and we measure the rate in terms of cycles per second, or Hertz. A cycle of any wave is a set of changes, first in one direction, then in the other and back to normal, which we can illustrate by the graph in Figure 8.2. The reason that we talk about a sound 'wave' is because the shape of this graph is a wave shape.

The frequency of sound is the number of cycles of changing air pressure per second measured in Hertz – one Hertz is one cycle per second. If the frequency is less than about 20 Hertz, we simply can't hear it, though it can still have disturbing effects. We can hear the effect of pressure waves in the air at frequencies above 20 Hertz, going up to about 15000 Hertz. The frequency of the waves corresponds to what we sense as the 'pitch' of a note. A low frequency of 80 to 120 Hertz corresponds to a low-pitch bass note. A frequency of 400 or above corresponds to a high pitch treble note. Human ears are not sensitive to

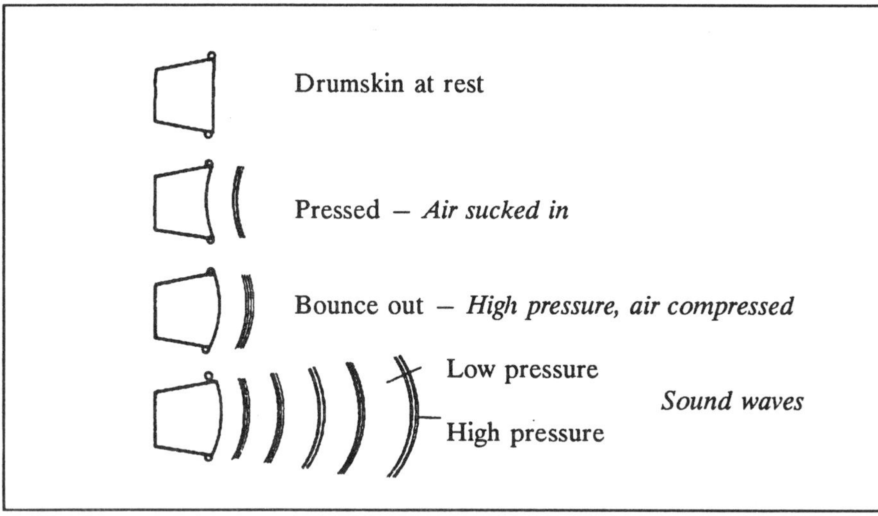

Figure 8.1
How a drum-skin produces sound by alternately compressing and de-compressing air.

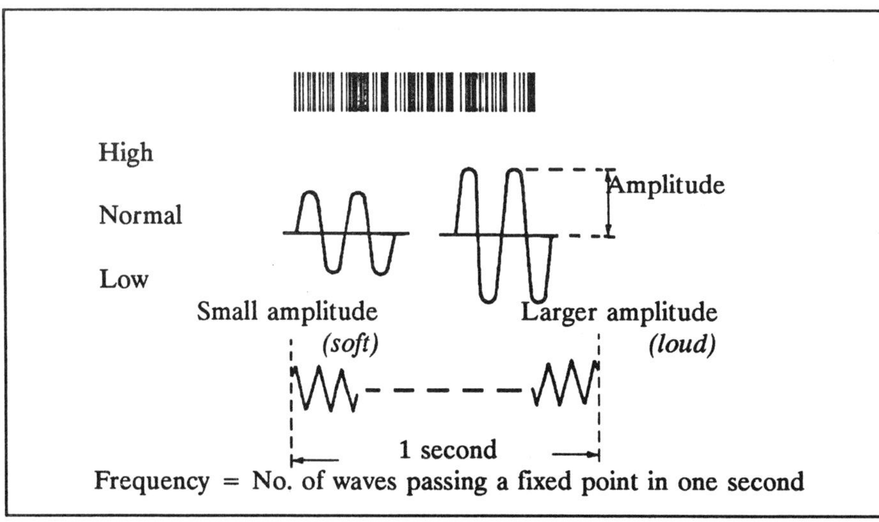

Figure 8.2
Sound waveforms that show how the pressure of the air changes during the time of a sound. The amount of change determines the loudness of the sound, and the rate of change determines the pitch of the note.

sounds whose frequency is above 20,000 Hertz (20 kilohertz), but many animals can hear sounds at and above this frequency.

The amount of pressure change determines what we call the loudness of a note. This is measured in terms of 'amplitude', which is the maximum change of pressure of the air from its normal value. For complete control over the generation of sound, we need to be able to specify the amplitude, frequency, shape of wave, and also the way that the amplitude of the note changes during the time when it sounds.

BASIC has three main sound instructions, BEEP, SOUND and PLAY. Of these three instructions, BEEP is a simple instruction, and the notes from it have fixed pitch and amplitude. As I mentioned earlier, this amplitude is controlled by the volume control of your monitor so that you can have it as loud or as soft as the circuits of the monitor permit. The SOUND instruction is a much more complicated one, though it needs only two numbers following it. What makes it more complicated is that several SOUND instructions are needed to set up one sound, and it's designed mainly to produce sound effects that can't be produced by the other commands. We'll keep SOUND until later, and concentrate on the other two for the moment, starting with BEEP.

BEEP doesn't have to be followed by numbers, it simply causes a short sound, the same as the on which you hear along with an error message. Fig 8.3 illustrates how you might use BEEP. There is a message appearing on the screen, and you want to make sure that the user looks at it. A long beep is produced by using a loop of ten beeps, and it makes a noise which is quite an effective attention-getter, especially if the volume control is turned up.

```
10 CLS:PRINT"message coming...."
20 FOR N=1 TO 2500:NEXT
30 PRINT"Hey, you, operator...."
40 FOR N=1 TO 10:BEEP:NEXT
```

Figure 8.3
Using the BEEP statement to produce a sound of fixed pitch and duration. Some versions of BASIC offer no more than this.

You shall have music ...

The BEEP instruction is very useful for its purpose, but BASIC has a lot more in store for you. A lot of computers are not really suited to working with music, because they require all of the instructions to be in number form. If you read music, or can work with sheet music, this is the last thing that you want. The ideal method of programming music would be to work with the named notes of music – and this is what the PLAY instruction of BASIC does. It might appear to be the obvious thing to do, but very few versions of BASIC for the PC do it, and some permit no more than a beep!

If you have no experience of music, however, this may seem rather puzzling to you. How do we go about writing down music? For each note, we have to specify what the note is (its pitch), how loud it must be, and for how long it is to be played. In written music, this is done by using a type of chart of lines and spaces for the pitch, and different shapes of markings (notes) for the duration. Loudness is indicated by using letters such as *f* (loud) and *p* (soft). More than one letter can be used, so that *fff* means very loud, and *ppp* means very soft. Each sound is indicated by a note, a shape on the chart, and the shape of the note gives some information about the duration of the note. In addition to this, each piece of music will start with some advice about the speed at which the notes are to be played. One of these methods is a metronome reading. The metronome is a gadget which ticks at regular intervals, and the metronome reading for a piece of music is the number of metronome ticks per minute. A more ancient way of

Symbol	*Time*	*Name*
𝅘𝅥𝅯	¼	Semiquaver
𝅘𝅥𝅯.	⅜	Dotted semiquaver
𝅘𝅥𝅮	½	Quaver
𝅘𝅥𝅮.	¾	Dotted quaver
𝅘𝅥	1	Crotchet
𝅘𝅥.	1½	Dotted crotchet
𝅗𝅥	2	Minim
𝅗𝅥.	3	Dotted minim
𝅝	4	Semibreve

Figure 8.4
The note symbols of written music, used to indicate the duration of each note.

indicating speed is the use of Italian words like allegro (fast), lento (slow) and so on. What these speed settings decide is how many unit notes will be played in a minute. The unit note is the crotchet, so if a piece of music is marked at a metronome speed of 60 (pretty slow), then there will be 60 crotchets played per minute, one each second. A more normal rate would be 120, two notes per second. The durations of all the other notes are decided in comparison to this unit, the crotchet. A minim sounds for twice as long as the crotchet, a semibreve for twice as long as a minim, which is four times as long as the time of a crotchet. The quaver sounds for only half the time of the crotchet. A semiquaver sounds for only half the time of a quaver, which is quarter of the time of a crotchet. The crotchets and other timed notes are indicated by the shapes of the written notes, as Figure 8.4 shows. In addition, symbols are used to indicate silences in the music, and these are based on the same idea of a unit duration of silence, and others which are twice, four times, half, or quarter. These silence marks are shown in Figure 8.5.

The pitch of a note is indicated in written music by placing it on to a kind of musical map which is called a staff (one staff, two staves) as shown in Figure 8.6. Piano music uses two of these staves, each consisting of five lines and four spaces. The upper stave is the treble stave, and it is used for writing the higher notes which will be played on the piano with your right hand. The lower stave is the bass stave, the lower notes, played with the left hand. Instruments which do not use a keyboard will normally have music written with only one staff. In

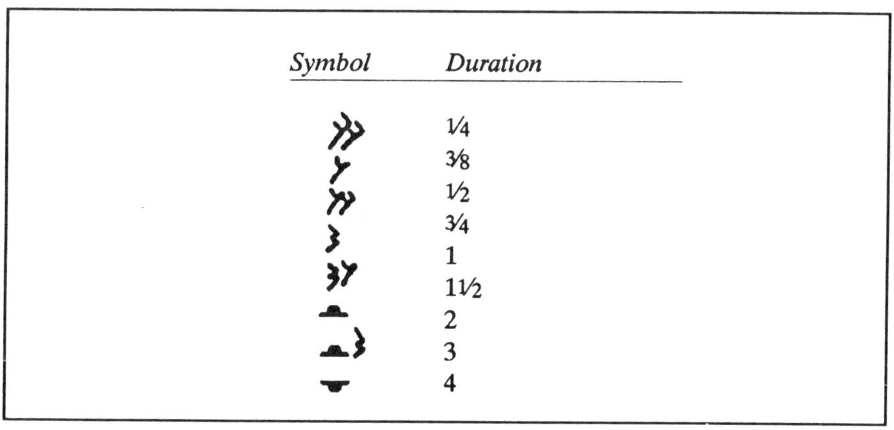

Figure 8.5
The silence (or pause) symbols for written music, which also use shape to indicate the timing.

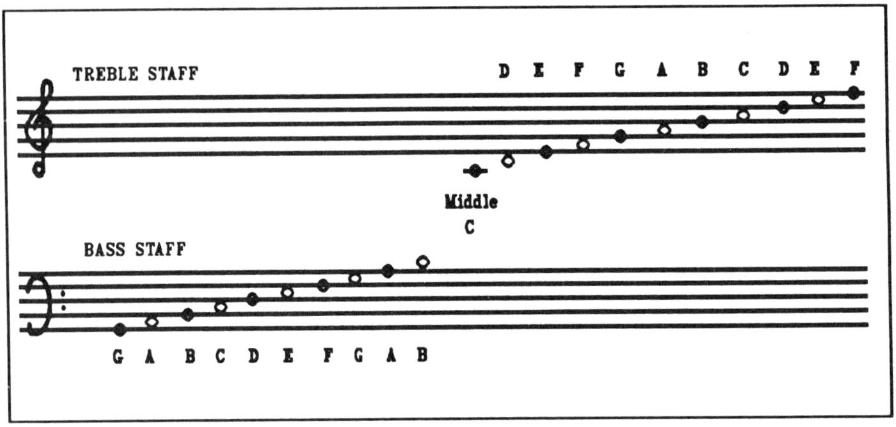

Figure 8.6
The stave, showing treble and bass staff as for a piano. This is a type of 'map' for musical notes. The position of a note on this map indicates the pitch of the note.

addition to this representation of notes by position on staves, we also use the letters of the alphabet from A to G to name the notes.

The piano is still the most familiar type of musical instrument, and its keyboard is set out so as to make it very easy to play one particular series of notes, called the 'scale of C Major'. The scale starts on a note that is called Middle C, and ends on a note that is also called C, but which is the eighth note above middle C. A group of eight notes like this is called an 'octave', so that the note you end with in this scale is the C which is one octave above Middle C. Because music (in the Western hemisphere, at least) is based on this group of eight notes, we use only the first seven letters of the alphabet in naming the notes. Why seven? Well, the eighth note is the end of one octave and the start of the next, so it bears the same name. The scientific basis of all this is that if you take Middle C, and find the frequency of the sound of this note, then the C which is the next octave above Middle C has precisely double the frequency value of Middle C. The C below Middle C has half the frequency of Middle C, and so on. That's why the ancient Greeks always thought that music was a branch of mathematics. Come to think of it, the way that the times of notes are related to each other in multiples of 2 corresponds exactly with the way that the computer deals with number values. Perhaps the ancient Greeks were right.

The appearance of these keys on the piano keyboard is illustrated in Figure 8.7. Middle C is, logically enough, at the centre of the keyboard, and we move right

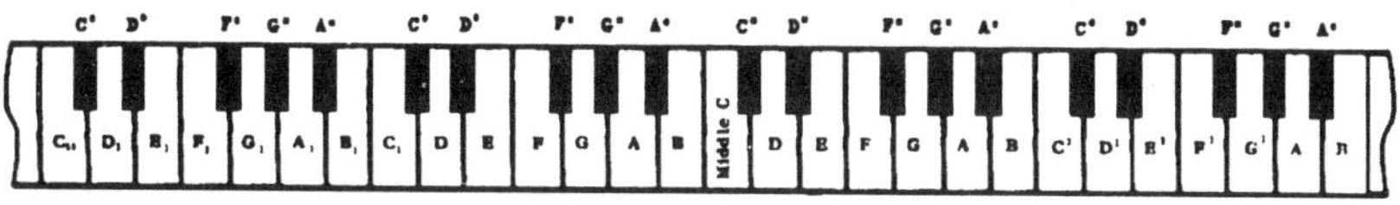

Figure 8.7

Part of the piano keyboard, showing Middle C. There is only one semitone between B and C and between E and F in the straightforward 'scale of C Major', starting with Middle C and ending with the B above it.

for higher notes, left for lower notes. One of the complications of music, however, is that the frequencies of the notes of a scale are not evenly spaced out. The 'normal' full spacing is called a 'tone' and the smaller spacing is called a 'semitone'. Each scale will contain two semitones. On written music, Middle C appears midway between the treble and bass staves.

The key instruction for playing music with BASIC on your PC computer is the PLAY instruction. Like DRAW, PLAY has to be followed by a string name. The string then contains all the information that is needed to produce the music. The notes are specified simply by their names, as used in music. These are the letters A to G, and we also use the signs + and -. The + sign or # sign means a semitone higher than the note indicated by the letter, so that A+ or A# is a semitone above A, the note a musician would call 'A-sharp'. Similarly, A- would mean a semitone below A, or 'A-flat'. In addition to the letter names of the notes, we can use other control letters to indicate the octave, length, tempo and pauses. The octave letter is O, and it has to be followed by a number whose range is 0 to 7. If you don't specify any O value, the computer will set itself to O4, which is the range of notes above Middle C. O0 means the lowest range of BASIC computer notes; O7 gives the highest, and O3 contains Middle C. This means that BASIC can play eight octaves of notes, which is more than the range of any ordinary musical instrument. One odd weakness in this system is that there is no provision for altering the relative volume of notes (though this is provided in some other varieties of BASIC that use almost identical instructions). We can, of course, still set the volume control to suit our own tastes. The letter L controls the length of all note, and has to be followed by a number in the range 1 to 255 (though the usable range is 1 to 16). This number does not behave in the way

```
10 A$="03CDEFGAB04C"
20 PLAY A$
```

Figure 8.8
Defining and playing a string of music subcommand letters.

you might expect, because the low numbers give the long notes, and the high numbers give the short notes. Figure 8.4 shows how these length numbers and also the pause numbers relate to the marked length of musical notes on sheet music. The pause or rest is a silent interval, and uses the letter P. It follows the same number scheme as note length, as Figure 8.5 indicates. If you don't specify any other values, the computer uses L4 and P4.

Time now for some illustrations. We'll start with Figure 8.8. This starts by defining a string A$. It consists of the notes that start at Middle C. How do I know? Well, Middle C on the BASIC computer is the first note in octave number 3, so by starting with 03 and C, the first note that we get is C. The other notes have been written in sequence, but we need to put 04 before the next C, If we don't, then we'll get Middle C again instead of the C above. The scale uses the default values of volume and speed (tempo).

This is a simple scale, but it's a good piece of music to illustrate what can be done with this BASIC command. Try Figure 8.9 now, to see what we can do to alter the way in which this scale can be played and the effect of the length L. The first thing that you have to know at this point is that T means 'tempo', and it controls the number of crotchets per minute – this in turn controls the speed of playing the string. The setting of tempo is always equal to 120 unless you

```
10 A$="T120L403CDEFL16GAB04L2C"
20 PLAY A$
30 PLAY"MN"+A$
40 PLAY"MS"+A$
50 PLAY"ML"+A$
```

Figure 8.9
Using MN, MS and ML to play the same note sequence in different styles.

change it. The range of T is a curious one, 32 to 255. The fastest tempo is obtained by using 32, the slowest by using 255. In the example, we have used the ordinary tempo, 120, but changed the and length of note settings. The reason for having separate tempo and length control letters is that you can get the tune sounding right by using L to select the length of notes, and then use T right at the start to set whatever tempo you like, If you want to speed things up, use a low value for T, if you want a funeral march, use a high value. You can even write the string without a T, and then add it in later by a command like:

```
PLAY "T100"+A$.
```

The length of a note can also be specified by using a number following the note, like C4 or A3, rather then the clumsier L4C or L2A. This allows you to use L to set the length of most of the notes and deal with any notes of different length by tacking a length number following them. In addition, you can lengthen a note by 50% by typing a dot following the letter, such as C. or A., which corresponds exactly to the notation that is used in written music.

The specification of timing and note length, however, does not tell us how the notes are played. You can play a set of notes in many different ways, depending on the spaces that you put between the notes. Rather than require you to put in these spaces for yourself, BASIC allows you to specify with three control codes, MN, MS and ML. MN means 'Music Normal', and will play the music string that follows it using short spaces between notes. MS means 'Music Staccato', and will play the notes as short bursts with longer pauses. ML means 'Music Legato', in which there are no pauses and each note runs smoothly into the next. The terms staccato and legato are standard musical names for these effects, which are demonstrated in lines 30 to 50 of Figure 8.9.

Figure 8.10 shows an example of a tune written using the PLAY instruction. Points to watch for here are the use of # for sharp notes, and the use of a dot following a note letter. When you use, for example, C., then this note will play for one

```
10 M$="03L4CC02B803C8D02A.G.FFE8F8G4D2E2L6F#GA.03D202L4G03CCC16
02B.A8G4"
20 PLAY"T90"+M$
```

Figure 8.10

A tune written for the PLAY instruction and using a tempo number that is inserted when the tune is played.

```
10 CLS
20 PRINT"What tempo would you like (1 to 255) ";
30 INPUT TEMPO%
40 PRINT"playing....":GOSUB 100
50 GOTO 20
100 M$="03L4CC02B803C8D02A.G.FFE8F8G4D2E2L6F#GA.03D202L4G03CCC16
02B.A8G4"
110 PLAY"T=TEMPO%;"+M$
120 RETURN
```

Figure 8.11
Using a variable within a string to control tempo.

and a half times as long as C with no dot. The dot is used in written music in the same way, so that being able to do this with BASIC as well makes it all the easier to transfer written music to the form of PLAY strings. Incidentally, you have the choice of playing music strings of up to 32 notes as foreground or background. If you pick foreground (which is a default anyhow, but can be commanded by starting your string with MF) then nothing can be done in BASIC until the music has finished. If you want the music as background, you start the string with MB, and the music plays away while the program moves on. This is possible only if the length of the music string is fairly short, however.

One last point on PLAY is that you can make items like the T number into variables, so that you can alter them more easily. Figure 8.11 illustrates this by using the music lines from the previous example. In line 110, the T=TEMPO%; will use as a value of T whatever number has been input for TEMPO% in line 30 – for simplicity no testing has been used, but you would normally check the input number to ensure that it was in the correct range. Note the semicolon in this statement – you will get an error message if this is omitted. Another item for which we have no space here is the use of sub-strings, which will be familiar from the previous chapter. If a melody contains a set of notes that is often repeated (well, you might be setting Beethoven's 5th for the PC), then you can assign this set of notes to a string variable such as RP$, and use the command XRP$; (don't forget the semicolon) in the main PLAY string.

Sounds unlimited

We now need to take a look at the third sound instructions of BASIC, using the SOUND command word. SOUND is an instruction which is used in a simple way, with just two numbers following SOUND. The first number in the SOUND command is a frequency number. The values that can be used here range from 37 to 32767, but the highest numbers are for the benefit of bats only and you won't hear them. The second number is a duration number for which a count of 18 plays the sound for one second. If you use zero for this number there will be no sound, and this can be a useful way of getting a silence.

Since the first number in a SOUND instruction is a frequency number, the effect of a change of number becomes less as the frequency increases. This is because an octave in sound corresponds to a doubling of frequency. For example, if we take the lowest note of frequency 37, then the octave above is obtained using 74. If you take the treble note whose frequency is 5000, then an octave above this needs 10000. In one case, the octave change used just 37 steps, in the other 5000. This is made clear in the example of Figure 8.12, which uses the SOUND instruction in a loop, playing notes by using the frequency numbers in the loop. Because the loop uses steps of 1, the frequencies change rapidly at first, but by the time you get to around Middle C, the notes change very slowly, and in the upper ranges it seems to take forever – use **CTRL-BREAK** when it becomes unbearable.

The main use for SOUND is in creating effects which would be tedious using PLAY. As an example, lend an ear to the example in Figure 8.13. This produces a warbling note by using two SOUND instructions in a loop, with the duration of each note as short as can be used. This is not short enough to convince anyone that the notes are being sounded together, however, but if you want to simulate telephone noises it could be useful. It can also at times be handy to know that you can produce a note of precisely controlled frequency. For example, SOUND 440,90 gives you five seconds of standard orchestral 'A' (got an oboe player in

```
10 FOR N%=37 TO 10000
20 SOUND N%,1:NEXT
```

Figure 8.12
A very long duration loop which shows the range of the SOUND statement.

```
10 FOR N%=1 TO 36
20 SOUND 264,1
30 SOUND 330,1
40 NEXT
```

Figure 8.13
Creating a warbling note with SOUND.

the house?) and allows you to dispense with tuning forks if you happen to use them.

Chapter 9

BASIC FILING TECHNIQUES

What is a file?

I have used the word 'file' in the course of this book to mean a collection of information of any type which we can record on a disk. Programs in BASIC are one type of file, and the only type, incidentally, which permits the use of the LOAD and SAVE commands, because MS-DOS programs and word-processor files are dealt with quite differently. In this chapter, however, I shall use the word 'file' in a narrower sense. I'll take it to mean a collection of data that is separate from a program. For example, if you have a program that deals with your household accounts, you would need a file of items and money amounts. This file is the result of the data-gathering action of the program, and it preserves these amounts for the next time that you use the program. Taking another example, suppose that you devised a program which was intended to keep a note of your collection of vintage 78 rpm recordings. The program would require you to enter lots of information about these recordings, such as title, artists, catalogue number, recording company, date of recording, date of issue and so on. This information is a file, and at some stage in the program, you would have to record this file. Why? Because when you load a BASIC program and RUN it, it starts from scratch. All the information that you fed into it the last time you used it has gone – unless you recorded that information separately. This is the topic that we're dealing with in this chapter, recording the information that a program uses. The shorter word is 'filing' the information. In this chapter, we look at the roots of the subject and at one type of filing that BASIC can carry out.

Knowing the names

You can't discuss filing without coming across some words which are always used in connection with filing. The most important of these words are 'record' and 'field', illustrated in Figure 9.1. A record is a set of facts about one item in the file. For example, if you have a file about vintage steam locomotives, one of your records might be used for each locomotive type. Within that record, you might have wheel formation, designers name, firebox area, working steam pressure, tractive force – and anything else that's relevant. Each of these items is a 'field', an item of the group that makes up a record. Your record might, for example, be the SCOTT class 4-4-0 locomotives. Every different bit of information about the SCOTT class is a field, the whole set of fields is a record, and the SCOTT class is just one record in a file that will include the Gresley Pacifics, the 4-6-0 general purpose locos, and so on. Take another example, the file 'British Motor-bikes'. In this file, BSA is one record, AJS is another, Norton is another. In each record, you will have fields. These might be capacity, number of cylinders, bore and stroke, gear ratios, suspension system, top speed, acceleration – and whatever else you want to take note of. Filing is fun – if you like arranging things in the right order. The importance of filing is that all of the information

File of FRIENDS

Record 1

Field 1: Name
Field 2: Name
Field 3: Name
Field 4: Name
etc.

Record 1

Field 1: Name
Field 2: Name
Field 3: Name
Field 4: Name
etc.

Figure 9.1
The meanings of the terms Record and Field as applied to data filing.

can be recovered very quickly, and that it can be arranged in any order, or picked out as you choose. If you have a file on British Motor-bikes, for example, it's easy to get a list of machines in order of cylinder capacity, or in order of power output, or any other order you like. You can also ask for a list of all machines under 250 cc, which ones used four-speed gearboxes, which were vertical twins, which were two-strokes. Rearranging lists and picking out items is something which is a lot less easy when the information exists only on paper.

Disk filing

In this book, because we are dealing with BASIC and its advanced filing systems, we'll ignore filing methods that are based on DATA lines in a BASIC program. Though you may be experienced with the use of filing with disk or even cassette systems on older types of machines, I'll explain filing from scratch in this chapter. If it's all familiar to you, please bear with me until I come to something that you haven't met before. To start with, there are two main types of files that we can use with a disk system, serial files, and random access files. The differences are simple, but very important ones. A serial (or sequential) file places all the information on a disk in the order in which the information is received, just as it would be placed on a cassette. If you want to get at one item, you have to read all of the items from the beginning of the file into the computer, and then select. There is no way in which you can command the system to read just one record or one field. More important, with such files you can't easily change any part of a record, or add more records in the middle of such a file. Any such action has to be done by reading the whole file and making alterations while the file is in memory, then re-recording the whole file. A random access file does what its name suggests – it allows you to get from the disk one selected record or field without reading every other one from the start of the file. You might imagine that, faced with this choice, no-one would want to use anything but random access files. It's not so simple as that, though, because the convenience of random access filing has to be paid for by a lot more complication. For one thing, because random access filing allows you to write data at any part of the disk, it would be very easy to wipe out valuable data with a program that was badly designed. There is also a problem of choosing which record to read. We'll start, then, by looking at serial files.

Serial filing on disk

We'll start by supposing that we have a file to record, called CAMERAS. On this file we have records (such as Nikon, Pentax, Canon, Yashica and so on). For each record we have fields like Model, Film Size, Shutter speed range, aperture range (standard lens), Manual or Automatic, and so on. How do we write these records? First of all, we need to arrange the program that has created the records so that it can output them in some order. Figure 9.2 for example, shows how we might arrange this part of a BASIC program so as to input a number of records, with five fields to each record. The number of fields is five, so the fields are input from the keyboard using a `FOR n%=1 TO 5` loop. The number of records isn't fixed, so we use a `WHILE..WEND` loop, which keeps putting out records until it finds one called "X" or "x", which is the terminator. If we need to make a test for the terminator at the start of a loop, then it's better to use a `WHILE..WEND` loop, but this deals with only one condition. If you want to terminate the input without having to put in dummy values for each of the five fields, you have to test the Record name input and then use a `GOTO` to take you

```
10 CLS:RC$="":X%=0:DIM FLD$(5)
20 REM Would need to open file here
30 PRINT TAB(35)"DATA ENTRY":PRINT
40 PRINT TAB(5)"Type X for record name to end entry"
50 WHILE RC$<>"X" AND RC$<>"x"
60 PRINT TAB(5)"Name of this record ";
70 INPUT RC$
80 IF RC$="X" OR RC$="x" THEN GOTO 150
90 REM Need to record this name
100 X%=X%+1:FOR N%=1 TO 5
110 PRINT TAB(5)"Field Item"N%;" is ";
120 INPUT FLD$
130 REM record this also - no array needed
140 NEXT
150 WEND
160 REM end of entries
170 REM need to close file
180 PRINT:PRINT TAB(5)"There are"X%;" records in this file."
```

Figure 9.2

How data needs to be gathered for a simple serial file program. The REM lines can be replaced later by lines that carry out the required actions.

to the WEND step. Note that we haven't used an array for holding these RC$ or FLD$ items, because an array has to be dimensioned, and we don't know in advance how many items we will have. Instead of storing the items in an array for future use, they will be recorded on disk. The points where the disk recording routine would be fitted are shown in the REM lines. Each item, field or record, is treated as a string. This is because strings are easier to work with and will lead to an ASCII file on disk that is compatible with the files of other forms of text. The name FLD$, incidentally, has been used because FIELD is a reserved name, and using FIELD$ will cause an error message.

Organising the fields in this way allows you to have the fields as long or as short as you like, and they will eventually be recorded on the disk in the same form. The main point of serial filing is that you can use fields of widely-varying lengths without the waste of space that you get when you need to declare a fixed length, and all shorter strings are padded out with blanks. The use of fixed length strings is, however, essential when random-access filing is needed, and we'll deal with it under that heading.

That deals with the organisation of the data for putting on to disk, but how do we actually put it on the disk? There are several stages, and the first one is to open up the file. This means assigning a reference number, otherwise known as a 'stream number', and a filename which will be recorded on the disk, and there are three varieties of this statement, one for writing, one for reading, and one for adding (writing) to an existing file. The stream number is a purely temporary thing which is used from the time that a file is opened until it is closed, and you might use a variable name for this purpose. Having assigned a stream number, you must not OPEN again with the same number until the first file that used the number has been closed. Apart from that, though, you are free to assign stream numbers as you please. The preferred range of numbers is 0 to 15, and for most purposes you can restrict yourself to 1 and 2 only. The OPEN statement will cause the disk to spin and the filename to be recorded, and a typical form is:

```
OPEN "b:myfile.dat" FOR INPUT AS #1
```

– with the hashmark used along with the stream number 1.

Once the file has been opened for writing, with the filename on the disk, you can place data on to the disk using a statement of the form PRINT#1 (or WRITE#1). The 1 in this example must be the same as the reference number or stream number that was used in the OPEN statement, because this is how the machine recognises files. Each time you want to make use of a file that has been opened, then, you must use this file stream number which has been established by the earlier `OPEN` statement. The difference between `PRINT#` and `WRITE#` is important only if you are using multiple items, like `PRINT#1,a$,b%`. In this type of use, the comma will have the effect of recording a set of spaces on the disk, corresponding to the use of columns on the screen. By using `WRITE#1`, you avoid this waste of space. If you are using single statements like `PRINT #1,a$`, then it doesn't matter whether you use `PRINT#` or `WRITE#`.

The purpose of using the filename and the stream number is to organise data. The disk stores all data in units of 512 bytes. It wouldn't make sense to spin the disk and find a place on the disk just to record one byte at a time, so when you record or read a disk, it's always one complete sector, or as much of a sector as possible, at a time. Some of the memory of the computer has to be used to hold data which is being gathered up for recording, or which is being replayed. The stream number is an identifying number for the piece of memory, called a buffer, that is being used, so that the machine finds the correct data in the correct part of the memory. Using this stream number avoids the need for you to have to allocate parts of the memory to use in this way as buffers. The memory which is used for this purpose is reserved by a command in a file that runs when the Master disk is used to load in BASIC. If you use a hard disk, the buffer and the data units are larger, but the principle is the same.

Opening the file

After that short diversion, back to our filing program. Before we start to gather the data together for filing, we need to 'open the file' for the data. This is done using the `OPEN "b:platters.dat" FOR OUTPUT AS #1` command. `OPEN` has to be followed by one of the keywords `INPUT`, `OUTPUT` or `APPEND`. When `OUTPUT` is used, a file will always be created and if a file of the same name exists it will be deleted. If `APPEND` is used, then if no file of that name exists one will be created, but if a file already exists it is added to. From this point of view, then `APPEND` is better to use than `OUTPUT` unless you deliberately want to ensure that you create a new file each time. In this example, we are opening a new file for output. The filename, note, includes the drive letter, b: in this case, as well as the full filename and extension. If you use a single floppy drive, then it's still useful to use the `b:` letter if you want to avoid having the BASIC program and the data file on the same disk. There's nothing wrong, however, in keeping them together, and in some applications this can be a decided advantage, as we'll see. When a large program can generate and file a large amount of data, then you really need to keep the program and the data disks separate. If you work with a hard disk then you can use a filename that includes path commands – for details see your manual or a good book on MS-DOS. The 'standard' filename extension for data is .DAT, so it makes sense to use this unless you have some pressing reason to use something else. When you are developing a program that will go through a large number of stages, it's a good idea to put the stage number into the main title as, for example, CAMERA01.DAT. When this first line is executed, the disk will spin for a short time, preparing for the file, and the filename will now appear on the directory/catalogue if you interrupt the program and type DIR. The buffer space will also be prepared in the memory and allocated to the stream number which in the examples has been 1.

Printing to the file

It's at this stage that we need to make use of the loops in the writing program. Within these loops, we need to have a line something like:

```
PRINT#1,FLD$
```

in which PRINT#1 means put the information out to the buffer whose stream number is 1, the stream number that was selected for the OPEN statement, so that PRINT#1 will eventually put out to the disk system the data that follows. The PRINT#1 statement can be used exactly as you would use the PRINT statement, and can be followed by strings, numbers, commas and so on just as a PRINT would be. WRITE#1 is more useful if you are recording more than one item in each statement. In this chapter, we will use PRINT#1 because WRITE#1 has no advantages for the type of examples used here. In this example, what is being printed to the file is FLD$. There is no need to use an array, such as FLD$(N%) here, because the items are recorded to the disk/buffer in order and no array is needed. We also need to write the 'record' name, and this is done within the loop, by using a line such as:

```
PRINT#1,RC$
```

Figure 9.3 shows the complete example of a very short and simple program of this type which has been adapted from the first example. The program is obtained from the listing of 9.2 simply by changing four of the REM lines, plus a routine for reading in title names on the assumption that this will be used to catalogue your valuable old LP's. You can enter anything you like into this, but it makes more sense to enter something that you can easily check. Since the file is called platters.dat, a set of items has been put into a DATA line to act as headings.

```
10 CLS:RC$="":X%=0
20 OPEN "b:platters.dat" FOR OUTPUT AS #1
30 PRINT TAB(35)"DATA ENTRY":PRINT
40 PRINT TAB(5)"Type X for record name to end entry"
50 WHILE RC$<>"X" AND RC$<>"x"
60 PRINT TAB(5)"Name of this record ";
70 INPUT RC$
80 IF RC$="X" OR RC$="x" THEN GOTO 150
90 PRINT #1,RC$:RESTORE
100 X%=X%+1:FOR N%=1 TO 5:READ NAM$
110 PRINT TAB(5) NAM$" :";
120 INPUT FLD$
130 PRINT #1,FLD$
140 NEXT
150 WEND
160 REM end of entries
170 CLOSE
180 PRINT:PRINT TAB(5)"There are"X%;" records in this file."
190 DATA Artist(e),Backing,Release date,Best chart
position,Delete date
```

Figure 9.3

A data-gathering and recording program based on the previous listing.

You can, of course, easily change this program so that it has another title that suits the information that you might want to use, and a completely different set of headings.

Before we move on, consider what this program has done. It has created a file called platters.dat on drive B:, and allocated a channel number of 1 to this file. It has then stored the data as it came along, in the sequence of RECORD, then FIELDS. Finally, the file has been recorded and closed by using CLOSE. This last step is very important. For one thing, you don't actually record on the disk any of the information in this short program until the CLOSE statement is executed. That's because it would be a very time-consuming business to record each item of a file at a time. What the filing system does, remember, is to gather the data together in memory. This is the 'buffer' piece of memory and its contents will be written to the disk only under one of two possible circumstances. One is that the buffer is full, so that there is a complete buffer-load to write. The other is that there is a CLOSE type of statement in the program. For a large amount of data, the disk will spin and write data each time the buffer is full. The CLOSE statement then writes the last piece of data, the one which doesn't fill the buffer. It also writes a special code number, called the end-of-file code (EOF). This can be used when the file is read, as we'll see later.

If you forget the CLOSE statement, you'll leave the buffer unwritten, with no EOF – and cause a lot of problems both in your programs and possibly with that disk. Forgetting the CLOSE is called leaving your files open, and you wouldn't like to be seen like that, would you? It's possible to use something like CLOSE #1, but since CLOSE – with no qualifying number – deals with any open files, this is easier and more certain. The biggest danger is when you are testing a program. If there is an error, such as a syntax error, which stops the program from running, there will be no CLOSE carried out, and the files will be open. If you had typed a lot of data, you would lose it if you then went on to correct the program and run it again. The correct procedure is to close all of the open files. In this example, it's easy – you only have to type CLOSE and press **RETURN**. For a large program, you would probably find it better to write an ON ERROR GOTO line which, when an error occurred, closed files and ended. This would automatically ensure that files are never left open. The CLOSE ensures that your data on all file stream numbers will be recorded.

When you use an INPUT statement, as in this example, to gather up the data, you can find that with a lot of data you will hear the disk start and stop at intervals. That's an indication of the buffer transferring data to the disk. You won't see on the screen what you type on the keyboard while the transfer is taking place, but the time that's needed to write a sector is fairly short, and no characters will be lost. In this example, there is nothing like enough data to fill a buffer. You will hear the disk spin when the OPEN command is executed, and again when the CLOSE command is executed, but not at any time between these two unless you enter a huge amount of data.

Getting your own back

Having created a file on disk, we need to prove that it has actually happened by reading the file back. You can read this file in quite a surprising number of ways, because it is an ASCII file. If you don't have BASIC running, you can use the DOS TYPE command which will display the file, taking one line for each item. You can also insert this file into any standard type of word-processor such as WordStar™. You can rename the file using REN oldname newname if you are using MS-DOS, but from BASIC you need to use NAME, which uses the syntax NAME "oldname" AS "newname" – the quotes around the names are needed because this is a BASIC command and not an MS-DOS command. To delete a file you can use the DOS commands ERA filename, DEL filename, or from BASIC KILL "filename" – once again, KILL is a BASIC command, and as such can be used within a program.

We need to look now at a BASIC program to read and make use of this file. A program which reads a file must contain, early on, a command which opens the file for reading. This will be something like:

```
OPEN "b:platters.dat" FOR INPUT as #2
```

– though you can use #1 again if you like since it is no longer in use. The OPEN command for reading use the same filename as was used to write the file. If we recorded a file using the name platters.dat, then we must not expect to be able to read it if we use cameras – or any other name. Mis-spelling can haunt you here, because if you specify a filename such as PLATTERS or PLATTERS.DAY you get only the response file not found, and your program promptly ends Remember that if a program crashes in this way you should close the open file by typing the word CLOSE (**RETURN**). Once the file has been opened, we can read data with INPUT#2 (or LINE INPUT#2), just to establish that we don't have to use the same number as we had when we recorded the file. This then will be followed by the variable name that we want to assign to each item. This statement reads an item from the disk, and will allocate it to a variable name, for printing the item or other use, according to what we have programmed. The number of reads can be controlled by a FOR..NEXT loop, if the number is known, or it can make use of the EOF marker, if the number is unknown. This marker is a number (ASCII 26) that is placed at the end of an ASCII file on disk, since this code can never occur in a file except as an end code.

By testing for NOT EOF(2), meaning not the end of file for file number 2, then, we can make the program stop reading the file at the correct place. The example of Figure 9.4 shows both methods in use. The number of fields has been five, so that a FOR..NEXT loop can be used to control the input of the fields. The number of records, however, has not be fixed by a FOR..NEXT loop, so that we have to keep reading the file until the EOF byte is found. This is done by testing EOF in a WHILE..WEND loop. If EOF is found, then the file is closed, and the program ends. The EOF test has been put into the WHILE..WEND loop, because EOF needs to be tested before another item is read. If you read again from a file like this, you will get the EOF Found error message, and the program will stop. Unless you have arranged for an ON ERROR GOTO line to close files for you,

```
10 CLS:OPEN "b:platters.dat"FOR INPUT AS #2
20 PRINT TAB(34)"DATA DISPLAY"
30 WHILE NOT EOF(2)
40 INPUT #2,NAM$
50 PRINT"Name of this disk ";NAM$:PRINT
60 RESTORE:FOR N%=1 TO 5
70 READ HEAD$:INPUT #2,DAT$
80 PRINT HEAD$;" - ";DAT$
90 NEXT:PRINT
100 PRINT"Press any key for next one"
110 K$=INPUT$(1)
120 WEND:CLOSE:PRINT"End of data"
130 END
140 DATA Artist(e),Backing,Release date,Best chart position,
Delete date
```

Figure 9.4

Reading back a file that has been created by the listing of Figure 9.3.

the files will still be open. Leaving a reading file open is not quite such a disaster as leaving a writing file open, but it's still very undesirable. Note that the disk does not spin each time you press a key to get another record. This is because a complete chunk of data is read each time, and if the information that you want is all in one buffer load, the disk need not be used. Sorry if I seem to be labouring this point, but a newcomer to disk filing sometimes finds it difficult to remember. If you now try out the reading program you can see that we have the essence of a useful filing system here. It's quite common to have the data gathering and writing part of a program separate from the reading and analysing portion like this, but you can have the two parts combined into one single program with a menu choice if you like. If you do this, then it's probably better for most purposes to use APPEND rather then OUTPUT in the writing part of the file.

Now this simple example shows a lot about serial filing that you need to know. What we have not actually tried so far is how to update a file. One method of file updating is that of adding more items to the end of the file, and as it happens, there is a particularly simple way of carrying this out by using the APPEND word in the OPEN statement. A simple serial file has a number of advantages, prominent among which is the ability to use variable length strings. In the past, however, serial filing systems have allowed only one way of altering the serial file – that of reading the file in, altering it and writing it out again. GW BASIC serial files have an advantage in this respect, in as much as items can be added (appended) to the end of the file by altering the file OPEN statement. If you want to edit an item in an existing part of the file or delete a record or field, then the old-fashioned method must still be used, and we'll look at them later. For the moment, we'll take a look at how APPEND is used.

There is just one line of the data entry program of Figure 9.3 that needs to be altered. In place of the existing OPEN line, edit in the replacement:

```
OPEN "b:platters.dat" FOR APPEND AS #1
```

in which the word OUTPUT has been replaced by APPEND. When this runs, assuming that the data disk is in place, new data will be added to the end of the existing file, and you can use the data reading program to check out that the new items have indeed been added. This is so beautifully simple that it invites the writing of a general entry subroutine in which you can pick (N)ew or (A)dd at an early stage. The reply to this can then be used to run either the OUTPUT line or the APPEND line, since this is the only difference between the routines, and the entry of data will take the same pattern as illustrated in Figure 9.3. Things are not nearly so simple when you need to make alterations to records that are in the middle of a serial file.

Updating the file

There are two answers to the problem of updating a serial file, other than by appending records. One possibility, which is the simplest one for short files, is to load the whole file into the memory of the computer, stored as an array or arrays, make the alterations (your BASIC program will have to be written so as to provide for this), and then write the file again, wiping out the earlier version. The other possibility is to open two files, one for reading and the other for writing. You don't need to have dual disk drives for this, though it makes life much simpler if you do, using a disk drive letter (A or B) at the start of the filename. You can work on one disk provided that there is space for both the old file and the new file on the disk. Working with two files open means that the computer will maintain two buffers. You read one record from the reading file and you can, if you want, display it. If it's all right, it's then written (to the buffer initially). If the record has to be modified, you can do so. If extra records have to be added, this is equally simple, and no great amount of computer memory need be taken up with large arrays, no matter how much data is involved.

Writing to a serial file

1) Open file in OUTPUT mode.
2) Write or append data from program variables using WRITE #, PRINT # or PRINT # USING.
3) Close file.

Reading from a serial file

1) Open file in INPUT mode.
2) Load data from file into program variables using INPUT # or LINE INPUT #.
3) Close file.

Figure 9.5

Outlining the methods that are needed for modifying a serial file by reading and re-writing.

Each time a buffer empties, the disk will spin and a read or write will take place. This 'simultaneous' operation is possible because of the use of different OPEN commands, which control different buffers. In practice, it's a matter of writing your program to suit. Figure 9.5 illustrates the programming methods that are needed. The principle is to read the items of a specified record, print them, and then change an item or items before re-recording the file. The main problem is to find a neat way of doing this. The program of Figure 9.6 shows one approach which I use in my own serial file programs. The editing is by the simplest possible method, asking you what you want to change specified by item number, rather than by searching for a name. Note that the file names have been chosen so as to make the revised file record as a temporary file under the filename temp.$$$. At the end of the program, the original file is renamed as a BAK file, and the temporary file is renamed as the main platters.dat file. One point we have to be very careful about, however, is closing files. The CLOSE statement is used whenever the program has finished, and is also used in the ON ERROR GOTO line so as to ensure that if an error is encountered in the program or its files, then all open files are closed. During the course of experimenting with serial files, you may corrupt files and wipe out end of file marks. This will cause trouble at the WHILE NOT EOF(6) stage, and the program will normally stop with an error message

Figure 9.6

Amending a serial file by reading and re-writing. If data only needs to be added, you can use the APPEND subcommand in the OPEN statement, but this routine allows you to change the file as much as you like. Remember that many files created by commercial programs are serial files.

```
10 ON ERROR GOTO 340
20 CLS:PRINT TAB(33)"Item to Change":PRINT
30 X%=1
40 OPEN "b:platters.dat" FOR INPUT AS #1
50 OPEN "b:temp.$$$" FOR OUTPUT AS #2
60 PRINT TAB(5)"Please specify record to be changed (number,
RETURN)"
70 PRINT"Number ";:INPUT REPLY%
80 WHILE NOT EOF(1)
90 FOR N%=0 TO 5:INPUT#1, DAT$(N%):NEXT
100 REM Treating as array here
110 IF X%=REPLY% THEN GOSUB 210
120 FOR N%=0 TO 5
130 PRINT #2,DAT$(N%):NEXT
140 X%=X%+1:WEND
150 IF X%<REPLY% THEN PRINT"No record of this number"
160 CLOSE
170 KILL "b:platters.bak"
180 NAME "b:platters.dat" AS "b:platters.bak"
190 NAME "b:temp.$$$" AS "b:platters.dat"
200 PRINT"End of program":END
210 CLS:J%=0:WHILE J%<>6
220 CLS:FOR N%=0 TO 5
230 PRINT TAB(3)N%;"  ";DAT$(N%):NEXT:PRINT
240 PRINT TAB(5)"Pick item to alter (0 - 5), 6 to end."
250 PRINT TAB(7)"RETURN key not needed."
260 A$=INPUT$(1):J%=VAL(A$)
270 IF J%=6 THEN GOTO 300
280 IF J%<0 OR J%>5 THEN PRINT"Incorrect choice- 0 to 5
only":GOTO 260
290 GOSUB 310
300 WEND:RETURN
310 PRINT:PRINT"new value for item ";J%
```

```
320 INPUT DAT$(J%)
330 RETURN
340 IF ERL=170 THEN RESUME NEXT
345 CLOSE:CLS
350 PRINT"Error number "ERR" in line "ERL
360 PRINT"closing files and ending program"
370 END
```

Figure 9.6 *Continued.*

and all files open. The ON ERROR GOTO ensures that files are closed and the source of the error printed if this happens. The danger here is that if files become corrupted, you could have no readable records on the disk.

The program in detail

The first line is the ON ERROR GOTO 340 statement, which will switch the program to line 340 if any error occurs. The lines from 340 on are intended to deal with one likely fault and any unanticipated ones. The likely fault is that when lines 170 is reached with its instructions to kill an old file, there may be no file of that name on the disk. Normally, this would stop the program dead, and you might have to create a dummy file just so that you could kill it!. However, by testing in line 340 for the line number (ERL) in which this has occurred, we can isolate this report, and cause the program to resume on the next line, that is line 180. This deals very neatly with a shortcoming of BASIC, that there is no way of checking whether a file exists before you try to delete it. The lines following 340 then deal with any other errors by closing all files, reporting error number and line number, and ending. If your ON ERROR GOTO lines are any more elaborate than this, you should make the first statement ON ERROR GOTO 0 in order to disable the error trapping once an error has been found. If this is not done, then any error that occurs while the error lines are running will cause a closed loop.

What follows line 10 is the filing part of the program. The input file is b:platters.dat, and the output file is b:temp.$$$. You are asked which record you want to change, and the assumption here is that you know the records by number. If you don't, then you could alter this section of the program so that you either looked at each record, or searched for some feature, such as DAT$(0) (the record title) having a value like “Midnight in Toledo”. Given that the number is the method used here, though, the main loop starts with the WHILE NOT EOF(1) line as usual. The principle is to read in the records, and increment the counter number X% for each record until X% is the number that you requested. If you have requested an impossible number, then the end-of-file will be met first, and the loop will stop. The test in line 150 will then cause the message to be printed and the program will end.

When the correct record has been read, the GOSUB 210 transfers control to the section that allows you to alter the record. This is a straightforward editing routine which displays the whole record with item numbers, and asks you to press keys **0** to **5** to alter some aspect of the record, or key **6** to end the editing. After any change, the record is displayed again, so that you can check the change and possibly make another change.

With the amendment made, the subroutine returns, and all records beyond the one you have edited will be read and re-written until the end of the file. The main loop ends at the WEND, and this is followed by the test which will print an explanatory message if you happened to ask for a record number higher than the number of records in the file. The files are then closed, and the renaming starts. When you first use this program, there will be no aircraft.BAK file on the disk, so the command to kill the old aircraft.BAK file must be used only if this file exists, and this has already been explained as one action of the ON ERROR GOTO routine. With this filename, if it existed, no longer on the disk, the original platters.dat file can be renamed as platters.bak, and then the new TEMP.$$$ file can be renamed as platters.dat. This leaves you with a copy of the amended file, and also a copy of the previous version, a very useful feature to build into any program that uses files.

Serial filing is often dismissed as primitive, but it is relatively free of complications, and has the enormous advantage of allowing you to use unrestricted string sizes. The read-then-write action that is necessary to alter a file can be tedious when large files are being used, but the machine is doing the work, and the time required is not so very great. For any type of data that requires only appending rather than amending, and can be kept in the order in which it was entered, serial files are preferable to other types. One useful point to note is that you can use the device names KYBD:, SCRN: and LPT1: in place of filename like B:platters.dat when you are testing programs. Obviously the keyboard can only be used in place of a file for INPUT and the screen or printer in place of a file for output – the EOF character is then **CTRL-Z**.

Chapter 10

RANDOM ACCESS FILING

Random access filing, as the name suggests, means that we should be able to get at any record (or set of records) on the disk without having to read all of the earlier records as well. This doesn't mean that we have to create a random access file by scattering bytes all over the disk (though we could), simply that it should be possible to locate and read any particular byte on the disk. As you might by now expect, this is not done by reading one selected byte but by reading one complete sector into memory and working on it there. In general, we will create a file initially, and record it, using much the same general techniques as we have used for serial filing. We can then add to the file, replace items, change items, and select items at random, using random-access techniques. The important point about such random-access filing is that it's possible to extend a file so that the file length is much greater than could be held in the memory of the computer. As an alternative, of course, we can use the random-access filing methods that we need for extending a file in order to create the file in the first place. With a random-access file, we can extract single items or groups as we please, amend or delete or replace items, all without the need to read the whole file into the memory and then back to disk as we did with the serial files. For most purposes, all that ever has to be read or written is one sector of the disk. This freedom, however, is bought at a price, and the details of the price are not easy to dig out of the manual.

Random access commands

The important random access commands of BASIC are OPEN, FIELD, PUT, GET and a set of field-positioning and number-conversion instructions, of which more later. Of these, the one that needs most explanation is FIELD, since this has no counterpart in serial filing. Random access filing is possible only if each record in the file consists of the same number of fields, and each field in the record is of a specified size. There's nothing magical about random access filing. The name of the file is stored on the disk directory, and the directory also contains the starting position of the file. From then on, it's easy. If you know that each record is 100 characters (bytes) long, for example, then it's easy to find the 4th record (numbering from 1) because it will start at the 300th byte in the file, and the 17th record will start at byte 1600. Similarly if the 100 byte record consists of four names each of 25 characters, then it's easy to find the third name in a record by getting to byte 75. Without these fixed lengths, random access filing is not possible, not in this comparatively simple form anyhow. The FIELD instruction exists to allow you to specify each field, its name in the file, and its length in number of characters/bytes.

The form of a FIELD statement is simple. It starts with FIELD #1 or FIELD #file%, for example, using the file stream (or reference) number. As usual, unless you have some rooted objection to the number, you might as well use 1. Using a variable such as file%, which can be assigned the value 1 at some earlier stage, allows you some freedom when you are designing a program, in case you want to change the stream number (to avoid conflict with another file, perhaps) without having to change all the statements that use it. Having used the FIELD statement and the stream number, you then put in each variable name that you want to use in the file and its maximum size. The syntax here is size AS name, and each name must be a string name. You can, for example have such items as 25 AS A$, 32 AS Add$ and so on. There must be one of these number AS string statements for each field that you will use, and they are separated from each other and from the start of the FIELD statement by commas. The FIELD statement cannot be run until the file has been opened.

The OPEN statement is more straightforward, because much of it is as you would use it for a serial file. The keyword OPEN is followed by the filename as for a serial file, and there is no INPUT, OUTPUT or APPEND this time, because a random access file permits two-way traffic. Following the name, then, comes AS and then the file stream number. A space separates this from the record size, in the form LEN=50, so that a complete OPEN statement would be like:

```
OPEN "B:daybook.rnd" AS #1 LEN=50
```

Any existing file of this name will be opened for random access by this statement and if no such file exists, one will be created. No BAK files are created when you use random-access filing, so there's nothing to stop you writing new data all over a valuable file if your program is badly designed. The length of the record, put in as `LEN=50` in this example, must match with the total of the lengths of the fields that will be used. As you might expect, chaos will result if these figures don't match!

The record length is fixed at 128 characters, the standard buffer size, unless you specify something different in the `LEN` part of the `OPEN` statement. For quite a surprising number of applications, 128 characters is a convenient record size, but if you are filing something small, perhaps only 10 characters per field, it would be a ridiculous waste of disk space to mark out a set of 128-character spaces each holding 10 characters. Problems arise, however, if you need a record length of more than 128 characters. If you specify this, you may find that you get an `Illegal function call` when the `OPEN` line is run, and your program stops. This is because the buffer size in GW BASIC is fixed at 128 bytes, and if you want to use records longer than this you need also to specify a larger buffer size. This *must* be done at the time when GW BASIC is loaded by using an addition to the BASIC name. For example, to load GW BASIC with a 256 byte buffer, you would start BASIC with `GW/S:256` in place of the normal `GW`. This can be such a chore to remember that you should place any random access file program that needs this step onto a disk that contains system tracks (formatted with `/S`), and write an `autoexec.bat` file (see Appendix B) containing the line:

```
GW/S:256 filnam.rnd
```

so as to load GW BASIC, set the buffer size, and load in the program whose filename is `filnam.rnd` in this example. Obviously, you can pick your own filename.

Padding

Since each field in a random-access file must be of a fixed length, what do we do if the information does not fit? To start with, we ensure that any number information will fit, by methods that we can look at later. The awkward items are strings like names and addresses. These will be chopped if they are too long and padded out with blanks if they are too short. Unlike some versions of BASIC, GW BASIC does not require you to write a lot of tedious loops in order to pad out short names. Instead, you can use three statements that will have a very familiar ring to anyone (like me) who used the good ol' TRS-80 disk system, or who have more recent acquaintance with MALLARD™ BASIC on the Amstrad PCW machines. These statements are LSET, RSET and MID$. The names indicate the action, but the syntax will be unfamiliar unless you have used a similar filing system. LSET, for example, sets a string to the left of its field, fills out the right-hand side with blanks, and assigns the field to the record. For example, using LSET A$=nam$ will assign A$ so that it contains nam$ followed by enough blanks to make up the correct field size, and put this field into place in its record. You cannot assign correctly to fieldnames other than by the use of these three commands, of which LSET is by far the most common. If the FIELD statement has used A$ AS 25, then the name in nam$ will be padded out to 25 characters, with the name at the start. As you might expect, if nam$ consists of more than 25 characters, it will be chopped to 25 characters by omitting characters at the right-hand side.

The word RSET works in a similar way, but will set the string over to the right, putting the padding blanks on the left. This is most likely to be used when you have converted numbers to strings and want the numbers placed to the right-hand side of a field. MID$ is rather more complicated, and is used mainly when you want to pad with characters that are not spaces. Used like this, MID$ is always preceded by RSET so that the name, or whatever you want to pad, is at the right-hand side of the field. Suppose, for example, that we used a field of 10 characters, and then assigned RSET A$="JIM", followed by MID$(A$,1,7)="##########". This would pick characters 1 to 7 from the string of hashmarks, and place them into the same positions in A$, giving #######JIM for A$. You would normally want to use this statement in the form MID$(A$,1,10-LEN(X$)), with X$ being the string that is later RSET as A$. You can't use LEN(A$) because the length of A$ is 10 characters, fixed by the FIELD statement.

Numbers are treated in a rather special way. Since each item that is stored in a random-access file must be a string, the obvious thing to do is to convert each number into a string by using STR$. This, however, is a slow action, and if you have to work with large files and a lot of numbers it can noticeably increase the time that you spend just waiting. In addition, the conversions that are made by STR$ are to quite long strings, particularly for double-precision numbers, and you have to make your fields long enough to hold all the characters. BASIC provides three sets of reserved words to cope with this conversion in a different and more useful way, once again familiar to former TRS-80 programmers. The principle is to convert into string form not the number itself, but the code that is used to store the number. The result of this will be strings that are often of very weird characters, if you try to print the result, certainly not recognisable as numbers. The advantage is that an integer always codes as a 2-character

```
10 A%=65:B%=16706
20 X=22.45
30 D#=216.45169#
40 A$=MKI$(A%):PRINT A$;"     ("LEN(A$)")"
50 B$=MKI$(B%):PRINT B$;"     ("LEN(B$)")"
60 X$=MKS$(X):PRINT X$;"     ("LEN(X$)")"
70 D$=MKD$(D#):PRINT D$;"     ("LEN(D$)")"
80 PRINT CVI(A$);"     "CVI(B$)
90 PRINT CVS(X$);"     "CVD(D$)
```

Figure 10.1

The effects of the MK and CV type of statements to convert numbers between number form and string form. The string form is NOT the same as is used by STR$, however, as this shows.

string, a single-precision number as a 4-character string, and a double-precision number as an 8-character string. Figure 10.1 illustrates this with a short program that uses the codings, prints the characters and the lengths of the strings, and shows how we can convert back into printable numbers.

The number-to-string conversions are done by `MKI$` (integers), `MKS$` (single precision) and `MKD$` (double precision), using fixed string lengths of 2, 4 and 8 bytes respectively. For an integer, you can see reasonably easily how the scheme works. The number 65 is character A in ASCII code, so when the string version of 65 is printed, you get an `A` printed. The next number, 16706, is more of a surprise, because it gives `BA`. The ASCII code for B is 66, with A being 65, and 16706 is 66+256×65. This corresponds with the way that larger integers are stored as two bytes. The strings that correspond to single and double-precision numbers are considerably more complicated unless you have a taste for mathematics. The program shows that the length allocated to each string has no connection with the number of digits in the number, and is fixed only by the type of number: integer, single-precision or double-precision. Finally, the conversion back to number form is carried out by using `CVI` (integer), `CVS` (single-precision) and `CVD` (double-precision) respectively. The use of these words allows us to work with numbers in random-access files using smaller fields than would be possible if we had to convert with `STR$` and `VAL`, and also with faster conversions.

An integer file

It's time to illustrate a random access file in action. The fact that this is a simple illustration should not put you off – the techniques are exactly the same as you will need if you choose to use random access filing for more serious purposes. The example is in Figure 10.2 and, as before, the first line is an automatic way of ensuring that files will be closed if an error is found. If an error is found as the program runs then instead of the program stopping with the usual error message, it goes to line 250, which will close files and end. The snag here is that

```
10 ON ERROR GOTO 250
20 REM close file on error
30 FILE%=1:LIMIT%=100
40 OPEN "b:integer.rnd" AS #FILE% LEN=2
50 FIELD FILE%,2 AS A$
60 FOR N%=1 TO LIMIT%
70 A%=1000-N%:REM recognisable number!
80 LSET A$=MKI$(A%)
90 PUT FILE%
100 NEXT
110 CLOSE
120 PRINT"Press any key to read"
130 K$=INPUT$(1)
140 OPEN "b:integer.rnd" AS #FILE% LEN=2
150 FIELD FILE%,2  AS N$
160 N%=1
170 WHILE N%<>0
180 INPUT"Item number, please (0 to end) ";N%
190 GET FILE%,N%
200 X%=CVI(N$)
210 PRINT"Number is ";X%
220 FOR J=1 TO 2000:NEXT
230 CLS
240 WEND
250 CLOSE:END
```

Figure 10.2

A simple random-access file program that contains both the recording and the read-back sections.

you get no error message in this simple application, and it's a good idea to omit this line while you are testing the program. Line 30 then defines two variables, `file%` assigned the value 1 to act as a stream number, and `limit%` to set a limit in a `FOR..NEXT` loop of items. The point of using variables for these quantities is to illustrate how easy it can be to adapt a program to other numbers when variables are used in this way. In this short example, of course, you could just as easily have used numbers 1 and 100 in the appropriate places.

Line 40 then starts the creation of the file, using the `OPEN` statement. The stream is as fixed by `file%`, equal to 1, and the name chosen for the file is `"integer.rnd"`. This suggests that the integers are random, but in this example they quite certainly are not for reasons that we'll look at in a moment. The last part of the `OPEN` statement fixes the record size at 2, since only 2 bytes are needed to store an integer. Following the opening of the file, which will start the disk spinning, the `FIELD` statement uses the stream number again, and states that the variable that will be filed is called `A$` and consists of 2 bytes only.

Having declared the sizes of record and of field, identical in this case since there is just one field per record, we can now put numbers into the file. The loop that does this starts in line 60, and uses the ending number set by `limit%`. In the loop, the numbers that are to be filed are assigned to `A%` in line 70, using `1000-N%`. The reason for doing this in a test is to provide easy recognition. If you use truly random numbers, you can't be sure when you replay the file if a given number is really the one that was originally filed in that position. By using a scheme like this, you can be sure that number 1 is 999, number 2 is 998 and so on, all easily recognised later. This is a useful tip for testing any filing system, because otherwise it's easy to miss a fault that makes the replayed item incorrect. Line 80 is the important one at this point. This line places the string version of the number `A%` into a string `A$`, and sets to the left. Since the string consists of only two characters, this looks rather un-necessary but it is essential. If you omit the `LSET`, you will find that `A$=MKI$(A%)` will run, but that you cannot find any numbers in the file when you replay it. The reason is that `LSET`, `RSET` and `MID$` are not just field padding statements, they are the statements that actually place the value of a variable into the file. You can't omit them! In normal circumstances, there would be several lines of `LSET`, `RSET` or `MID$` statements to place the fields into the record in correct form, and following these you need to put the record on to the file. This is done in the following line here, using `PUT file%`. If the record is of the default size of 128 bytes, this statement will place the data on to the disk, but if the records are small, as they are in this example, the records are stored in a 'buffer' piece of memory until the total length is around 128 bytes, upon which the assembled records are filed. Figure 10.3 shows a summary of these processes. At the end of the loop, the file is closed by using the `CLOSE`

1) Open file using channel number and file name. Include record length if default of 128 characters not suitable.

2) Set FIELD values to define field sizes.

3) Use LSET to load data into field together with left justification and padding spaces.

4) Use PUT to load record into the file – disk activity will only take place when file file buffer has been filled.

Figure 10.3
A summary of the processes involved in random access filing programs.

statement. Once again, `CLOSE file%` could be used, but `CLOSE` by itself closes all files.

The second part of the example shows how such a file can be read back. One golden rule here is that unless you are trying to do something very clever (or risky), you should try to use statements in the same form when replaying as you did when recording. Accordingly, the replay program starts with the same form of `OPEN` as the recording program used. Note that the `OPEN` statement is identical, no matter whether we are writing, reading or extending the file. We can once again use `FIELD` to declare the form of the fields, and this time we have used `2 AS N$`, with a different variable name. The variable name of `A$` need not be used this time – all that is going to be done is to take two characters from the file and assign them to a string variable, and provided that you declare some variable, it doesn't matter what the name is so long as it does not conflict with anything else that you use. With the file open and the `FIELD` statement executed, you can then use the file. In this case, we are going to read the file, and to do so we have to specify which record we want to read. This is done by record number, and this is the weakness of random access files of this form. Unless you know the record numbers, you can't read the records. If the records that you are using will have some 'natural' number, like an employee record number, all is well. If not, then you have to find some way of associating each record with its accession number, as this is called. In this simple example, of course, you simply type a number between 1 and 100, and the number appears. Since you know that the number that appears should be 1000-record number, you can check that the numbers are the correct ones. Asking for a number greater than 100 is not an error, you merely get the result of zero, assuming that the disk contains no other files. This is important, because it means that a random-access file can make use of more disk space that you might have intended, and if this could be a problem, then your programs will have to include steps that limit the number of records that can be used.

Now before we leave this example, it's important to point out that random access allows much more than is illustrated here. Once the file is opened and the `FIELD` statement executed, we can amend or extend the file as we like. This is done by specifying a record number with `PUT` in the same way as we have used `GET` in line 190. In other words, if you assign something to `N$` in this second part of the program, you can use a statement like `PUT file%,45` to change record number 45 to some other number. You can also use a statement like `PUT file%,120` to create a record that did not exist in the original. Neither the `OPEN` nor the `FIELD` statement puts any limit on the number of files that you can create, and there's no restriction about the order in which you create them. The system that is followed is that if `PUT` is used with no record number, then the records are put into the file in order starting with 1, or with any specified number that is used in a preceding `PUT` statement. This freedom can cause difficulties, however, because it's quite possible to specify a record number that cannot be filed because there is no more room on the disk. Because of this, random access files have to be planned carefully, usually by setting a limit to the number of entries and making a dummy file with this number in order to clear space on the disk.

A longer example

Our investigations of random access filing have, so far, been confined to simple programs, and these simple illustrations do not really bring out the peculiar advantages and disadvantages of random access methods. The main disadvantage for many purposes is the need to refer to each item by number, the accession number as it is called. For some purposes, the use of an accession number can be a positive advantage if the item would be numbered anyhow, so that if your program keeps track of works personnel by using works number, or of references in a book indexed by page number, then you have the number principle built-in, and all's well. For a lot of other files, however, including the very common name and address file, you would not want to have to remember a number in order to read a file. For such a case, there are established methods which are noted briefly (a full description would fill another two chapters) at the end of this chapter.

The example which will be developed here is a natural for accession number – a day memo book. Since each day of the year is numbered starting at 1 for January 1st, then we can make the day number equal to the record number. For a daybook, you might not need anything apart from a note, but this program will allow for a cash input and a cash output entry, a birthday name, and also for a 'Meeting at ...' section that can be used when reading to indicate that this is an important event. Each record will therefore consist of a note string, a string for a name (birthday name), the 'meeting at' string, cash in and cash out, and the day number will be added in case you need to know it, though it isn't used in the readout. Since the file is a random one, it follows that you can make an entry for any day in the year, and also read any entry that has been made. A further step would be to allow addition to a string or amendment of any string, or the summing of cash for a given month – but for the moment we'll concentrate on the essentials. As a sideline, we need to be able to convert from the more familiar 26/4/87 type of date format into a day number – and that needs some planning.

Like all programs, this starts as a core routine which is illustrated in Figure 10.4. This allows for screen setup, initialisation (particularly of records), menu display and then choice, the chance to repeat a menu item, and closedown. From this

```
10 REM setup
20 GOSUB 1000
30 REM initialise records
40 GOSUB 1200
50 REM menu
60 GOSUB 1300
70 REM choose
80 GOSUB 1500
90 REM Another?
100 CHOICE$="menu item"
110 GOSUB 1600
120 IF K$="Y" OR K$="y" THEN GOTO 60
130 REM close and end
140 GOSUB 10000
150 END
```

Figure 10.4

A core program for a daybook random-access filing program.

simple core, quite a considerable program has grown. This allows the creation of a file for one year, with one year per disk as presently constituted. Once a file for a year has been created, items can be entered for each day in the year. These items can also be read, with one item displayed per screen. No provision has been made for hard-copy, or for more elaborate displays or editing, and the menus are straightforward pick-number types. In short, this is just a starter to which you can add as much as you like to make it more useful or more appealing to you. The record size is 210, and this requires you to use the `/S:256` command when you load in BASIC. A blank file is created for each year when the program is first run for that year, so as to ensure that each space in the file is correctly allocated. This avoids the problem of reading rubbish from a file that has been placed on a disk that was previously used for other files.

The complete listing is shown in Figure 10.5 – spread over the next five pages, having grown considerably from the core outline. Much of this is because of mugtraps and other routines, notably the routine for converting a date in DD/MM format into a day number, allowing for leap years. The daybook is configured up to 1997, but could be used beyond this date with no adjustment needed for the foreseeable future (until the `year%/400` test for an additional leap year becomes applicable).

To make the task of examining this program easier, we'll look at it in the order of the listing of the routines, though this is not the order in which they were written. The original listing has been renumbered so as to make it easier for you to type using the `AUTO` command. The subroutine in line 160 deals with the printing of the title and the brief instructions. These actions are straightforward, and need no further explanation. The real meat of the program starts with the initialising subroutine at line 250, which contains the important variable initialisations. Variables `FILE%` and `NOTE%` are used as stream numbers. `FILE%` is used for the main random access file, and `NOTE%` is used for a small serial file that holds the year and whether or not it is a leap year. The other variable in the first line of this subroutine is the assignment of 365 to `LENYR%`, the normal length of a year. Leap years are dealt with by using a quantity `LEAP%`, which will be false (0) or true(–1), by subtracting `LEAP%` from `LENYR%` – since subtracting a negative quantity is the same as adding a positive quantity, then `LENYR% + LEAP%` gives 366 on leap years and 365 on other years.

The next step is the filling of an array that will be used in calculating day numbers. The principle here is that if the month is January, month 1, then the day number is just the number of the day in January. If the month is February, then the day number is 31 + date, because the number of days in January has to be added to the number of days in February, and so on. The array `MON%(J%)` therefore

Figure 10.5

The complete daybook program. Approach this one subroutine at a time so that you can see what is being done.

```
10 REM setup
20 KEY OFF:GOSUB 1000
30 REM initialise records
40 GOSUB 1200
50 REM menu
60 GOSUB 1300
70 REM choose
80 GOSUB 1500
90 REM Another?
100 CHOICE$="menu item"
110 GOSUB 1600
120 IF K$="Y" OR K$="y" THEN GOTO 60
130 REM close and end
140 GOSUB 10000
150 END
1000 CLS
1010 PRINT TAB(36)"YEARBOOK":PRINT TAB(36)"========"
1020 PRINT:PRINT TAB(3)"This program allows you to set up a
notebook for an entire year."
1030 PRINT TAB(2)"You use Option 1 only once each year, and
from then on use the other options"
1040 PRINT"to enter items or read items. These are classed
as general notes, meetings,"
1050 PRINT"birthdays, cash in and cash out. You specify
dates in the normal way and they"
1060 PRINT"are converted to day numbers. The day number and
year will be stored in each"
1070 PRINT "record.":PRINT:PRINT"Press any key to proceed."
1080 K$=INPUT$(1):RETURN
1200 FILE%=1:NOTE%=2:LENYR%=365
1210 DIM MON%(12)
1230 FOR J%=1 TO 12:READ MON%(J%):NEXT
1240 DATA 0,31,59,90,120,151,181,212,243,273,304,334
1250 TRUE%=-1:FALSE%=0
1260 RETURN
```

```
1300 CLS:PRINT TAB(38)"MENU":PRINT TAB(38)"====":PRINT
1310 PRINT TAB(5)"1. Create a file for a NEW YEAR.":PRINT
1320 PRINT TAB(5)"2. Write to this years diary.":PRINT
1330 PRINT TAB(5)"3. Read a days notes.":PRINT
1340 PRINT TAB(5)"4. End.":PRINT
1350 PRINT"Please choose by number (1 to 4):"
1360 RETURN
1500 K%=0:WHILE K%<1 OR K%>4
1510 K$=INPUT$(1):K%=VAL(K$):WEND
1520 ON K% GOSUB 2000,2500,3000,10000
1530 RETURN
1600 CLS
1610 PRINT TAB(2)"Do you want another "CHOICE$" (Y/N)?"
1620 K$="X":WHILE INSTR("YyNn",K$)=0
1630 K$=INPUT$(1):WEND
1640 RETURN
2000 CLS:PRINT TAB(34)"NEW YEARBOOK":PRINT
TAB(34)"============"
2010 PRINT:PRINT TAB(5)"What year, please (1987 to 1997)"
2020 YEAR%=0:WHILE YEAR%<1987 OR YEAR%>1997
2030 INPUT YEAR%:WEND
2040 IF YEAR%/4=YEAR%\4 THEN LEAP%=TRUE% ELSE LEAP%=FALSE%
2050 OPEN "b:notes.dat" FOR OUTPUT AS #NOTE%
2060 PRINT #NOTE%, YEAR%,LEAP%
2070 CLOSE #NOTE%
2080 PRINT TAB(5)"Year noted in file"
2090 PRINT TAB(5)"Please wait for daybook creation."
2100 OPEN "b:daybook.rnd" AS #FILE% LEN=210:GOSUB 5000
2110 FOR J%=1 TO LENYR%-(LEAP%)
2112 LSET DAY$=STRING$(2,0):LSET COMMENT$=STRING$(160,0)
2114 LSET MEET$=STRING$(20,0):LSET BDAY$=STRING$(20,0)
2116 LSET CASHIN$=STRING$(4,0):LSET CASHOUT$=STRING$(4,0)
2120 PUT #FILE%,J%
2130 NEXT
2140 CLOSE #FILE%
2150 PRINT"Daybook file for New Year ready for use now."
2160 GOSUB 9000
```

Figure 10.5 *Continued*

```
2170 RETURN
2500 OPEN "b:daybook.rnd" AS #FILE% LEN=210:GOSUB 5000
2510 CLS:PRINT
2520 PRINT TAB(32)"Write to Daybook."
2530 GOSUB 4000:REM find year
2540 GOSUB 4500:REM get day number
2550 GOSUB 5500:REM write to record
2560 GOSUB 9000:CLS
2570 CHOICE$="write action"
2580 GOSUB 1600
2590 IF K$="Y" OR K$="y" THEN GOTO 2530
2600 CLOSE #FILE%
2610 RETURN
3000 OPEN "b:daybook.rnd" AS #FILE% LEN=210:GOSUB 5000
3010 CLS:PRINT
3020 PRINT TAB(35)"READ DIARY":PRINT
3030 PRINT TAB(3)"You can now read your entry for any day."
3040 GOSUB 4500:REM get day number
3050 GOSUB 6000:REM read entry
3060 CHOICE$="read"
3070 GOSUB 1600
3080 IF K$="Y" OR K$="y" THEN GOTO 3040
3090 CLOSE #FILE%
3100 RETURN
4000 OPEN "b:notes.dat" FOR INPUT AS #NOTE%
4010 INPUT #NOTE%,YEAR%,LEAP%
4020 CLOSE #NOTE%
4030 RETURN
4500 CLS:PRINT:PRINT TAB(5)"Please enter date now -"
4510 PRINT TAB(5)"Use format DD/MM or DD-MM"
4520 BAD%=TRUE%:WHILE BAD%=TRUE%
4525 MYDATE$=""
4530 LOCATE 7,5:FOR J%=1 TO 5
4540 K$="":WHILE K$=""
4550 K$=INKEY$:WEND
4555 PRINT K$;
4560 MYDATE$=MYDATE$+K$:NEXT
```

Figure 10.5 *Continued*

```
4570 FOR J%=1 TO 5:K%=ASC(MID$(MYDATE$,J%,1))
4580 IF (K%>47 AND K%<58) OR J%=3 THEN BAD%=FALSE%
4590 NEXT
4600 IF BAD%=TRUE% THEN LOCATE 7,5:PRINT SPACE$(79);
4610 WEND
4620 DNO%=VAL(MID$(MYDATE$,1,2)):MNO%=VAL(MID$(MYDATE$,4,2))
4630 IF MNO%<1 OR MNO%>12 THEN PRINT" Bad month
number":GOSUB 9000:GOTO 4500
4640 IF (DNO%>28) AND (MNO%=2) AND NOT LEAP% THEN GOSUB
7000:GOTO 4500
4650 IF (DNO%>29) AND (MNO%=2) THEN GOSUB 7000:GOTO 4500
4660 IF (DNO%>30) AND ((MNO%=4) OR (MNO%=6) OR (MNO%=9) OR
(MNO%=11)) THEN GOSUB 7000:GOTO 4500
4670 IF (DNO%>31) THEN GOSUB 7000:GOTO 4500
4680 DAYNR%=MON%(MNO%)+DNO%
4690 IF LEAP% AND (MNO%>2) THEN DAYNR%=DAYNR%+1
4700 RETURN
5000 FIELD #FILE%, 2 AS DAY$,160 AS COMMENT$, 20 AS MEET$,
20 AS BDAY$, 4 AS CASHIN$, 4 AS CASHOUT$
5010 RETURN
5500 GOSUB 8000:REM edit
5510 PUT #FILE%,DAYNR%
5520 RETURN
6000 GOSUB 4000:REM Get year
6010 GET #FILE%,DAYNR%
6020 CLS:PRINT
6030 PRINT TAB(29)"Date: "DNO%"/"MNO%"/"YEAR%:PRINT
6040 PRINT TAB(3)"Comments: ";COMMENT$
6050 PRINT
6060 PRINT TAB(3)"Meeting at: ";MEET$
6070 PRINT
6080 PRINT TAB(3)"Birthday of: ";BDAY$
6090 PRINT
6100 PRINT TAB(3)"Cash in: "CVS(CASHIN$)
6110 PRINT
6120 PRINT TAB(3)"Cash out: "CVS(CASHOUT$)
6130 PRINT:PRINT"Press any key to proceed."
```

Figure 10.5 *Continued*

```
6140 K$=INPUT$(1):RETURN
7000 PRINT" Bad day number - please try again "
7010 GOSUB 9000:RETURN
8000 CLS:PRINT:PRINT TAB(3)"Please enter as prompted."
8010 PRINT TAB(5)"Pressing RETURN by itself makes no
entry.":PRINT
8020 LIMIT%=160:STRLEN%=161:WHILE STRLEN%>LIMIT%
8030 PRINT TAB(5)"Comments for today (2 lines max.) "
8040 PRINT TAB(5);:LINE INPUT REP$
8050 GOSUB 8500:WEND
8060 LSET COMMENT$=REP$
8070 LIMIT%=20:STRLEN%=21
8080 WHILE STRLEN%>LIMIT%
8090 PRINT TAB(5)"Meeting at (20 characters max.) ";
8100 LINE INPUT REP$:GOSUB 8500:WEND
8105 LSET MEET$=REP$
8110 LIMIT%=20:STRLEN%=21
8120 WHILE STRLEN%>LIMIT%
8130 PRINT TAB(5)"Birthday today for (20 characters max.) ";
8140 LINE INPUT REP$:GOSUB 8500:WEND
8150 LSET BDAY$=REP$
8160 PRINT:PRINT TAB(5);
8170 INPUT"Cash in today..";REP
8180 LSET CASHIN$=MKS$(REP)
8190 PRINT:PRINT TAB(5);
8200 INPUT "Cash out today...";REP
8210 LSET CASHOUT$=MKS$(REP)
8220 PRINT:PRINT TAB(3)"Please check this entry
for";DNO%"/"MNO%"/"YEAR%"."
8230 PRINT TAB(5)"Press N key to repeat this entry, any
other to proceed."
8240 K$=INPUT$(1): IF K$="N" OR K$="n" THEN GOTO  8000
8250 RETURN
8500 STRLEN%=LEN(REP$)
8510 IF STRLEN%>LIMIT% THEN PRINT"Too long- please try
again":GOSUB 9000
8520 RETURN
```

Figure 10.5 *Continued*

```
9000 FOR X=1 TO 1500:NEXT:RETURN
10000 CLS
10010 CLOSE
10020 PRINT"END."
10025 KEY ON
10030 END
```

Figure 10.5 *Continued*

consists of the cumulative number of days, using 0 for January, 31 for February, and so on. Leap years are catered for by adding 1 for months following February, as we shall see later. The last item is the assignment to TRUE% and FALSE%, since these are not preassigned in this version of BASIC.

The menu and choice subroutines follow conventional paths, and we need not spend any time on them. The important main subroutines are the first three choices in the menu, used respectively for creating a new file, writing to a file, and reading a file. The final choice simply closes all open files and resets the function keys display. This closing subroutine at 10000 is also used in several escape points within the program, and is not a true subroutine in the sense that it never returns. Both the reading and the writing routines make use of a subroutine for converting dates into day numbers for the chosen year.

The create subroutine, starting at 470, will be used only once on each data disk, since it sets up the serial file noting year and LEAP%, and then a dummy random-access file, filled with blanks, for a daybook for one year. The year is requested at the start of the subroutine, and is tested to find if it divides evenly by 4, because this would make it a leap year. The variable LEAP% is used in a TRUE or FALSE way as an indicator from that point on. To ensure that this data is available each time the daybook for that year is used, the year and the variable leap are recorded in a serial file called b:notes.dat. Obviously, you may want to alter the drive letter if you are using a hard-disk machine, but the use of B: is suitable for either a single or dual floppy machine. Once this serial file has been closed, the main random dummy file is opened. This will wipe out any other file of that name on the disk, so that you are not allowed to create another file for the same year on one disk. The length is specified as 210, allowing for the planned sizes of comment (160 characters), meetingplace and birthday (20 each), cash in and cash out (both real numbers using 4 bytes each), and day number (integer of 2 bytes) which is unused but might come in handy. A FOR..NEXT loop then records the strings, assigned with LSET to blanks, into each record of this file, using FOR J%=1 to LENYR%-(LEAP%) in order to make the file extend to 365 for normal years and to 366 for leap years, remembering that LEAP%=-1 for a leap year and 0 for others. This action takes some time, so a 'Please wait' notice has been placed on screen while this is being done. The file needs about 78K, so that it would be perfectly feasible to have more than one year on a disk, but the complications of altering filenames make it hardly worth while. The file is closed, then a message informs you when the file has been created, and the subroutine then returns you to the menu if you answer Y to the question. The disk now contains blocks of 210 bytes (356 of them, or 366 in a leap year), and you can place data into any of these blocks using the writing routine that starts on line 680.

The writing subroutine starts by opening the file that should have been previously created, but will not fail if no file exists. The only reason for creating the dummy file is to ensure 'clean' disk space so that reading an unwritten day does not result in reading left-over rubbish from the disk. The main parts of this subroutine are then carried out by three more subroutines, at 910, 950 and 1200 for finding the year, finding the day number and writing the record respectively. Of these, the year find routine at 910 simply opens up the serial file and reads the year and the value of LEAP%. The subroutine at 950 is the one that gets the day number from the date that is to be entered, and is used also by the file reading routine, so we'll deal with it first, though its action is nothing to do with random access filing, because it illustrates how a set of well-known rules can be put into program form.

The day number routine starts in line 950 with a request to enter the date in DD/MM form. In fact, any form of divider can be used, so that DD.MM, DD,MM, DD–MM and so on are all equally acceptable. The important point is that this reply must consist of five characters, so that the first of September is entered as 01/09 and not as 1/9. This date entry is carried out within a WHILE loop so that it can be tested for incorrect entries like 1/12 or 234/5. The input uses an INKEY$ loop which has been used in preference to INPUT$ in this case because we want to see on the screen whatever is typed, and INPUT$ does not permit this option. If the date is of the wrong format, the use of ?SPACE$(79) wipes out the line so that another attempt can be made. So far, however, nothing prevents the acceptance of a date such as 32/13, and this has to be tested for separately.

The next section of the routine tests month and day numbers. Since the previous section has ensured that the date is in the correct format, we can use string slicing and VAL to get the day and the month numbers as variables DNO% and

MNO%. These are then tested in a set of IF lines which are arranged so that if the test fails a message is printed and the date entry is restarted. The first test will reject month numbers less than 1 or more than 13, and the remaining tests are to establish the correct day number. This is complicated by the use of unequal numbers of days per month, and is done on the basis of the old rule of '30 days hath September, April June and November'. The first line, however, deals with Month 2, February. If the month number is 2 and the number of days exceeds 28 and the year is not leap, then we have an error, and the usual routines are invoked. The next line tests for a February with more than 29 days, with the same result if the test is true. The following line rejects months with more than 30 days if they happen to be months numbered 4, 6, 9, or 11 (April, June, September, November), and then a final line rejects any month with more than 31 days.

Since the array MON% has already been created in the initialisation section, the number of days from January 1st can now be calculated by adding the variable DNO% to MON%(MNO%). This is adjusted for leap years and month number greater than 2 in the following line to allow for the 366-day years. The end result is the number DAYNR% because this will be used as the accession number for the record whether for reading or writing. The following routine, starting at 1200 will now make use of this number to write data to a chosen record.

The write day routine starts with an editing subroutine of a very simple type which asks for inputs and tests for length of input. This rejects any input that is too long (you have to type it all again, which is far from ideal), and if the input is simply the **RETURN** key no assignment is made. The string or number replay is the assigned using LSET and MKS$ as appropriate, into the record. An improvement on this would be to make the LSET steps conditional on the string length exceeding zero, so that pressing the **RETURN** key with no entry could be used to keep a field of an existing record intact. Following the entry of all of the data, the record is placed in the file using PUT #FILE%,DAYNR% in the usual way.

Reading a record

The steps for reading a record follow so closely the steps for writing a record that most of the subroutines can be reused, which is the whole point of having subroutines. The subroutine at line 420, in fact, has been used several times, with part of the message assigned to CHOICE$ each time. The record reading routine starts at line 800 by opening the random access file and running the filed sizes subroutine. The reading routine then uses the day finding subroutine at line 950 which accepts the input of a date and converts it into a day number for use as a record number. The main part of the reading routine is the subroutine which starts at line 1230. This uses the subroutine at 910 to read the year and the value of variable `LEAP%` from the serial file. Since the random access file is open, the `GET` statement can then be used with `DAYNR%` specifying the record number. This reads the record and in the following print section, the fields are extracted and printed to the screen. By using a print `#STREAM` type of statement, you could start such a read with the 'Printer or Screen' choice, and assign a suitable stream number so that the data was sent to whichever output device you wanted to use. You are given the choice of repeating the read actions as often as you want.

This example, though comparatively lengthy, is really only a starter for a much more elaborate program. No attempt has been made, for example, to do more than look at each record, and you might want to add routines that allowed you to make additions to a record you were looking at, or to make use of the day number coded into each record, or of the cash amounts. You might, for example, want to write a routine which asked for two dates and then printed the cash in and cash out totals between these dates. Since all the subroutines for date conversion already exist, the addition of such routines is comparatively simple – but make sure that the main routines are working correctly.

Just one final point. I get a lot of letters asking if there are errors in printed routines, and listing error messages that have appeared. No program is perfect, but the printed routines in this book have all been run and tested, the listing made, and the book has used this listing directly. If this or any other program in the book drops out with an error, the first place to look is at your own typing. Always disable any `ON ERROR GOTO` lines before trouble-shooting in this way, because syntax errors are often hidden by `ON ERROR GOTO`. If you are absolutely certain that your program is giving some unique problem that did not occur on the original, then write in by all means, but please enclose a listing or the program on disk so that I can sort it out. Try as I may, I can't help much if the message I get is simply that the program didn't run – I need to know where it failed, what the error message was, what files are on the disk, to name just three points. One of the advantages of writing a book for PC owners, however, is that readers can generally be relied on to type well and sort out their own syntax errors!

Indexed sequential action

Serial files are very useful for a lot of purposes, but not if you want to be able to obtain one record out of a very large number. The obvious alternative is random access filing, and we have just dealt with that topic. Random access filing, however, in BASIC, suffers from one considerable snag. Unless you know the number of a record, you cannot get random access to that record. You can't, for example, get the record for TAYLOR,J, just by typing this name, and unless you happen to know that this is record number 273, that's it, you will have to search through the records one by one just as you would with a serial file. Programming with random-access filing so that you can recover items by name, or so that you can quickly list in alphabetical order of name, is by no means easy – but these are often precisely the actions for which we most need random access!

The solution to the problem was, however, developed a long time ago, and is called by various names like indexed random access, relative filing, ISAM (Indexed Sequential Access to Memory) and so on. In the space that we have here we can only look briefly at the principles – but they are, in fact, quite simple. In an ISAM filing system, each time a random access record is written, a serial file is also written. Into the serial file is put some key item, which is often the first six letters of the main field of the random access record. For example, if your random access record dealt with names and addresses, you could extract the first six letters of the surname, and this would be files on a serial file along with the record number.

Now when you want to search for a name you don't have to search each record in the random access file, only the much shorter serial file. As an improvement on this, you could arrange a subroutine that read the serial file into an array each time the program was being closed down, and sorted the items into alphabetical order. Since each item is recorded along with its record number, the rearrangement of the items in the serial file does not jumble the record numbers. you could then use a very fast binary search routine to find the name you wanted in the serial file, and the program would read the record number and use it to get the record from the random access file. When you feel confident in using both types of file, have a go at this for yourself.

Chapter 11

EDITING, FAULT-TRACING AND MISCELLANY

In a computer BASIC which permits as many commands as GW BASIC does, it's impossible in a book of this size to cover everything in detail. As your experience and confidence grows, however, you'll find that you learn new tricks faster, and that there are some instructions which only start to look useful when you have come up against a problem that can't be solved easily any other way. In this chapter, we'll be looking at a lot of the instructions that can be used for making your programming easier, or for tracing faults, or which just didn't fit anywhere else.

To start with, there is the `AUTO` command. A lot of published programs are written with line numbers that ascend in tens. If you type `AUTO` (then **RETURN**), or just press the **Alt-A** keys, then the word `auto` appears on the screen – and so does the line number 10. You can then type your line 10, and when you press **RETURN**, the next line number, 20, will appear. Using this scheme, you don't have to type any line numbers, which is good news if you find that you tend to forget them. Suppose you want to start at line 100? No problem, just type `AUTO 100` or **Alt-A** 100, then **RETURN**, and your first line number will be 100. You want lines that go up in fives, not tens? Then use `auto 50,5` and you find that your first line is 50, the next is 55 and so on. It's a very useful dodge when you have a lot of lines to enter. At the end of the program, just press **CTRL-BREAK**, and the automatic line numbering will stop. One particularly useful feature of `AUTO` is that it will detect lines that already exist. If you use `AUTO` to write a program, having forgotten that you already have a program in the memory, then each line number produced by `AUTO` will be followed by an asterisk if there is already a line of this number, like 100*. This allows you to escape and list so as to check what you have.

As well as entering lines automatically, it's often useful to be able to delete lines automatically. If, for example, you have a program with a useful subroutine which you want to save on disk, it's useful to be able to delete lines 10 to 4500, and be left with the subroutine which uses lines 5000 to 5050. Just type `DELETE 10-4500`, press **RETURN**, and it's done. You might wonder how anyone could manage without it. The answer is – not very well!

There's another command which is closely related to these. Suppose that you have a program which is neatly numbered in tens, and that you remove three lines, 240 to 260 inclusive. This might be because you have been able to use a subroutine instead of these three lines. Your program now has a hole in it. Even more likely is that you have to add lines like 126, 127 to a program just to get something extra in. The BASIC computer allows you to make everything neat again by using the `RENUM` command to renumber your lines. Using `RENUM` (then **RETURN**) will number your program starting at 10 and numbering in tens. `RENUM 100,10,5` will start your line numbers at 100, and number in fives. You can renumber just as you want to, and you don't have to renumber all of a program. If, for example, you type `RENUM 2000,160,10`, then press **RETURN**, you'll find that your program is as it was as far as line 150, but the next line is 2000, and it's numbered in tens from then on.

Now what do you do with a subroutine when you want to use it in another program? One useful answer is to save it on disk. Saving subroutines has a very useful purpose, because of the `MERGE` command. Suppose, for example, that you have a subroutine called `b:mysub.bas` recorded with the `,A` option – we'll imagine that this is a subroutine which uses line 5000–5200. Now use `NEW` to clear the machine, and then type a few lines which have lower line numbers than the lines of your subroutine. For example you might type lines 10 to 100. Now type `MERGE "b:mysub.bas"`, using the filename that you picked for your subroutine. Press **RETURN**, and you will hear the disk spin and soon after, the '`O.K.`' appears. Now list, and you will see that you have a merged program. Your lines 10 to 100 are now joined with lines 5000 to 5200 of the subroutine. This sort of thing, which is not available on all computers, even some at fancy prices, encourages you to program in the way that I have outlined in chapter 6, using subroutines. You can keep a stock of useful subroutines on disk, ready to use. I find that there are subroutines that I use in all of my programs. There's always a 'press-any-key' routine, usually some sound effects, often something that sorts words into alphabetical order. You, too, will find that you have favourite subroutines, and you'll greatly treasure this useful set of commands. One thing you need to watch, though, with GW BASIC is that the subroutines you load in this way do not have line numbers that already exist in the existing program. They must also be saved in ASCII format, using `"filename",A`.

Other loading and saving

BASIC allows a large number of variations, some useful, some interesting, and some rather odd, on the theme of loading and saving of programs. In addition to the saving that uses the `,A` for ASCII files, you have in GW BASIC also the ordinary `SAVE "filename"` which uses codes for the reserved names, and `,P` for a protected program. A protected program can be loaded and run, but not listed. On the loading side, you can use `LOAD "filename",R` to make the program load and run. This will also allow any files that were open to remain open and in use, so that if you put a `LOAD "getfil",R` instruction as the last step in a program, it will have the effect of loading in the `getfil` program, running it, and using the files that were opened by the first program. There are several other statements of this type for allowing one program to call and run another. The `RUN "filename"` command will load and run a program, and the addition of `,R` will also have the effect of keeping files in use.

Both `LOAD` and `RUN`, in all their varieties, will delete whatever program is in the memory at the time when the command is executed. As we have seen, there is also `MERGE` which will load one program file on top of another. This requires the merged files to be in ASCII format, and if there is a conflict of line numbers, then the line numbers in the `MERGE` file prevail. A form of command that is more flexible is `CHAIN`, which allows one program to load and run another, keeping all the variable values of the previous program intact. Figure 11.1 shows a simple example. Type the listing of (b) and record, using `SAVE "b:second",A` – the use of A for an ASCII file is important. Now type and save the listing in (a). With the main program section in the memory, run and watch the screen. You will see the values of `example 6` appear on the screen from the main program, and then '`New example 12` caused by the running of the second program, into which the variable values `A` and `b$` have been passed.

The variable passing in this example uses `ALL` in the `CHAIN` statement to specify that all of the variables shall be passed – unless this is specified, no variables will be passed. The commas have to be included in the statement because there is provision for placing a line number between the commas, as in `CHAIN "b:second",20,ALL`. In this example, the program 'second' that is chained will start running at line 20 rather than at its first line, which is the default. If you

(a)

```
10 REM main
20 A=6:B$="example"
30 PRINT B$;"   ",A
40 CHAIN MERGE"b:second",,ALL
50 END
```

(b)

```
10 REM second
20 X=2*A
30 C$="New "+B$
40 PRINT C$;" ";X
50 END
```

Figure 11.1 (a & b)
How CHAIN MERGE can be used to pass variable values from one program to another.

don't want to pass on all of the variables, the CHAIN statement can include the names of the variables that are to be passed. Suppose that these were the string A$, a number variable TOTAL and a string array DATE$. At the start of the main program, or near its start, you would declare these variables as common to all chained programs by a line such as:

```
COMMON A$,TOTAL,DATE$()
```

– and then the form of the CHAIN statement would then be simply:

```
CHAIN"b:newone"
```

– to which you might want to add a comma and a line number if some lines in the chained program were to be skipped.

Another possibility is the use of overlays. In this system, a main program stays resident in memory, and a number of routines are loaded in and used as need be, but without deleting the main program. This can, for example, be used to load and run 'help' pages, and this is often done using the function keys, making use of the ON KEY(n) type of instruction noted in chapter 7. Suppose, for example, that your main program uses lines 10 to 5000, and you want to load and run lines that start at 6000. A statement such as:

```
CHAIN MERGE "Over1",6000
```

will load in this piece of program, and start it running at line 6000. If this particular piece of program uses lines 6000 to 7000, then when you wanted another overlay, you would want to delete this one first by using:

```
CHAIN MERGE "Over2",6000, DELETE 6000-7000
```

Finally, there are some important differences between the actions of CHAIN and of CHAIN MERGE. When CHAIN MERGE is used the effect of any DEFINT, DEFSNG, DEFDBL, DEFSTR or DEFFN statements that have been included in the main program will continue into the merged program, and any files that have been left open by the main program can be used by the merged program. When CHAIN is used without MERGE, all files in the main program are closed when the merge takes place, and all the DEF-type statements are void. If variables are to be passed to a chained section then the names of the variables must include their type (like T%,A$,d#) because this cannot be passed on by the use of DEFINT, DEFSTR and so on. you could, of course, have the same DEFINT, DEFSTR, etc., lines in the chained section, in which case there would be no problem.

Editing antics

Editing means changing something that has already appeared on the screen. Any feature of a line, including its line number can be changed by editing. The editing process can be carried out:

(a) While a line is being entered, before **RETURN** has been pressed,

(b) At a later stage, after a line has been entered, but before the program is run,

(c) When an error is signalled during running.

For any form of editing, the line that you want to edit must be visible on the screen. It doesn't matter where about on the screen it appears, or what other lines or commands are placed around it. If you can see it, you can edit it!

Dealing with these in order: while a line is being entered, all of the editing commands, below, can be used. Editing is completed by pressing the **RETURN** key. This works even if you are using auto line numbering.

When the line has been entered, but the program has not been run, you must make sure that the line is on the screen. If it is not, then type `LIST xxx`, where `xxx` is the line number, and press **RETURN**. Remember that the key **F1** gives you the word `'LIST'`. After editing, and pressing **RETURN**, you should then be careful to use the cursor down-arrow key to move the cursor below the last line on the program before using `LIST` or `RUN`. If you do this before pressing **RETURN**, the editing changes will not be carried out. Be careful where the cursor is placed before you type anything.

When the program stops with an error message, the line in which an error has been traced will be put on to the screen, along with the editing cursor. This does not always mean that there is an error in this line. For example, if the line contains `READ X`, and only strings can be read, an error will be signalled in this line, because this is where the `READ` takes place. You need to alter a `RESTORE` or a `DATA` line, so press **RETURN** without typing anything.

Editing commands

1. Cursor movement. The cursor (arrowed) keys of the keyboard of the PC computer allow you to move the cursor around the screen in the direction indicated on each key.

2. To replace a letter, simply place the cursor over the error and type the correct letter. The editing default is replacement, meaning that one typed character replaces the one on which the cursor rests.

3. To delete a letter, place the cursor over it and press the **DEL** key – the one next to the **INS** key at the bottom right hand side of the keyboard.

4. To insert a letter, place the cursor over the letter that will follow the insertion. Press the **INS** key, and then type the letter. You can then

Where the effect of a control key is the same as a standard graphics character this will be shown as G, so that G1 means the same character as CHR$(1). The Ctrl key is shown as ^ in the list.

Ctrl-Key	*Effect*
^A	G1
^B	Move to start of previous word
^C	Move to start of next line
^D	G4
^E	Delete line, return cursor to start
^F	Move cursor to bottom right hand corner (End)
^G	No effect
^H	Delete character under cursor
^I	Tab across 8 spaces
^J	New line
^K	Move cursor to top left hand corner (Home)
^L	Clear screen , home cursor
^M	RETURN (key)
^N	Move to end of line
^O	G15
^P	G16
^Q	G17
^R	Alter cursor to insert cursor
^S	G19
^T	G20
^U	G21
^V	G22
^W	G23
^X	G24
^Y	G25
^Z	G26
^6	Up one line
^[	Delete line
^]	Move the end of previous line
^–	Move down one line

Figure 11.2
Using the Ctrl key combinations in the GW editor.

type several more characters without pressing **INS** again. Pressing **INS** again stops insertion. Insertion is also stopped when you press the cursor controls or the **RETURN** key. When the cursor is being used for insertion, it changes to a larger block size. Watch out for this, because it's a good way of checking that insertion will actually take place. It's annoying to think that you are inserting when you are, in fact, replacing letters!

5. Pressing **CTRL E** (**CTRL** key and **E** key together) will delete everything in a line to the right of the cursor. 'Line' in this sense means a complete numbered BASIC line, which may take several lines on the screen.

6. The **CTRL I** key pair moves the cursor five spaces to the right. You can also use the **TAB** (usually next to **Q**) key to do this.

7. Pressing **RETURN** ends editing, and places the line into memory. If you don't press **RETURN** after editing a line, but only move to another line by using the cursor controls, then no editing is carried out.

Figure 11.2 lists the uses of the **CTRL** and other keys pressed together. Many of these actions duplicate others. You can obtain these effects in a program by using an instruction such as `PRINT CHR$(12)`, which clears the screen and homes the cursor to the top left hand side of the screen, like `CLS`.

Digging out the bugs

In computing language, a fault in a program is called a 'bug', getting it out is called debugging, and someone who puts the faults there is called, of course, a programmer. Your programs can exhibit many kinds of bugs, and a lot of these are indicated by the error messages that you get when you try to run a program. Some of these messages are pretty obvious. `Undefined line number`, for example, means that you have used a command like `GOTO 1000` or `GOSUB 1000` and forgotten to write line 1000. It can also appear if you have tried to `DELETE 1000` with no line 1000, or if you have a `THEN 1000 ELSE 2000` following an `IF` somewhere.

The most common fault message is `Syntax error`. This means that you have wrongly used some of the reserved words of BASIC. You might have spelled a word incorrectly, like `PRIBT` instead of `PRINT`. You might have missed out a bracket, a comma, a semicolon, or put a semicolon in place of a colon. Machines can't tell find out what you meant to do, they can only slavishly do exactly what you tell them. If you haven't used BASIC in exactly the way the machine expects, you'll find a syntax error being reported. Another common error is `Illegal function call`. This usually means that something silly has happened involving a number. Anything that makes use of numbers, like `MID$`, `LEFT$`, `RIGHT$`, `INSTR`, `STRING$` and others can have an incorrect number used – and this will cause the `Illegal function call` error. You will also find that using a negative number in `SQR(N)`, a negative or zero value in `LOG(N)`, and other mathematical impossibilities will cause this error message. The cause shouldn't be hard to trace, because the machine tells you which line caused the trouble. The most elusive one is one we have dealt with already – when an `OPEN` line for a random access file uses a record size of more than 128 bytes when BASIC has been started without specifying a more suitable size.

A lot of errors can find their way into programs, even when you are entering a program that has been printed in a magazine. In general, the programs that you find in the monthly computing magazines are pretty reliable, but some are printed in a way that makes it difficult for you to enter them correctly. The main problems arise when the author of the program has used I (capital I) or l(small L) as a variable name, or has used a printer which does not have slashed zeros. Of these, confusion between `O` and `0` is the worst. A line like:

```
IFM=100RJ=40RD=2
```

can cause a lot of trouble. If it had been printed as:

```
IF M=10 OR J=4 OR D=2
```

all would have been clear. You have to be particularly careful with sound programs, because of the use of `O` to mean Octave. In your own programs, beware of using letters `O` and `I` as variable names.

Even when you have eliminated all of the syntax errors and illegal function calls, you may still find that your program does not do what it should. BASIC does what any programming language of the '80s should do – it gives you a lot of ways of finding out exactly what has gone wrong. One of the most powerful of these is the **CTRL-BREAK** key combination. This, as you know, stops the action of the machine when you press it, and restarts it when you type `CONT` and press **RETURN**. This, as we'll see later, can be very useful for graphics bug-hunting, but for other programs, leaving the program stopped is more useful – though beware of open files. This stops the program, and prints the line number in which the program stopped. What you probably don't know, however, is that

```
10 FOR N=1 TO 1000
20 PRINT N
30 FOR J=1 TO 1000:NEXT
40 NEXT
```

Figure 11.3

Breaking into a count and resuming after changing variables.

you can print out the values of variables, and even alter values while the program is stopped, and then you can make the program resume by using `CONT`. Suppose, for example, you try the simple program in Figure 11.3. This is a slow count, and you should run it, and then press **CTRL-BREAK** at some early stage. The program stops, and you get a message like `Break in 30`. That line number, 30, is important, because this is where the program has stopped. You can start the program again at that line, using `CONT`, providing you don't edit, delete or add to any of the lines of the program. Try typing `?N,J` and **RETURN**. This will give you the value of `N` and `J`. Now try `N=998` and press **RETURN**. Type `CONT`, then **RETURN**. You will then see the count start again – but at 999!. This is an excellent way of testing what will happen at the end of a long loop. Testing would be a rather time-consuming business if you had to wait until the count got there by itself. You can even make this testing process automatic! Take a look at Figure 11.3. This uses line 10 to make sure that a subroutine is run whenever the **F10** key is pressed. In this case, the effect will be to print the values of `N` and `J`, alter the value of `N` to 995, and then continue. To cancel the effect of line 10, we use `KEY(10)OFF` in line 50, just before the program ends.

Tracing the loops

One way in which a program can be baffling is when it runs without producing any error messages – but doesn't run correctly. This is really a sign of faulty planning, but sometimes it's an oversight, and the `ON key(10) GOSUB` method of tracing a fault can be very useful, because it allows you to print out the state of the variables at any stage in the program, and then carry on. Sometimes you want a simpler form of tracing, though. If your program contains a lot of `IF..THEN..ELSE` lines, it often happens that one of these does not do what you expect. In such a case, the BASIC computer provides help for you in the form of two commands `TRON` and `TROFF`.

```
10 ON KEY(10) GOSUB 1000 :KEY(10) ON
20 FOR N=1 TO 1000
30 PRINT N
40 FOR J=1 TO 500:NEXT
50 NEXT:KEY(10) OFF
60 END
1000 PRINT N,J:N-995:RETURN
```

Figure 11.4
Setting up key f10 so that it will make a subroutine run when pressed.

TRON (how did you think the film got the name?) means TRACE ON, and its effect is to print on the screen the line number of each line as it is executed. The line numbers are put between square brackets, and they are printed at the start of a screen line, in front of anything the program prints. Try typing TRON and then running the program of Figure 11.4. TRON is particularly useful if you aren't sure what a program is doing, and it can be very handy in pointing out when something goes wrong with a loop. Remember that you can combine TRON with other de-bugging commands. You can, for example, stop the program, alter the variables, and then continue, with TRON showing you which lines are being executed. Typing TROFF (then **RETURN**) switches off this tracing process. TRON and TROFF are available on function keys **F7** and **F8** respectively.

The programmed keys

The programmed keys are the keys which are marked **F1** to **F10** on the keyboard. Each of these keys can put in a keyword for you, without the labour of typing out the complete word. The actions of the keys are summarised in the line at the bottom of the screen. Typing KEY LIST (**RETURN**) will give a list of all the commands which have been assigned to the keys. – don't forget the space between KEY and LIST. As we have seen in the course of this book, typing KEY OFF will delete the key reminder strip, and KEY ON will restore it.

Keys **F3** and **F4** each give commands that need to be followed by other information (a filename at least) and then by pressing **RETURN**. The keys that are marked with a left-facing arrow in the keystrip, however, have the 'return' action built in, so pressing the key completes the action. Key **F2**, for example, will RUN a program with no need to press **RETURN** or add anything. These keys are, however, programmable, which means that you can alter them to suit yourself, and key **F9** is set up for this purpose. Suppose, for example, that you want key **F10** to give you MID$(TEST$, for use in a program that makes a lot of use of this piece of slicing. All you have to do is type:

```
KEY10 "MID$(TEST$,"
```

and then press **RETURN**. you can get the word KEY by pressing **F9**. You will see the display at the foot of the screen confirm the change, and **F10** will give you this action for as long as the computer is switched on. You can get the effect of the **RETURN** key also by using CHR$(13), with no quotes, and this is often a useful addition to LIST if you always want a complete list. All you need to do is type:

```
KEY(1),"LIST"+CHR$(13)
```

You can use up to fifteen characters on each of these keys, and by careful selection, you can save yourself a lot of typing. It's useful, for example, to have PRINTTAB (on a key, and SOUND can be another useful word in some programs. Any of the F-keys can be turned off by a statement such as KEY(3),"", and when this has been done, the keys will return rather peculiar results when you use them with an INKEY$ loop. Try the little listing shown in Figure 11.5, which makes key **F10** a blank, and then enters an INKEY$ loop. When you press **F10**, you find that K$ prints as 'D', but gives zero for ASC(k$) and for VAL(k$). This is because a CHR$(0) exists in front of the 'D' code, and though this is ignored by PRINT K$, it totally confuses ASC and VAL. As shown here, you can make the test using CHR$(0)+"D", or you could use ASC(RIGHT$(K$,1)). The key code numbers range from 59 to 68 for keys 1 to 10 respectively, with each code prefaced by a CHR$(0).

```
10 KEY 10,""
20 WHILE K$=""
30 K$=INKEY$:WEND
40 PRINT K$, ASC(K$),VAL(K$)
50 IF K$=CHR$(0)+"D" THEN PRINT"YES"
```

Figure 11.5

The key codings after the function keys have been 'turned off'.

That's the end of this particular road for me, but only the beginning for you. Any BASIC is a fascinating bag of tricks, all of which you will gradually learn to unlock. This book should have unlocked some of the secrets for you, and the rest is now up to you. By this time, you should be able to cope with the way in which commands are described in the Manual. From now on, each time you settle down to write a program, you will be learning more about BASIC and its uses. This is something that you can never acquire from running programs, or even from studying programs that were written by other people. By all means look carefully at programs in the magazines. You will find that a lot of programs that are written for the MSX computers can be adapted for this BASIC computer, and programs in BASICA of the IBM PC will run without modification unless they contain PEEK and POKE statements (omitted here for a variety of reasons). Very soon, you will find a huge variety of program ideas which are available for you to use. Happy programming.

Appendix A

ALT-KEY EFFECTS

The Alt key is used in many programs to obtain a set of characters by holding down the **ALT** key and typing a number on the numeric keypad at the right hand side of the keyboard. In the table below, the graphics and other characters that are produced should be detailed in your computer manual, and are indicated by 'Gr'. Where there is no effect, a blank has been left. The KEYBUK program had been run when the computer was first turned on.

Alt key	*Effect*	*Alt key*	*Effect*
1	Gr	16	Gr
2	Home cursor	17	Gr
3	Return	18	Flashing block
4	Gr	19	!!
5	–	20	Gr
6	End of screen	21	Gr
7	Beep	22	Gr
8	–	23	Gr
9	Tab	25	Gr
10	Return	26	Gr
11	Home cursor	27	Clear line
12	CLS, home cursor	28	–
13	Return	29	Backspace
14	–	30	Up line
15	Gr	31	Down line

Appendix B

AUTOEXEC.BAT FILES

PLEASE NOTE: In this appendix it is assumed that you are working with a *working copy* of the system disk and that you are *sure* you know what you are doing. If in doubt, don't!

An AUTOEXEC.BAT file is a type of file called a batch file, which is a set of instructions to the operating system of the computer. This has nothing to do with BASIC, so that our only interest in this type of file is that it can provide the correct conditions for using BASIC. In particular, it makes it possible to create a disk which will, when the computer prompts for for a System Disk, load in MS-DOS, carry out any special actions that are needed, and then load and start GW BASIC. The form of such a file is a simple set of instructions with no line numbers, one line per instruction. The instructions of such a file can be written using EDLIN, any word-processor that creates ASCII files, or even GW BASIC (by creating a serial file). The important points are that the file must be in ASCII codes only, with each instruction ended by using the **RETURN** key.

The file I used for GW BASIC in the course of this book consisted of four lines of instructions:

```
echo off
keybuk
rtc
GW/S:256
```

Note: some versions of GW BASIC use the filename BASICA rather than GW.

Some editors or word processors require you to state in advance what the filename is to be. You can use AUTOEXEC.BAT directly, or pick some other name with the aim of changing it once you are certain that the file is free of errors. In such a simple file, it's hardly worth the extra bother, so you can name the file as AUTOEXEC.BAT directly. The file must be typed as shown, and recorded on the disk that you use for loading up your BASIC. This disk must have been formatted as a *system* disk, carrying the MS-DOS tracks, and also COMMAND.COM. If you do not have the system tracks in place, then format a new disk, using FORMAT/S, and copy BASIC to it after formatting is complete. You will then have to copy your AUTOEXEC.BAT file, and also any files that are called for in AUTOEXEC.BAT. In the example above, these are RTC.COM and KEYBUK.EXE. RTC is the file that is needed to ensure that BASIC runs a clock that is synchronised to the computer's own clock on an Amstrad PC1512. If you have a clock in your computer then there will be a similar program. If not, just leave the instruction out. KEYBUK is the file for ensuring that the keyboard uses the UK character set.

You also need to copy over the file CONFIG.SYS, which selects other features of the use of the computer, including the setting of the Ram-disk. For use with BASIC, you will find the config.sys file that is already on your MS-DOS Master disk totally suitable – you can look at the contents of this field by using TYPE CONFIG.SYS if you like. A CONFIG.SYS file is created in exactly the same way as an AUTOEXEC.BAT file, but it is used during the setting up of the MS-DOS system rather than afterwards.

Once your autoexec.bat file is on the disk, along with the files it calls, you can then load and run BASIC by inserting this disk as you would insert the MS-DOS Master disk when the machine is being started up or reset. If you use a program along with GW BASIC, a random access file program perhaps, you can add the program name following GW or GW/S:256 (separated by a space) so that when you use this disk you will get GW BASIC loaded, then the program loaded and running. When you leave a BASIC program you will then be back with GW BASIC, and if you leave GW BASIC (by typing SYSTEM **RETURN**), you can then use the computer for other work that involves programs that run under MS-DOS. You can get back to BASIC by inserting your disk, and typing AUTOEXEC.BAT – there is no need to reset unless you have been using DOS-Plus.

Index